The Learning Fractals

The Learning Fractals
A playbook for perpetual learners on digital journeys

Anubhav Pradhan
Sekhar Subramanian

ISBN: 978-1-83556-163-8

Cover design by:

Shivani Srivastava

For Shivani, Gahan and Gatik
- Anubhav

For Appa, Amma, Anna, and Nivedita
-Sekhar

Table of Contents

Foreword

David Morris
Global Head of People Capability at HSBC
https://www.linkedin.com/in/david-morris-5652461/

I am as far from being a mathematician as you can imagine, but I've always been fascinated by the concept that everything is essentially mathematical. Early in my career I would look at the hourly sales forecasts for our stores. They were almost always accurate even though it would be entirely different human beings buying the products. Repeatable patterns that were more predictable the more they scaled.

Perhaps more exciting than hamburger sales was science fiction legend Isaac Asimov's concept of Psychohistory. From his Foundation[1] universe, it combined history, sociology and maths to predict the future, on a galactic scale. Very cool to read about as a teenager, but also what has ultimately been the basis of my own career; exploring, and perhaps influencing (or more realistically nudging), human behaviour at an individual and organisational level.

It's in my capacity as a talent professional that I have the privilege of knowing Anubhav Pradhan. When I first met him, I was immediately struck by, and a little in awe of, his expertise in the technology learning landscape. Here was an experienced L&D leader who had honed his skills at one of the world's largest digital services organisations, a company with an exceptional reputation for training and skills development. Whilst I was lazily reading science fiction, Anubhav was publishing books and articles to help educate fellow technologists. We were extremely fortunate when Anubhav joined our organisation and we've benefited massively from one of the best practitioner-educators in the field, as well as one of the nicest and collegiate colleagues you could wish for.

When Anubhav told me he was writing a new book about digital learning, using the metaphor of fractals, my interest immediately peaked. Complex patterns, repeating, evolving, scaling. I've long seen corporate learning and development as a sort of Trojan Horse for influencing business culture and so was intensely interested in a handbook that codified exactly that, especially against the backdrop of technological changes and digital skills. L&D departments will always be several steps behind the consumer platforms that colleagues are well used to. L&D teams are reliant on enterprise HR tools catching up (sometimes decades late) or piggybacking off other corporate employee platforms. Anubhav and Sekhar's book provides insights, frameworks and approaches that enable learning agility and a growth mindset in an increasingly complex landscape for learners, leaders, and learning practitioners.

I found myself nodding (often vigorously, even when there was no one else around) throughout the book. I was particularly struck by the concept of the Learning Triad; logic, data, and imagination. Logic is (mostly) plentiful in corporations. Data, although it requires much more effort to be genuinely insightful, is always in strong demand. But how wonderful to see imagination as the third element. Back to my love of science fiction once again; it's curiosity, creativity and possibilities that enable learners and leaders to craft new futures.

The book further examines how these foundations help build a learning ecosystem, and how that ecosystem has a rhythm, with "vibrations" at individual, enterprise and learning team level. Those of us that have been in the game a while are probably aware that these vibrations should be synchronised, monitored and adapted, but here is a map that shows us how to do so with more purpose and intentionality, for far greater effect, and I suspect, job satisfaction.

And so back my other favourite author, Issac Asimov;

"I believe that scientific knowledge has fractal properties, that no matter how much we learn, whatever is left, however small it may seem, is just as infinitely complex as the whole was to start with. That, I think, is the secret of the Universe."

If, like me, you believe that business learning and development is much more than providing access to a corporate learning catalogue, then it might just be that Anubhav and Sekhar have crafted their own sort of guide to the Universe (hitchhiking[2] optional).

David Morris
London, 2024

References

1. Foundation, Issac Asimov, 1951
2. The Hitchhiker's Guide to the Galaxy, Douglas Adams, 1979

Preface

"Fractals offer us a new way of looking at the world, a way of seeing the beauty in the intricate and the complex."

- Michael Barnsley

The room was silent, but soon it would be bustling and every seat would be taken. We were expecting more than 50 participants from across different departments within our organization. Each of them were experts in their own areas, and were tasked with leading large teams that built software for some of the biggest Fortune 500 companies. As our participants walked in, we recognized many of them. Among them, there were business leaders who manage clients across various industries such as financial services, healthcare, and manufacturing; there were software architects who have designed and built software that impact millions of people; and there were some senior leaders who were experts at leading teams that worked with a variety of technologies across areas such as Artificial Intelligence, Big Data, Cloud, Cyber, Web Development, Mobile App Development, Infrastructure, Testing, and many more. We stood there thinking again about what we were going to tell them that is new for them? What is something that is worth their time? And what are they looking to learn from us? And then for a split second we looked back to see how we got here!

A little less than 3 months ago, the then head of learning at our previous organization, presented us with a problem. Having taken the reins of our department recently, his insights about the customers we serve i.e. the experts in the room awaiting our session, was unique and refreshing. He expressed that our business leaders, architects and technology experts, were of often specialists in their own areas of work and had deep invaluable expertise. However, what they needed to impact change and accelerate growth was to be able to understand the breadth of digital offerings that our organization provided, and piece together how they are all connected with one another. The solution that we came up with was this session - a masterclass - one that provided the audience with a unified view of the ever-changing landscape of digital skills that they all operate in. This masterclass offered them a holistic view of the landscape of digital skills used by various teams across our organization to build modern digital experiences, and helped them charter their learning journey to not only dive deeper into each area but also appreciate the interconnectedness between various skills.

As of the time of writing this book, we have run this masterclass well over a hundred times; since its first run late in 2017. Each time we have met with new faces (and some familiar ones from the previous sessions too) who are enthusiastic about what we offer them in these sessions. However, every instance of the masterclass continues to have that tiny blemish of nervousness. We are constantly thinking about how we can cater to a diverse audience who are not only experts in the various areas that we speak about individually, but also collectively represent everything that we offer them in these masterclasses. As our audience nods along, smiles, quizzes us, debates with us and each other, actively engages with us during these sessions, and shares their positive feedback afterwards, we continue to grow in confidence that what we offer them is rich and unique.

We have observed how and why these masterclasses are a huge hit among our audience. Most of them instantly connect with how we present the unique unified view of the digital skills landscape through the "lens of digital experiences". They tell us that it helps them look back at their digital journeys so far and understand the role that various tools and technologies play in crafting modern digital experiences. They also appreciate how it offers them a peek into the future waves of evolution and sets them up for continued success along their digital journeys. As leaders and experts of various work streams within an enterprise, they often find value in how this masterclass helps them and their teams gain a perspective of the ways in which different parts of digital products, platforms, and services leverage the connections between these various digital skills to form wholesome modern digital experiences. And above all, they appreciate how these sessions provide them with a framework to define meaningful learning objectives for their teams to stay abreast with the ever-changing landscape of digital skills, and synchronize their learning momentum with the pace of digital transformation.

This book finds its roots in the ideas that we presented in these masterclasses. The ideas that we share in this book are very close to our heart, but we must confess they weren't originally in the shape that you are going to see them in; as you read this book. We knew that the content of our workshop is special and wanted to share it with everyone. But at the same time, we also wanted to weave it along with a simple, yet powerful metaphor as the theme, so that it's easy to consume and can be adopted by everyone who comes across it. Months of research, ideation, and discussions ensued before our eureka moment happened. Just as they say, great ideas come when you let your mind wander. We stumbled upon fractals by chance when we read about how they are being used in various areas of computing and science. Fractals weren't new to us, for we have been amazed with the different ways in which they occur in nature and are applied in science. However we had never before seen them in the context of learning, which we are about to share with you in this book. Early in our writing journey, we formalized the seed thought for this book in this LinkedIn blog[1], and then we germinated it further to grow it into the principles, practices, and tools around learning digital skills that you will come across in this book. We take you into the world of how fractals can inspire you to become a perpetual learner and thereby help you succeed in your digital journey. You will see how drawing inspiration from fractals helps you better understand the overarching landscape of digital skills (yes, the one that we share in our masterclasses!), paves the way for you to master this ever-changing digital landscape, and also enables enterprises to support individuals like you and the teams that you work with to thrive on your digital journeys.

Digital journeys of individuals and enterprises go hand-in-hand with the waves of digital transformation that we all experience. Digital transformation may refer to several things such as adopting new technologies, refining business processes, leveraging data to drive decision making, creating a safe and privacy-friendly ecosystem of digital products and services, or in most cases all of these. However at its core, we believe that digital transformation is fundamentally centered around people and the skills they possess. To be able to craft the digital products and services that enterprises envision, and grasp the context and complexity of these digital transformations, individuals and teams have to learn a plethora of technologies which not only ride their own waves of change but are also interconnected in myriad ways. This book offers individuals and enterprises the fractal-inspired learning principles, practices, and tools to succeed on their digital journeys.

This book is for the benefit of everyone, irrespective of what role they play within an enterprise today, and serves as a guide for their continuous learning. We have written this book with a variety of personas in mind and we believe it would benefit them as follows:

- For beginners in the world of everything digital, or the future-workforce that is currently equipping themselves with skills required by modern enterprise, this book offers a comprehensive view of the landscape of digital skillsthat make up the modern digital experiences which they presently consume, and will eventually go on to create.

- For those who work with these digital skills on a regular basis, this book offers a unique perspective inspired from fractals which not only strengthens their understanding of the evolving landscape, but also helps them explain technology and guide others on their learning journeys.

• For the leaders and learning professionals within enterprises, this book offers fractal-inspired learning principles, practices, and tools that can help them build a sustainable learning ecosystem that fosters a thriving learning culture, to benefit the people they lead and/or influence.

• For academicians at the helm of building the next generation of workforce, this book provides them with the insights that can help them understand the nuances of the digital skills that they help their students/learners prepare for. This book can serve as a reference guide on how to build learning programs that help nurture the key elements required for an individual's success on their digital journeys.

This book emphasizes the need for learning for everyone amidst the continuous waves of digital transformation, lays out the various challenges that hinder success on their journey, and guides them on to overcome these challenges by drawing inspiration from fractals. As we cruise through this book you will discover how learning journeys of enterprises and individuals exhibit fractal patterns, explore how fractals can be used to demystify the complex and ever-changing landscape of digital skills, appreciate how the fundamental properties of fractals can inspire the design of learning ecosystems in modern enterprises, and how fractals hold the key to nurturing a sustainable rhythm for lifelong learning.

This book is divided into five chapters viz. The Learning Fractal, The Learning Spectrum, The Learning Foundations, The Learning Ecosystem, and The Learning Rhythm. In the **first chapter** i.e. The Learning Fractal, we will establish the theme of this book by understanding the fundamental characteristics of fractals, exploring how learning exhibits fractal properties, discovering the fundamental fractal that is central to all learning, and describing the various learning related challenges that enterprises and individuals face on their digital journeys. We will briefly discuss how drawing inspiration from fractals can help overcome these challenges and set the stage for the latter chapters of the book.

In the **second chapter**, we will get introduced to our fractal - The Learning Spectrum - which represents the ever-changing landscape of digital skills that enterprises and individuals encounter on their digital journeys. This chapter will present the time-tested, unique, and comprehensive view of this overarching landscape which we shared with numerous leaders of enterprises in our masterclasses. To view this spectrum, we will rely on the *prism of digital experiences* that is pivotal to the digital journeys and transformations. By understanding the nuances of what constitutes modern digital experiences and exploring its various aspects, you will be able to visualize the underlying spectrum of digital skills which come together to craft these experiences. You will understand the broad purpose of each digital skill in this vast spectrum, and explore the connections among these skills which ultimately helps craft the modern digital experiences that you consume today. By the end of this chapter you will be able to appreciate the fractal properties that the learning spectrum exhibits as you explore the breadth of digital skills it constitutes and the interconnections between them.

In the **third chapter**, The Learning Foundations, we will zoom in and zoom out of our fractal (the learning spectrum) to unearth its foundational aspects that underpin the mastery of the digital skills landscape. These foundational aspects interplay with one another to form thefundamental fractal - *the learning triad* - which is the seed for the learning spectrum. As you go through this chapter, you will once again rely on the prism of digital experiences to discover the learning triad, explore its elements and the interplay among them. You will also delve into how each of the elements of this triad plays a role in the overall learning spectrum and gain an insight into how each element can be mastered. By the end of this chapter, you will walk away with the secret sauce that is the essential ingredient to mastering the entire learning spectrum and staying abreast with its evolution.

In the **fourth chapter**, The Learning Ecosystem, we will explore how fractals can help design a learning ecosystem that is equipped to sustain a future-ready workforce along its digital journey. We will draw inspiration from fractals to understand the key tenets that any learning ecosystem should aim to fulfill. As we go through this chapter, we will discuss the archetype of any learning ecosystem, understand its key aspects, and then delve into a reference learning architecture that can be used as a framework within enterprises to construct their own learning ecosystems. As an individual learner going through this chapter, you will walk away with a framework to organize your learning effort and recognize the role that a learning ecosystem plays in your learning journey. As a leader, you will be able to appreciate the framework as a guide that helps you influence, support and advance the learning within your teams and enterprise. By understanding the framework of the learning ecosystem, you should be able to promote and channelize the learning efforts thus championing the success along your enterprise's digital journey.

In the **last chapter,** The Learning Rhythm, we will discuss how various learning rhythms nurture the learning fractal which in turn sustains the learning momentum in individuals and enterprises. As we go through this chapter, we will explore the bias for action that individuals and enterprises must have towards learning in order to succeed on their digital journeys. We will also understand the nuances of the various learning rhythms that play a part in ensuring that thelearning sticks, and individuals stay on track to achieve their learning goals. As a learner, you will understand the various factors that influence your learning journey and walk away with practices that help you stay focused towards meeting your learning goals. As a leader, you will learn about various tools that can be used to measure the efficacy of learning within your teams and the enterprise, and take away various practices that you can use to nurture a progressive learning culture.

Within these five chapters, we have attempted to cover a wealth of experience and learning that has helped us transform several enterprises into continuous learning organizations, and influence the learning journeys of numerous individuals. Most of the concepts presented here are time tested, and have been covered in our masterclasses and conversations with several leaders in the context of enriching learning within enterprises. Further, we acknowledge that we may not be able to access and engage with each one of you personally to have these conversations, however to make up for it we have attempted to replicate that spirit with the diagrams and illustrations in this book. You will find that these are mainly hand-drawn, just the way they would be if we were to engage with you in conversations and share these ideas. We also recognize the need for deeper conversations on some of these concepts and welcome your thoughts and questions to that end through email or LinkedIn.

We hope you enjoy reading this book as much as we loved writing it for you!

Anubhav Pradhan
pradhan.anubhav@gmail.com
https://www.linkedin.com/in/anubhavpradhan/

Sekhar Subramanian
sekharsubramanian@gmail.com
https://www.linkedin.com/in/sekhar-subramanian/

Acknowledgements

This project has been in the making for a while now, since 2017 to be precise. We held the first of our masterclasses in 2017, and continue to iterate over it even now. The idea to collect those concepts into the form of a book too has been around at least since 2018. And between then and now in 2024, we have had the chance to share this journey with several amazing people who we will remain eternally grateful to for their wholehearted support and encouragement. This book would be incomplete without acknowledging their contributions. We would like to extend our sincere appreciation to a number of people, mentioned below in no particular order, without whom this project couldn't have been possible.

To start with, we would like to acknowledge the immense contributions of Dr. David Knott, CTO of the UK Government, for thoroughly reviewing the content of this book and sharing his profound insights which helped us immensely improvise on how we presented the subject matter and the content of this book. Further, we would also like to thank him for writing the epilogue to this book, and sharing how the ideas in this book resonated with him and thereby offering guidance to our readers on how to apply these ideas into their learning journey.

We are also highly indebted to David Morris, Global Head of People Capability at HSBC, who not only inspired us to record our thoughts on designing sustainable learning ecosystems and appreciated our humble efforts to contribute to the learning universe, but also graciously provided the foreword for this book. We are grateful for his insightful perspectives on the key concepts discussed in the third, fourth, and fifth chapters. His contributions were instrumental in validating our ideas and, we hope, will offer you valuable insights into navigating the challenge of scaling enterprise learning with both passion and purpose.

We would like to extend our gratitude to several leaders across the organizations we worked at for helping us shape the various ideas, and frameworks that we have presented in this book. We would specifically like to thank Pramod Prakash Panda - Chief Learning Officer (Tech Mahindra), Thirumala Arohi - EVP - Global Head of ETA and Service Offering Head (Infosys), Satheesha B Nanjappa - SVP and Head of Education, Training and Assessments (Infosys), Balasubramanian Ganesh - Advisor to Startups, Global Capability Centres & Banks, and Brad Hilborn - Managing Director, Group Head of IT Strategy & Transformation at HSBC, for their invaluable advice and guidance as we implemented the various principles, practices and tools that we describe in this book. Further, we would also like to thank Pradeep Menon - MD & CEO of HSBC Technology India, Atul Soneja - COO (Tech Mahindra) and Shaji Mathew - Group Head of Human Resources (Infosys) for strongly advocating and sponsoring our masterclasses, and thereby encouraging us to develop these ideas further and share them with the wider community.

We are deeply thankful to Shivani Srivastava for designing the concept of the cover of the book and to Azmi Mohamed Khan, Artist and Founder of Art Alternative, for bringing the cover design to life, and for formatting and typesetting the print version of the book. We also want to thank Hammad Khalid from HMDPublishing for his support and guidance which made the publication of this book smooth and seamless.

Having the support of our friends and colleagues during the process of drafting the manuscript has been extremely crucial in shaping the book into the form that it is now. We would like to thank J.A. Eswaran, Director - Engineering Talent Academy, Bosch Global Software Technologies, for his review and critical comments that helped improve the manuscript. In addition, we would like to extend our appreciation to Sekhar Babu Tatavarti (HSBC), Patrick Andrews

(L&T Technology), and Divyansh Tripathi (UIPath) for their constant support, honest feedback, and being a soundboard for our ideas.

We also want to express our heartfelt gratitude to the participants of our masterclasses for engaging with us through lively discussions that have greatly influenced the breadth and depth of the content of this book.

Finally, we want to express our gratitude to perpetual learners like you who have chosen this book as part of your learning journey, and for continually inspiring us with your curiosity and zeal for learning. This book is a testament to the collective learning and growth that we all share.

Thank you!

Chapter-1
The Learning Fractal

Fractals are truly a source of beauty, creativity and surprise!

You may observe fractals as patterns that nature repeats in flowers, trees, snowflakes, waves, coastlines, mountains, and in the formation of galaxies. For example, Romanesco broccoli is a fractal which grows in a golden spiral pattern where the spiral gets wider by a factor equal to the golden ratio[2] for every quarter turn it makes. As you can see in Fig 1.1a, each bud of the broccoli grows smaller buds, and even the smallest bud resembles the whole broccoli; the whole broccoli looks just like a bud too. Similarly, Snowflake designs, as shown in Fig 1.1b, also follow fractal patterns. When you look closely at a snowflake, you will notice that it has branches spawning side-branches which further spawn side-branches, and so on repeatedly. If you look closely, lightning bolts and veins of leaves also branch out repetitively and exhibit fractal patterns in a similar manner.

Fractals are not just limited to nature; one may find them in art forms as well. Ba-ila housing settlements, as shown in Fig 1.2a, in southern

Fig 1.1a: Romanesco Broccoli[3]

Fig 1.1b: Snowflake

Zambia are a testimony to how ancient African civilizations used fractal patterns to architect their homes and towns[4]. These housing settlements are shaped as a ring of rings with an increasing status gradient that one can observe as one moves from the front to the back of each ring, and of the overall settlement. You may also find several fractal patterns in ancient Indian temples such as when you observe the shikharas (spires) of Khajuraho, or the intricate sculptures of deities in Madurai. The shikharas of the Khajuraho temples, as shown in Fig 1.2b, are made up of smaller shikharas, which in turn are made up of even smaller shikharas, and so on. In Madurai, you can observe fractal patterns in the intricate carvings that adorn the gopurams (tower gateways) and mandapams (pillared hallways) of the Meenakshi Amman temple.

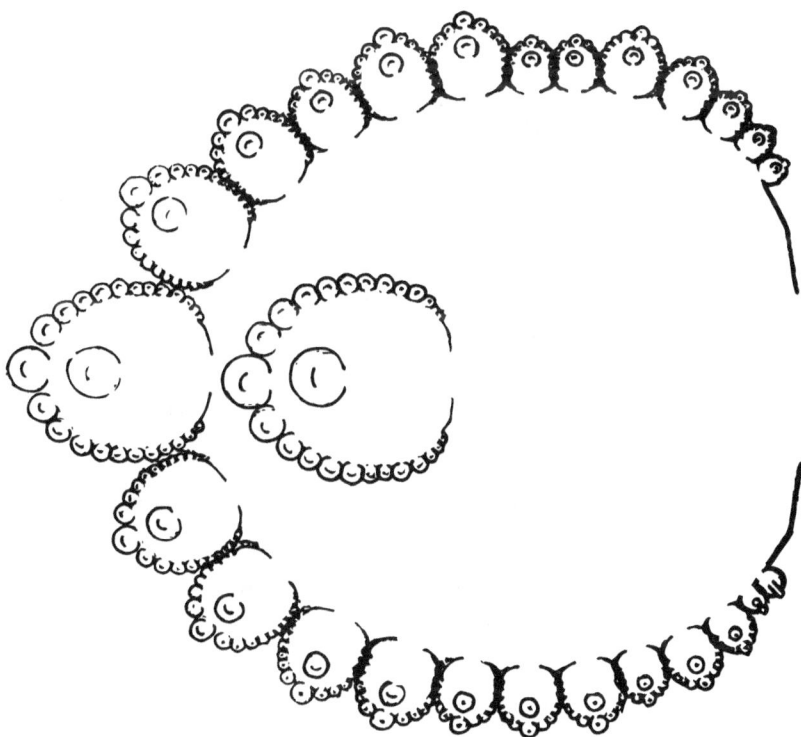

Fig 1.2a: Ba-ila Housing Settlements

Fig 1.2b: Shikharas of Khajuraho[5]

Did you know that when you went to the movies to see Inception(2010), Doctor Strange(2016), or Matrix Reloaded(2003), you were watching virtual environments that were generated using fractals? In the field of music too, fractals are used to create melodies by picking a segment of an already composed music, stripping it down to a basic framework, and creating an all new composition using specialized software. Fractals are being used in a similar vein to unlock the mysteries of the music of great composers like Bach and Mozart.

Fractals are used in Physics, Biology, Ecology and Social Sciences. They are used to model turbulence, fluid dynamics, polymers and gels. Computer science experts are also exploring fractal networks to train machine learning models for solving specific types of real-world problems. Conventionally, such problems are solved using artificial neural networks or other machine learning algorithms.

Although fractals have been in existence since time immemorial, the term 'fractal' was coined by mathematician Benoit Mandelbrot in 1975. He famously wrote "Clouds are not spheres, mountains are not cones, coastlines are not circles, and bark is not smooth, nor does lightning travel in a straight line" in his book, "The Fractal Geometry of Nature". He presented a case to celebrate the chaos and irregularity of the world, which he referred to as roughness. He pioneered the usage of fractals in mathematics which inspired practitioners of many disciplines such as engineering, medicine, genetics, cosmology, art and music.

Even before Mandelbrot's pioneering work, other artists, painters, architects, mathematicians have all had a tryst with fractals. Mandelbrot noted that Gustave Eiffel had intuitively incorporated the idea of fractals in the design of the Eiffel tower where the tower is not built of solid beams but of colossal trusses which have sub-trusses and eventually the trusses have the same strength of cylindrical beams but are much lighter. In another example, he has noted that paintings of the Japanese artist, Katsushika Hokusai too display fractal patterns[6]. You can see that the famous painting "The Great Wave Off Kanagawa" (shown in Fig 1.3) by Katsushika Hokusai in the early 1800s shows

Fig 1.3: The Great Wave off Kanagawa by Katsushika Hokusai[7]

a large ocean wave breaking off into smaller and smaller waves. The works of mathematicians such as Gaston Julia, Georg Cantor, Helge von Koch and Felix Hausdorff all inspired the work of Benoit Mandelbrot with fractals.

The Mandelbrot set[8] (shown in Fig 1.4) named after Benoit Mandelbrot can be generated by iteratively visualizing the output of the mathematical function:

$$z_{n+1} = z_n^2 + C,$$

where C represents a complex number and z starts from 0

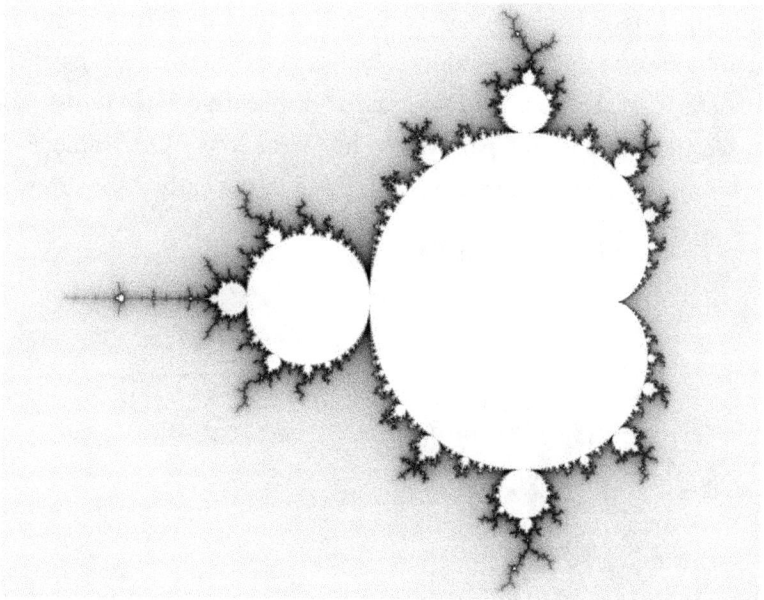

Fig 1.4: Mandelbrot Set[9]

Similarly, several other fractal patterns such as Koch Snowflake[10], Sierpinski Triangle[11], and Julia Set[12] can be visualized using mathematical functions. Fractals, both natural and simulated, not only help us peek into the underlying mathematics of nature and arouse our creativity, but also serve as both an inspiration and a tool to solve complex real world problem

Fig 1.5 illustrates the growth of a simple tree using a fractal pattern. It depicts how a simple tree of 2 branches (extreme left) grows to become a large complex tree (extreme right), with numerous branches and sub-branches. It further depicts how in each iteration of growth, the branches (and its sub-branches) repetitively spawn sub-branches.

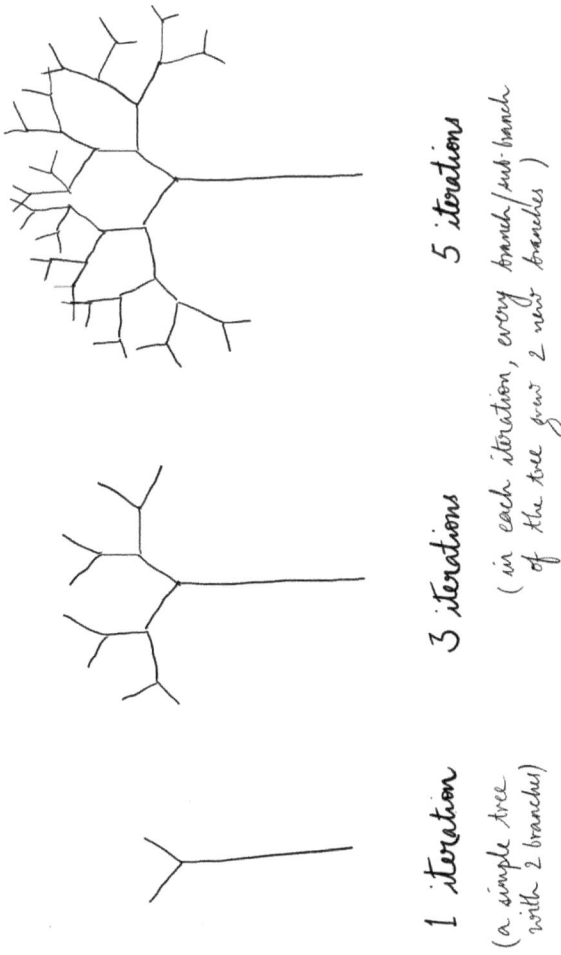

Fig 1.5: A Fractal Tree

5 iterations

3 iterations

1 iteration

(a simple tree with 2 branches)

(in each iteration, every branch/sub-branch of the tree grows 2 new branches)

When we closely examine any fractal pattern (such as the one illustrated above), we can see that it exhibits the following three fundamental characteristics:

1. The part we are looking at resembles the whole; and when we zoom out the whole looks very much like the part.

2. The fractal patterns are created by repeating a simple pro cess over and over in an ongoing loop.

3. The various parts of the overall fractal pattern connect with each other, and eventually everything links together.

Fig 1.6 depicts this triumvirate of eternal (infinite), self-organized, and connected characteristics which reflects the nature of fractals.

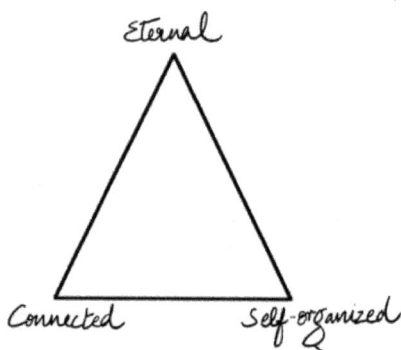

Eternal

Connected   Self-organized

Fig 1.6: Key Characteristics of Fractals

Fractals are **eternal** in the sense that the image of the fundamental fractal can be found at various scales of the pattern. This can be observed when we zoom in and zoom out of the pattern. For example, in our fractal tree (shown in fig 1.5) we observe that at any scale of the tree the image looks similar to the fundamental fractal (a simple tree with 2 branches).

Fractals are **self-organized** in the sense that however large and complex the pattern may seem, it is created by repeating the fundamental fractal over and over. For example in our fractal tree, in each iteration, every branch/sub-branch of the tree grew 2 new branches. Repeating this fundamental pattern a number of times (potentially eternally) eventually produced the full blown complex fractal tree.

Fractals are **connected** in the sense that every new iteration connects to at least a part of the previous pattern and eventually forms the overall fractal. For example, in our fractal tree the new sub-branches were linked to their parent branches and eventually formed a part of the whole tree.

If you recall our earlier examples of fractals in nature such as the Romanesco broccoli and snowflake, we can evidently observe that they exhibit these three characteristics - eternal, self-organized and connected. For example, If you observe the broccoli, it can theoretically continue to grow new buds that further grow buds eternally (infinitely). Each bud (part) looks very much like the whole broccoli and the whole broccoli looks very much like the part. You also observe the self-organized nature when you understand that fundamentally it's a simple process of repeating the growth of buds in a spiral pattern that creates the seemingly complex shape/pattern of the broccoli. It is of course hard to miss that the buds are in turn connected with one another to form the whole broccoli. To quote Benoit Mandelbrot here, "Bottomless wonders spring from simple rules repeated without end". We can see that these three characteristics of any fractal viz. eternal, self-organized and connected, lends it its beauty, creativity and surprise!

When we came across fractals amidst our search for a simple, yet powerful metaphor to express the various concepts that we describe in this book, it almost instantly struck a chord. We instinctively knew that we stumbled upon something that can captivate our readers and tie well with our thoughts and ideas. As we thought more deeply about these three characteristics of fractals, we began to see how learning journeys of individuals and enterprises too exhibit fractal patterns In our vocation as learning professionals spanning a few decades, we have helped several enterprises and numerous individuals learn digital skills, create digital experiences, and most importantly foster a curious, collaborative and continuous learning culture. We could look back at our journey and evidently see that fractal patterns underpin not only the behaviors of life-long learners but also are foundational to the culture of continuous learning organizations.

When we think about these learning journeys and correlate them with the three fractal characteristics, we can see that learning is like a true fractal pattern, where the parts resemble the whole and the whole resembles the parts; yet of course the whole is much more than the parts. We have observed that this is the crucial element of the attitude that perpetual learners and continuous learning organizations must have towards learning. They must never be content with acquiring just a part of knowledge (which may seem like whole at that time), but pursue learning the whole, ardently by going wider and deeper. Education can have a formal start and end, but learning must be **eternal**. We are learning organisms and all of us are on a life-long learning journey.

Fractals are self-organized images of dynamic systems that are created by repeating a simple process over and over in an ongoing feedback loop. Although they may seem complex at first, if we look closely we will glean that they are created by repeating the fundamental fractal over and over. Similarly, we have seen that although a well-intended learning journey may seem overwhelming initially, it can be mastered over a period of time by leaning on just a few fundamental constructs. Learning too is **self-organized**, wherein a learner chooses a preferred way to learn, and hones the craft over time by repetitively applying learning constructs; supported by continuous feedback received along the learning journey.

Fractals are formed as the patterns intricately get connected with one another and by virtue of this interaction feedback gets disseminated; eventually everything connects to everything else. Similarly, we have observed that learning journeys thrive when **learning efforts are connected** with one another. Learners must not only seek to explore the breadth and depth of the parts that they learn, but also learn to appreciate the connections between various elements and gradually progress towards seeking the whole.

These three properties viz. eternal, self-organized, and connected, lend beauty, creativity and surprise to learning; just as they do to any other fractal pattern. Knowing these properties of learning not only adds wonder to such a fundamental aspect of our lives, but also guides us to acquire the virtues of perseverance, discipline and curiosity which are crucial to our success as life-long learners. Fig 1.7 depicts **The Learning Fractal** which represents these virtues in tandem with the properties of fractals. Eternity inspires a learner to acquire perseverance and continuously grow with learning, self-organized leads to discipline as it emphasizes the importance of a fundamental process being performed repeatedly, and connectedness instills curiosity where the learner appreciates how learning accumulates and compounds with time.

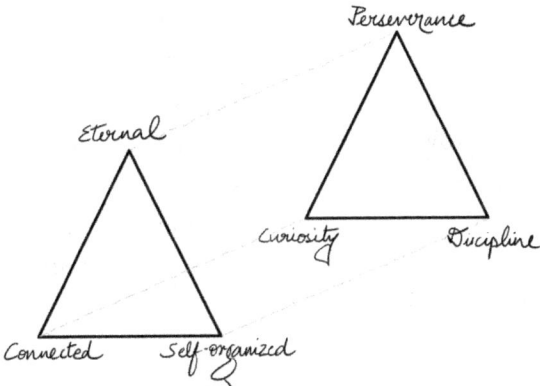

Fig 1.7: The Learning Fractal

In our experience as learning professionals, we have often observed that enterprises and individuals are typically awed by the eternity of learning journey ahead of them as they strive to acquire skills to stay relevant and prepare for the future. They regularly face this pertinent question when they introspect on their learning journeys - "Are we learning enough?". As Josh Waitzkin, author of The Art of Learning, says "The key to pursuing excellence is to embrace an organic, long-term learning process, and not to live in a shell of static, safe mediocrity. Usually, growth comes at the expense of previous comfort or safety.". **Perseverance is the key here.**

Individuals and organizations must stay true to their learning journeys and strive to enhance their skills and capabilities enthusiastically. They must ask themselves - "Are we consistent in our learning?", and adapt nimbly on their learning journeys with commitment. As Abigail Adams, former first lady of the United States of America has aptly put it, "Learning is not attained by chance, it must be sought for with ardor and attended to with diligence". **Discipline is the key here.**

Individuals and organizations frequently encounter a myriad of new skills and capabilities as they progress on their learning journeys. Along their journey they come across different paths and are often puzzled with the question - "What should I learn?", and realize that everything they don't know is something they can learn. They should remember to explore everything that they come across, and be assured that eventually all the dots get connected to swiftly propel their learning journey towards achieving the 'Whole'. As Doris Lessing, a British-Zimbabwean novelist and Nobel prize winner in literature eloquently put it – "That is what learning is. You suddenly understand something you've understood all your life, but in a new way". **Curiosity is the key here.**

In his play, "As You Like It", Shakespeare vividly represents drudgery in the context of formal education as "And then the whining schoolboy, with his satchel, And shining morning face, creeping like snail, Unwillingly to school". Unfortunately, this image of learning continues to persist, casting a shadow on the joy of acquiring knowledge. However, we believe that when learners embrace the learning fractal by imbibing the virtues of perseverance, discipline and curiosity, learning blooms to life. The learning fractal has the potential to shape learning journeys and act as the force that transforms learning into an organic and sustainable process. The learning fractal holds the key to unlocking our learning potential as it serves as a guide which helps bring order to the chaos in our learning journeys.

It is important to note that the learning fractal we just described is pretty generic and can be applied to amplify one's learning potential in virtually any area of learning. From sports to science, music to meditation, or art to engineering, one can learn to master anything by inculcating the virtues of perseverance, discipline and curiosity and navigate the eternal, self-organized and connected learning journeys associated with it.

Just as fractals are being used in various areas such as physics, mathematics, architecture, medicine, geology and finance to solve complex problems, in this book we will use the learning fractal to address the complexity associated with learning digital skills. We have envisioned this book as a playbook for perpetual learners to successfully navigate their digital journeys. And we specifically delve into how the learning fractal can guide individuals to acquire digital skills, and enterprises to build an ecosystem that promotes digital skills learning and fosters a progressive learning culture. It is important to note that digital skills are not just technology skills, it is always about technology + people skills. As Ray Kurzweil says "Our technology, our machines, is part of our humanity. We created them to extend ourselves, and that is what is unique about human beings."

Digital skills are key to the success of individuals in any enterprise today. This is because irrespective of what kind of products or services an enterprise offers, it is fundamentally a technology enterprise on a digital journey. As Christopher Little, a software executive and one of the earliest chroniclers of DevOps, said, "Every company is a technology company, regardless of what business they think they're in. A bank is just an IT company with a banking license." Technology is permeating every arm of today's enterprises and any enterprise that shies away from adapting to the technology advancements typically pushes itself behind, if not setting itself up for failure.

Although each enterprise is unique and so is its digital journey, what is common is the need for a workforce equipped with the right digital skills. The sustainability of such a workforce in the ever changing landscape of technology hinges upon its ability to learn and adapt. Thus every enterprise on its digital journey should aim to become a learning organization that is both robust and nimble to evolve with time.

To become a learning organization, enterprises have to overcome three key challenges:

> 1. They have to come to terms with the vast expanse of ever changing technologies that they encounter on their digital journeys. Individuals in today's enterprises have to not only acquire a wide variety of digital skills to navigate the modern technology landscape but also be able to nimbly adapt to the evolving technology trends and consumer demands.

> 2. They have to adapt to the growing expectation of talent archetypes - which is changing from becoming a specialist to becoming a generalist to becoming a versatilist. To elaborate further, earlier enterprises sought individuals who could specialize in a given area and bring in deep expertise in the field. Soon, as the technology landscape expanded, they sought individuals who could be generalists with knowledge and skills across a wide range of areas to bring in a broader perspective.

Today, given the ever changing and rapidly evolving landscape of technology, enterprises seek individuals who are versatile enough to adapt to changing circumstances and quickly acquire new skills. For example, Infrastructure engineers today are expected to grow into SRE (Site Reliability Engineer) roles where they fuse their knowledge and skills of infrastructure with the nuances of software engineering to enhance the reliability, and stability of enterprise systems.

3. And finally, enterprises and their learning teams must create and foster a sustainable learning ecosystem which nurtures a progressive learning culture. Individuals, enterprises and learning teams must be able to not only recognize the need for learning, but also have a bias for action to create an environment that is conducive for learning which eventually bolsters their agility and catalyzes innovation.

In this book, we will explore how individuals, enterprises and learning teams can overcome these three challenges by drawing inspiration from the learning fractal. Fig 1.8 depicts the overall learning journey of this book. So far, in this chapter, we have already seen how learning exhibits fractal properties and how the learning fractal, and its virtues of perseverance, discipline and curiosity, hold the key to mastery in any learning journey.

In chapter 2 of this book, we address the first challenge of coming to terms with the vast expanse of ever changing technologies that enterprises and individuals encounter on their digital journeys. We have observed that in the realm of technology, as enterprises and individuals progress on digital journeys they are required to master a plethora of digital skills to navigate the vast and complex landscape of technology. The potpourri of technology terms such as Generative AI (Artificial Intelligence), Deep Learning, Blockchain, Extended Reality, Quantum Computing, Microservices, DevSecOps, Containers, and many such buzz words, may seem daunting at first. But we

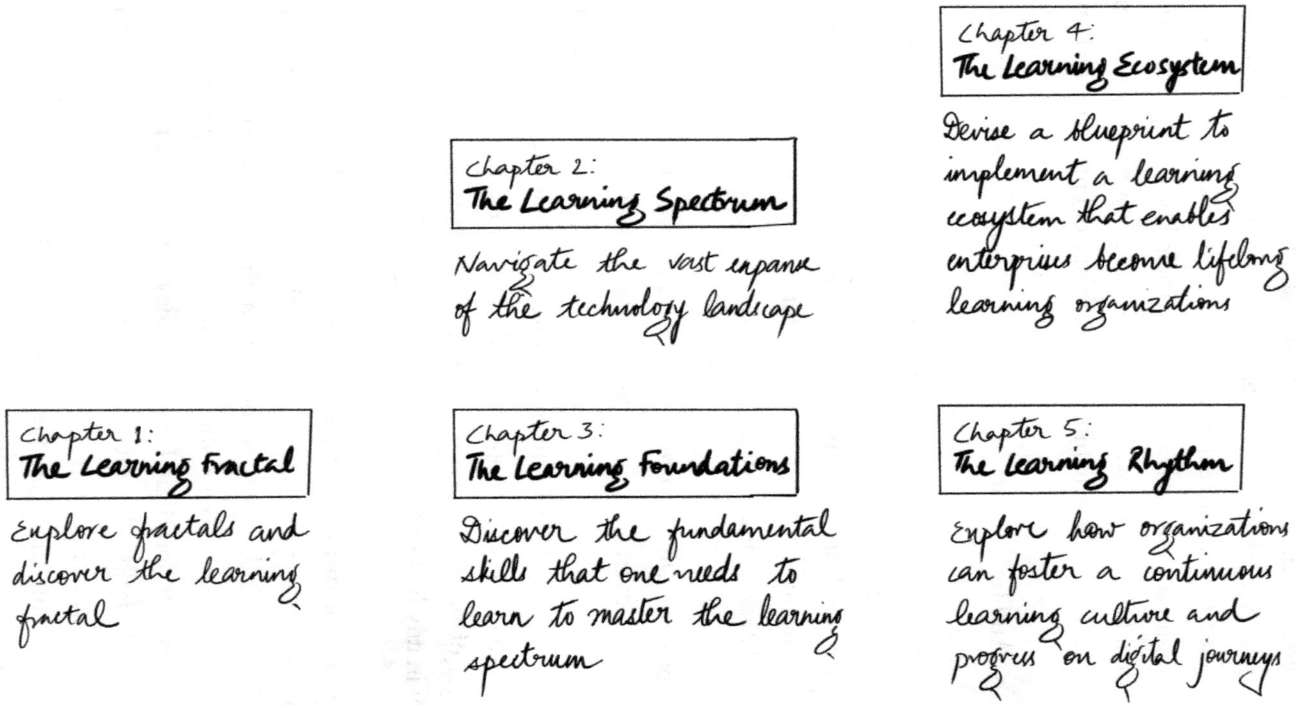

Chapter 4:
The Learning Ecosystem

Devise a blueprint to implement a learning ecosystem that enables enterprises become lifelong learning organizations

Chapter 5:
The Learning Rhythm

Explore how organizations can foster a continuous learning culture and progress on digital journeys

Chapter 2:
The Learning Spectrum

Navigate the vast expanse of the technology landscape

Chapter 3:
The Learning Foundations

Discover the fundamental skills that one needs to learn to master the learning spectrum

Chapter 1:
The Learning Fractal

Explore fractals and discover the learning fractal

Fig 1.8: Learning Journey of this book

will draw inspiration from the fundamental characteristics of fractals to navigate this complex technology landscape. To start with, when we delve deeper into understanding the digital journeys, we observe that it ultimately boils down to the digital experiences that end users look and feel. Which is why, we consider digital experiences as the true pivot to discover and navigate the digital skills that one encounters on their digital journeys. Using the prism of digital experiences, we will visualize the vast and complex learning spectrum of digital skills which too exhibits fractal properties. We will observe how the learning spectrum - our learning fractal, is eternal as we explore the breadth and depth of its various areas. We will also observe its connected nature as we zoom out to appreciate how the various areas of the spectrum intertwine with one another to bring digital experiences to life.

Comprehending the intricacies of the learning spectrum brings the second challenge of evolving talent archetypes to the fore. To start with, learners may already be dabbling with the pertinent question of how to enhance their skills and specialize deeply in one of the areas of the spectrum, and at the same time command a view of how the breadth of the spectrum grows and evolves. Peering into their own future in the context of the vast learning spectrum could very well leave them perplexed and wondering as to how they can become a versatilist who is equipped to weather changes and disruptions. In chapter 3 of this book, we will explore the fundamental building blocks that one must master in order to equip themselves to ride the waves of change and disruptions. We will start by zooming into the learning spectrum to discover the fundamental fractal that repeats all over the spectrum; representing the self-organized nature of our learning fractal. We will then observe how the fundamental fractal appears in the different areas of the spectrum and learn to master it in order to successfully navigate our learning journey.

Ultimately, to catalyze their digital journeys through continuous learning, enterprises must overcome the third challenge of building and sustaining a learning ecosystem which fosters a progressive learn -ing culture. In chapter 4 of this book, we will explore the key aspects of a holistic learning ecosystem which is essential to build and sustain a future-ready workforce. We will explore a reference learning archi- tecture that can be used as a blueprint to create the foundation of the learning ecosystem. We will also discuss how enterprises and their learning teams can foster a progressive learning culture that sup- ports life-long learning which is crucial for the learning ecosystem to thrive. The learning ecosystem essentially forms the breeding ground for germinating and nurturing the learning fractal. In chapter 5, the last chapter of this book, we will explore the various rhythms that need to be orchestrated in unison to harmonize the eternal, self-orga- nized and connected learning rhythm. We will learn about the bias for action which individuals, enterprises and learning teams should have in order to shape the learning.

" काक चेश्ट बको ध्यानं, श्वान निद्रा तथैव च ।
अल्पहारी गृह त्यागी, विद्यार्थी पंच लक्षणं ।। "

" Kaak Cheshta, Bako Dhyanam, Shwan Nidra Tathaiwa Cha I
Alpahari, Grihtyaagi, Vidyarthi Panch Lakshnam II "

" The perseverance of a crow, the concentration of a crane, the alertness of a dog, exercise self-restraint with respect to food, and denounce the world of comfort in the pursuit of knowledge, are the five qualities that a learner should possess."

This is a profound and timeless Sanskrit shloka which elucidates the attributes that every learner must strive to attain. "Kaak Cheshta" refers to the persistent efforts of the crow in the fable where a parched crow (kaak) comes upon a high and narrow neckedpitcher with very little water at the bottom. Using its wits, the crow persistently picks and drops pebbles into the pitcher to raise the level of water and quench its thirst. Learners too must put persistent efforts like the crow and be relentless in their efforts to quench their thirst for knowledge.

"Bako Dhyanam" refers to the behavior of a crane (bako) that demonstrates remarkable focus and discipline while waiting for the perfect opportunity to catch a fish. The crane understands that trying to catch small fish will not only leave it unsatisfied but also disrupt the water, warning the larger fish of its presence. Instead, the crane patiently waits for the right-sized fish to come along before making its move. Learners too should be disciplined in their pursuit of learning and strive for excellence.

"Shwan nidra" refers to the alert nature of the dog (shwan). Dogs are typically light sleepers and are alert to the circumstances around them. Learners too should stay alert and curious about the world around them and always be ready to soak in new knowledge.

"Alpahari" translates to abstemious and refers to practicing abstinence or exercising moderation in consumption of food. Similarly, in the context of learning, one must be disciplined to moderate their negative thoughts and feed their mind with positivity in order to make steady progress in their learning journey.

Finally, "Grihatyagi" refers to the practice of students in India during the vedic times leaving the comfort of their homes to study under teachers(gurus) in Gurukul. In this context, it refers to learners stepping out of their comfort zones to actively explore and pursue new learning.

The learning fractal, just like the shloka, encourages learners to inculcate the virtues of perseverance, discipline and curiosity, and serves as a guide for individuals, and enterprises along their learning journeys. It is the key to demystifying the spectrum of digital skills, discovering the underlying foundational skills, designing a robust learning ecosystem, harmonizing the learning rhythms, and ultimately fostering a progressive learning culture.

Chapter-2
The Learning Spectrum

The Grand Canyon, Arizona, USA is a wonder of the natural world that is probably on every nature lover's travel wishlist. Its majestic and dramatic rock formations, stunning colors and textures, and rich ecological diversity contribute to its status as a must-see destination. The Colorado river had a great role to play in the formation of the canyon. Over millions of years, as the river flowed across the plateau it gradually eroded the rock formations, cut channels and carved the canyon deeper. The deepening of the canyon changed the course of the river too, and led to the formation of meanders (or bends) which gradually grew larger over time.

Several parts of the landscape of the Grand Canyon resemble fractal patterns[13]. Firstly, just like any fractal pattern, at the first glance, the Grand Canyon too may seem infinite (eternal) and overwhelming. Secondly, when we zoom into any part of the Grand Canyon, we can observe the self-similarity in the rock formations formed by repeated erosion, and we may be able to correlate this with the self-organized nature of fractals. Finally, the Canyon is made up of several segments that were formed in different eras[14] which eventually got connected to become the current path of the Colorado river, reminding us of how different parts of a fractal connect with one another to become the whole. And just like a complex fractal pattern (such as the Mandelbrot set), the Grand Canyon offers different views and experiences based on where you are looking at it from.

Modern digital experiences that every one of us interact with today have some striking resemblances to the Grand Canyon. For instance, modern digital experiences offer unique, varied and personalized experiences to the end users who consume them, just like how everyone who visits the Grand Canyon comes away with their own unique impression. Also, interestingly, like the Canyon, modern digital experiences too are ever changing and continuously evolving (of course, not comparable in the time scale!). Finally, just like how the Colorado river forms the life force of the Canyon and continuously crafts it, a spectrum of digital skills form the underlying force responsible for crafting these modern digital experiences.

There is a wide gamut of digital experiences that you regularly interact with and often the role of technology in bringing them to life is obvious. You might find yourself acknowledging its role when you read a book (digital version), plan your next vacation (maybe to the Grand Canyon!), connect on social media, choose entertainment options, explore the night sky, or maybe even find your soulmate. Technology permeates several aspects of our lives already and is set to transform more of our experiences as the difference between the digital and physical worlds blur.

If you were to zoom in on a popular digital experience - online shopping (like we zoom in to see the rock formations of the canyon), you will encounter a variety of features and attributes that come together to shape it up. For most people, this experience is fairly routine and they navigate it without second thought. However, if you pause for a moment and think about how this experience is brought to life, the complexity that underpins it starts becoming more apparent and may be overwhelming to fathom at one go. To elaborate, you may be intrigued by the various technologies that enable you to shop online anytime and anywhere over a web browser or mobile app in a secure manner, the insightful recommendations that personalize your shopping experience, the myriad ways through which you can pay instantly, the real-time tracking of your shipment, and many more. Contemplating the underlying spectrum of digital skills and technologies that are used to construct this experience might seem daunting at first. However, if we zoom in further and take inspiration from the characteristics of fractals, we should be able to demystify these components one piece at a time, explore the connections between them, discover the underlying fundamentals, and marvel at the simplicity of its core.

In this chapter we will use the prism of digital experiences to view our learning fractal - the learning spectrum. Digital experiences form the core of the digital journeys of enterprises and individuals, and therefore is the true pivot to discover and navigate the spectrum of underlying digital skills used to create them. By navigating the different parts of any digital experience we will be able to discover the different parts of the learning spectrum and in turn explore the vast expanse of digital skills that come together to create modern digital experiences. We will start by demystifying the various attributes of digital experiences and then we will explore the different parts of digital experiences to uncover the different parts of the underlying technology landscape. Eventually we will visualize the entire learning spectrum and appreciate the connections between its various parts.

Although this chapter which explores our learning fractal - the vast and interconnected learning spectrum - may seem daunting at first, we will find relief when we discover its simplicity in the next chapter - the learning foundations.

The Prism of Digital Experiences

Online shopping is a very popular digital experience that all of us consume today. The earliest examples of online shopping dates back to the Boston Computer Exchange[15] founded in 1982. It was one of the first examples of an online marketplace for buying and selling used computers. Sellers would upload their inventory to the marketplace's database and buyers could browse it from a public access system and then place orders using a telephone and pay for it. Eventually, the company created a fully automated online auction and trade system, and became an Internet-based business too. The online shopping marketplaces of today are very different from those of yesteryears; they have evolved to the needs of consumers like us. The online marketplaces of today connect us with sellers around the world from the convenience of a variety of devices such as desktops, mobile phones, and even smart home assistants. They not only offer a wide range of products but also allow us to pay for our purchases securely and instantly. Further, by offering recommendations on products and forecasting when our order is likely to be delivered, these modern online shopping experiences are transforming our shopping behaviors and influencing our choices.

Contemplating the different facets of such a modern digital experience may seem intangible or unfathomable at first, however if we look closely, any compelling digital experience can be broken down into 7 key attributes, as depicted in Fig 2.1.

Intimacy lies at the forefront of any digital experience and characterizes the belongingness of the users with the digital experiences. It ensures that users repeatedly seek to engage with the experiences and ultimately stay connected to the brands that provide them. You may remember the time when most of us were shy to even purchase a shoe online, however today enterprises are building rapport with us through simple, friendly, and secure digital journeys which make us comfortable to even purchase a wedding ring over an online shopping app.

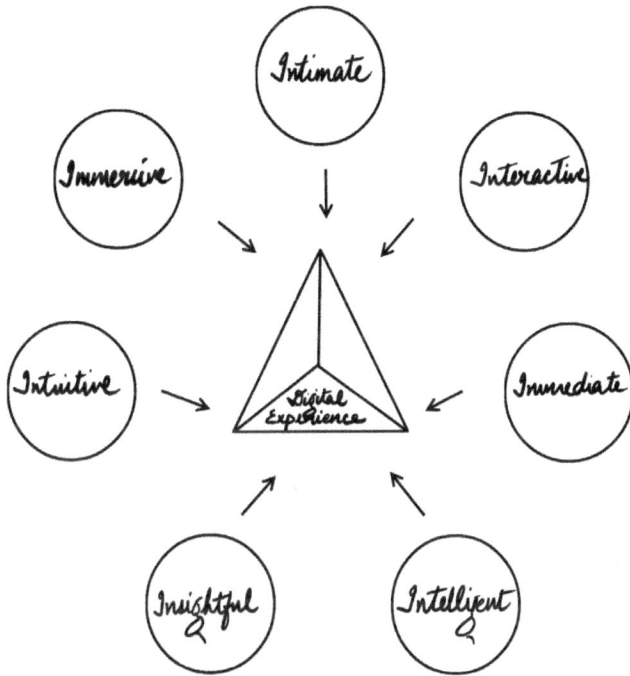

Fig 2.1: The 7 Key Attributes of Compelling Digital Experiences

Modern digital experiences are expected to cooperate with the users and delight them in every single **interaction**. Interactive digital experiences respond to a range of inputs from users such as gestures or voice commands making the interaction not only comfortable but also as natural as possible for the users. Adding various interactive elements also helps the brands to draw the attention of the users in several ways and in turn establish a bond with them. You would agree that the variety of interactive options in modern experiences such as scrolling, right swiping, left swiping, pinching, tapping, etc. delight you more in contrast to dull and boring yesteryear's digital experiences that provided only limited interactive elements. We can evidently observe this in modern online shopping apps that allow you to swipe to see more images of a product or explore different items in a catalog, pinch and zoom into product images, and scroll or click/tap to view more details, making the whole experience highly interactive. What's more, with the adoption of AR/VR (Augmented Reality / Virtual Reality) technologies, the way users interact with digital experiences could see a remarkable change where the interactive elements would respond to eye movements, hand gestures and/or voice commands.

Users of modern digital experiences typically seek instant gratification and expect the experiences to provide **immediate** responses or feedback to their actions. Brands that build digital experiences must recognize the key role that immediacy plays in ensuring that users are continuously engaged with the experiences. You may be able to correlate this desire for immediacy with your experience of selecting a payment gateway during online shopping; where in you are more likely to repeatedly choose those payment options that are quick to send an OTP (one time password) and those apps that provide instant access to this OTP from your messages onto the payment screen. Further, immediacy is not just prevalent in how digital experiences respond to user actions, but it is also permeating into how users desire immediate outcomes in the real world too. You may have observed that you often tend to choose those online shopping apps which offer faster delivery options such as next-day or same-day delivery. This immediacy in the real world too is powered by underlying technologies.

Digital experiences that demonstrate **intelligent** behavior by contextualizing their responses to the user and her environment elevate the overall experience of the user. Brands embed such intelligent behavior to treat users consistently and personally irrespective of the channel from where the experience is consumed - web, mobile, voice assistant, etc. You might have enjoyed this intelligent behavior while receiving pertinent search results when looking for a product in an online shopping app just by providing a relatively small set of keywords. You may also have enjoyed this intelligent behavior in other digital experiences such as when receiving the quickest/best route to a destination, or next word suggestions while responding to emails.

At the heart of every digital experience is its **insightfulness**. Compelling digital experiences engage the users with profound insights and ensure that users are presented with relevant data and perspectives to act upon. Brands harness the power of data that they source from user behaviors and actions to mine such insights and present them to the user. You would have observed that such insightful recommendations form a crucial part of your experience while shopping online, or choosing entertainment options.

Any highly usable and desirable digital experience has to place the users at the center and provide a natural segue to appropriate user journeys in order to enjoy advocacy from its users. Brands ensure this by making their digital experiences highly **intuitive** so that the users can quickly discover the important features provided as part of the experience. You might relate to this by observing a pattern across your favorite digital experiences in terms of the visual cues from the icons used, the position of various features such as search, navigation bars, etc., consistent responses to various gestures and actions, and many more. In an online shopping app, typically the cart is to the top right/bottom right, the navigation pane is on the left, and the various icons used make it easy to comprehend the action to be performed.

Finally, as digital experiences are increasingly becoming a part of the users' lives the differences between the physical and digital worlds are blurring. Brands are making their digital experiences **immersive** to ensure that users become a part of the experience, just as much as the experiences become a part of their lives. You might have been pulled into this immersiveness while exploring the night sky through sky gazing apps or kickboxing on a gaming console. In terms of online shopping, you may be amazed by the ease with which you can place an order for an item through a conversation with a voice assistant or try out how a new couch looks in your living room using your phone's camera with the help of AR/VR.

Various digital experiences such as online shopping, social media, gaming, banking, and even learning fundamentally exhibit these seven attributes of intimacy, interactivity, immediacy, intelligence, insightfulness, intuition and immersiveness. Having explored these key attributes of digital experiences, you may now be able to observe the presence (or absence) of them in the digital experiences that you interact with in your day-to-day lives. You may also be able to appreciate why some digital experiences are more compelling than others.

Let us now use the prism of digital experiences to demystify the learning spectrum (our learning fractal), which enterprises and individuals need to become familiar with in order to progress on their digital journeys.

The Breadth and Depth of the Learning Spectrum

Sir Isaac Newton did not just stop at passing a beam of sunlight through a prism to observe its constituent colors, he went a step further to recombine the spectrum back to demonstrate that white light is composed of colors and further established that color is a property of light and not of the object itself.

Just like how the colors on a rock are a property of the light and not the rock itself, the 7 attributes that we observe in the various features of modern digital experiences, as outlined in the previous section, are caused by the components of our learning fractal - the learning spectrum.

If we further attempt to demystify the learning spectrum using the prism of digital experiences, we will observe that like a normal spectrum, the learning spectrum too contains visible and invisible parts, as depicted in Fig 2.2. These visible and invisible parts are made up of a plethora of digital skills that one has to fathom in order to explore the breadth and depth of the learning spectrum.

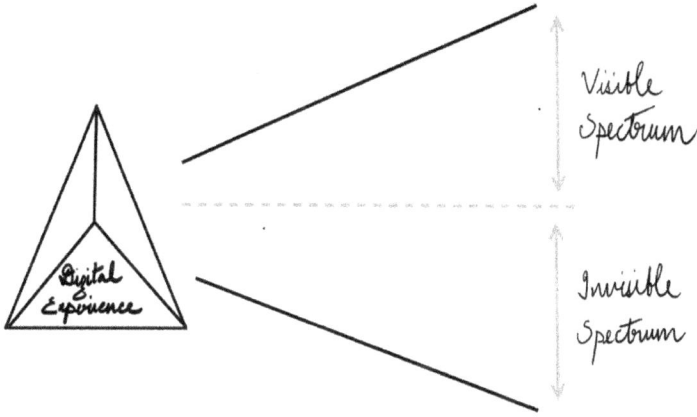

Fig 2.2: Visible and Invisible parts of the Learning Spectrum

The visible part of the spectrum represents the digital skills required to build those aspects of digital experiences that we see and/or feel as we consume them. For example, in the online shopping app that we discussed earlier, the skills and technologies that form the visible spectrum help create the app that users can access anytime, anywhere on their mobile devices. Further, the components of the visible spectrum also take center stage in making the experience insightful for the users by providing personalized recommendations and enhancing the shopping experience.

The invisible part of the spectrum comprises the skills and technologies that are employed under the hood to enable the full capabilities of digital experiences. For example, in the online shopping app, while the visible spectrum is responsible for showing the products that a user can buy or recommend those that the user could be interested in, the invisible part of the spectrum is responsible for all the activities and processes that happen under the hood. To elaborate, these activities and processes may include maintaining an inventory of products, processing the payment from the user against an order, fulfilling the order to ensure that the user gets the product that she ordered, and handling returns if any. The invisible part of the spectrum comprises several intricately connected digital skills that perform the heavy lifting, and are key to building digital experiences.

Discovering the visible and invisible parts of the learning spectrum by exploring it using the prism of digital experiences serves two purposes. First, it helps us understand what goes into crafting modern digital experiences i.e. what constitutes a digital experience, the parts that we can observe, and the parts that lie under the hood. Second, it serves as a guide on our learning journey, forming a map to navigate the breadth and depth of digital skills that we should become familiar with to create compelling digital experiences.

The Visible Spectrum

The visible part of the learning spectrum comprises the technologies and skill sets that are used to build those parts of digital experiences that users typically see and/or feel (or both). Exploring the visible spectrum entails learning the subset of the technology landscape which enables access to these experiences and makes them insightful while we are consuming it, as depicted in Fig 2.3.

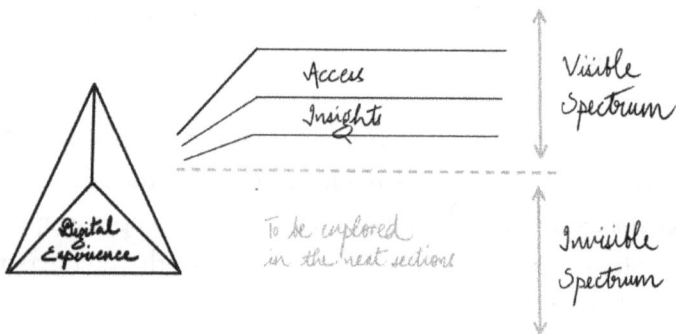

Fig 2.3: The Visible Spectrum

Access points

You may have noticed the trends in the different ways that we all have been consuming digital experiences over the last few decades. For example, online shopping has been there for decades now and the earliest experiences only offered an online catalog for users to browse through a web page and then buy items using a telephone. Over time, as technology progressed and enterprises leveraged digital skills, online shopping expanded to include features such as the shopping cart, processing payments online, and even further optimizing the apps for mobile devices, activating voice search, and many more. Not just online shopping but various other digital experiences have evolved from being accessed through simple web pages to immersive mixed realities and everything in between, from the time they first appeared during the dotcom era more than 3 decades ago. Modern digital experiences are accessed over a wide variety of touchpoints such as web, mobile, wearables, conversational interfaces, and extended reality interfaces, as depicted in Fig 2.4.

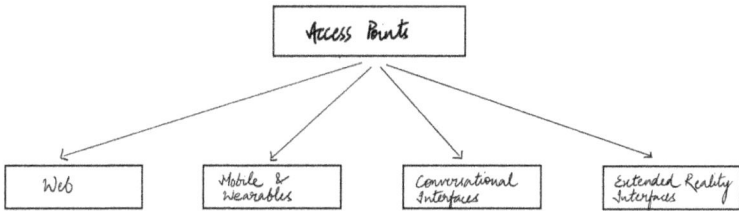

Fig 2.4: The access points

Building experiences for these myriad access points demand learning different technologies and skillsets. While some technologies and skill sets might be common across access points, others would be unique given the nature of the access points.

As we explore this part of the spectrum (and the other parts of the spectrum) we will encounter a wide variety of technologies and skill-sets. Each section would be a rapid survey of the key concepts of that part of the spectrum and would help you understand the landscape of digital skills and create a map to navigate your learning journey (using the references provided). Although these sections are primarily aimed at learners who may be a novice in either some or all of these areas of the spectrum, for those familiar with technology, these sections may seem fundamental, but can provide an insight into how to explain technology to others and guide them on their learning journeys.

Web

Web as an access point refers to connecting with digital experiences over browsers such as Google Chrome, Mozilla Firefox, Apple Safari, Microsoft Edge, etc. on various devices such as televisions, desktops, laptops, tablets, or even mobile phones of varied screen sizes. These experiences have been typically referred to as webapps/websites/portals.

The origin of the web can be traced to the time when Sir Tim Berners-Lee developed a system of interlinked hypertext documents and created the HyperText Markup Language (HTML) to improve information sharing among scientists when working at CERN. Digital experiences on the Web have come a long way in the past 3 decades. From being a mere collection of simple static interconnected pages typically consumed on a desktop computer, to becoming rich, interactive and indistinguishable from mobile apps that can be consumed across a variety of devices.

Based on the Digital 2023 report, as of Jan 2023 there are 5.16 billion users who consume the internet and on an average they spend 6h and 37m online.

Source: https://datareportal.com/reports/digital-2023-global-overview-report

If you look at Amazon's web page from 1995 (shown in Fig 2.5 below), and compare it to what you see today, you would observe how much it has changed. You will notice that the present web application is rich with images and media, contains interactive elements like navigation bars, buttons, carousels, etc., and is personalized for every user, and is far more sophisticated in comparison to the web page from 1995 which was a simple interface containing only text and links.

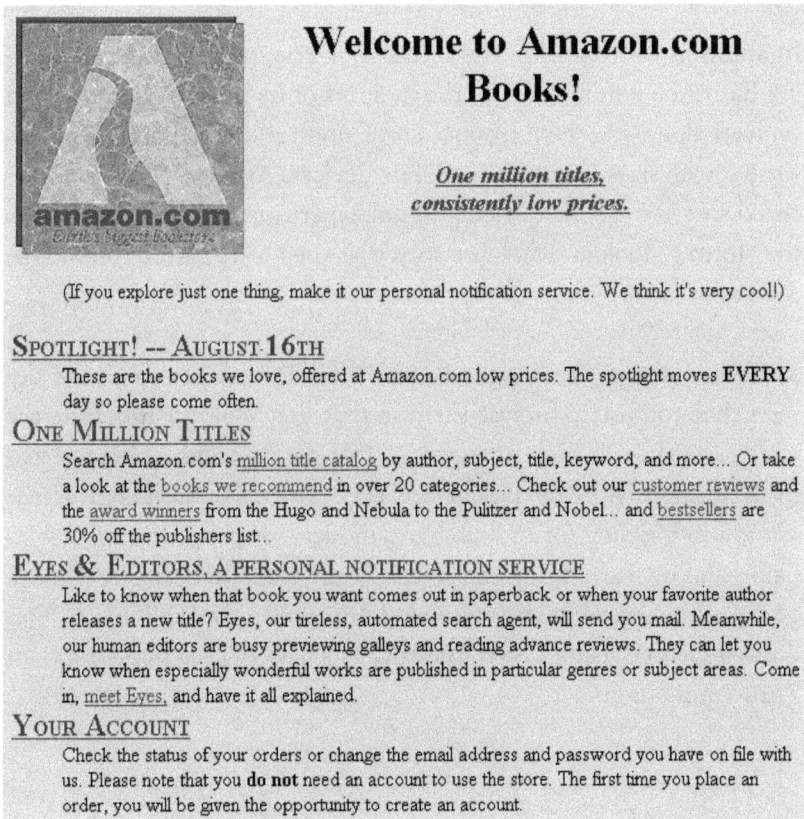

Welcome to Amazon.com Books!

One million titles, consistently low prices.

(If you explore just one thing, make it our personal notification service. We think it's very cool!)

SPOTLIGHT! -- AUGUST 16TH
These are the books we love, offered at Amazon.com low prices. The spotlight moves **EVERY** day so please come often.

ONE MILLION TITLES
Search Amazon.com's million title catalog by author, subject, title, keyword, and more... Or take a look at the books we recommend in over 20 categories... Check out our customer reviews and the award winners from the Hugo and Nebula to the Pulitzer and Nobel... and bestsellers are 30% off the publishers list...

EYES & EDITORS, A PERSONAL NOTIFICATION SERVICE
Like to know when that book you want comes out in paperback or when your favorite author releases a new title? Eyes, our tireless, automated search agent, will send you mail. Meanwhile, our human editors are busy previewing galleys and reading advance reviews. They can let you know when especially wonderful works are published in particular genres or subject areas. Come in, meet Eyes, and have it all explained.

YOUR ACCOUNT
Check the status of your orders or change the email address and password you have on file with us. Please note that you **do not** need an account to use the store. The first time you place an order, you will be given the opportunity to create an account.

Fig 2.5: Snapshot of Amazon.com's website from 1995[16]

Although there is a great deal of transformation in how digital experiences on Web look today in comparison to those of yesteryears, you may be surprised to know that the rich and varied experiences of billions of websites are almost all built using the same technologies: HTML[17], CSS[18] and JavaScript[19] that were introduced three decades ago. Mastering this underlying technology trio is key to learning to build modern digital experiences that are accessed over the Web access point. As you delve into mastering these technologies, you will learn that the functional content and layout of web pages is composed using HTML (HyperText Markup Language), the styling of the content and layout is enhanced with CSS (Cascading Style Sheets) and the rich interactions are powered by JavaScript (JS).

In addition to mastering the technology trio, a great deal of learning has to be emphasized on the nuances of its modernization which evolved alongside the introduction of smarter access points with diverse screen sizes, specifically mobile devices. As more consumers adopted smarter mobile devices, digital experiences on the Web had to transform to look and feel like apps that they were used to on mobile devices.

Modern webapps are designed to be fluid and adapt to suit the devices that you use to browse them so that they look great despite the screen size/type they are accessed in. This design technique is referred to as Responsive Web Design(RWD)[20] which is considered as the minimum baseline for building any modern webapp. It employs resizing and/or rearranging the layout of the webapp based on the real estate of the screen/device it is viewed in, as depicted in Fig 2.6. This is implemented using CSS frameworks such as Twitter Bootstrap[21] or Zurb Foundation[22].

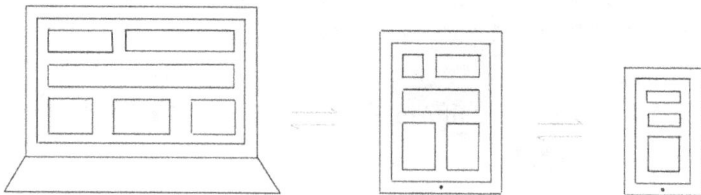

Fig 2.6: Responsive Web Design Illustration

In contrast to older webapps that used to load/refresh the entire view and data for each action performed by the user, modern webapps are more agile to load only the relevant section of view and data upon user action. This rich interactivity and immediacy that you feel in modern webapps which almost give them a native/mobile app like experience is achieved through Single Page Application (SPA)[23] design techniques implemented by modern JavaScript frameworks such as Angular[24] or React[25].

Single page applications typically load the user interface of the application first upon request and then (asynchronously) load the data required based on the user's interaction. For example, a web app built using either Angular or React for booking a hotel, would initially launch with a simple interface that allows the user to choose the dates of stay and the location they want to stay in. The app would then load a finite set of results (perhaps 30) based on the user's input. If the user scrolls down further indicating that she wants to see some more results, then the app would fetch and load the next set of finite results (maybe another 30). And while all of this happens, the user does not observe any change in the page and only experiences a relatively short wait time to load the new set of results. In contrast, traditional web apps, would perhaps have displayed each set of results on a new web page and the user would observe the interface and the results load together with a significant wait time between loading two sets of results.

As of March 2024, approximately 42.13% of top 10k websites use React and about 5.18% use Angular.

Source: https://trends.builtwith.com/javascript/React & https://trends.builtwith.com/framework/Angular

---

As you may have noticed, building Web based access points for digital experiences requires one to learn technologies such as HTML, CSS, JavaScript, Angular or React, Bootstrap, Zurb Foundation, and a few other supporting libraries or frameworks. If you zoom in further, you will notice that all these technologies are eventually connected with the primary technology trio of HTML, CSS and JavaScript. Ultimately, when you examine closely, you will learn that building web based access points ultimately boils down to two broad aspects - defining the position of the user interface elements and styling them (using HTML and CSS), and describing their behavior when users interact with them (using JavaScript).

Mobile and Wearables

Consuming digital experience on mobile devices is almost second nature to all of us. The spontaneity, ubiquity and indispensability of mobile has shifted digital experiences from the confines of a desk to the convenience of anytime and anywhere, making mobile as the most desirable medium to access digital experiences. Mobile app marketplaces and mobile-friendly webapps have seen immense growth since the introduction of the Apple iPhone in 2007.

Mobile apps that are downloaded from online app marketplaces such as Google Play Store or Apple App Store and installed on mobile devices are typically referred to as native apps. These apps are designed to run on a specific mobile platform (e.g. Apple, Android, etc.) and have access to the underlying capabilities (e.g. hardware sensors, NFC, etc.) of mobile devices. In order to build native mobile apps one needs to learn platform specific technologies such as Kotlin[26] & Android SDK[27] (Software Development Kit) for Android, and Swift[28] [29] & iOS SDK for Apple.

In 2023 alone, mobile app stores such as Google Play and Apple App Store recorded a cumulative of 257 billion global app downloads.

Source: https://www.statista.com/statistics/271644/worldwide-free-and-paid-mobile-app-store-downloads/

On the other hand, mobile friendly webapps leverage RWD and SPA principles and are built using the web technologies discussed in the previous section. While mobile friendly webapps have an advantage over the native apps that they can be accessed across diverse devices and have a single underlying codebase, they may fall short when it comes to speed, native look-and-feel, and access to the underlying device capabilities.

Hybrid apps bring together the best of both the worlds (native and web). They are built using web technologies that allow a single codebase to support a diverse set of mobile platforms, and at the same time exploit the underlying device capabilities. Facebook React Native[30], or Google Flutter[31] are some of the popular technologies used to build hybrid apps. These apps are then packaged and deployed onto online app marketplaces for users to download from and install on their mobile devices just like native apps.

The choice of the approach to building digital experiences on mobile, as depicted in Fig 2.7 depends on the range of devices to be supported, device capabilities to be leveraged, and the magnitude of speed and native look-and-feel desired. Typically enterprises opt for a mix of these approaches to deliver digital experiences for their consumers.

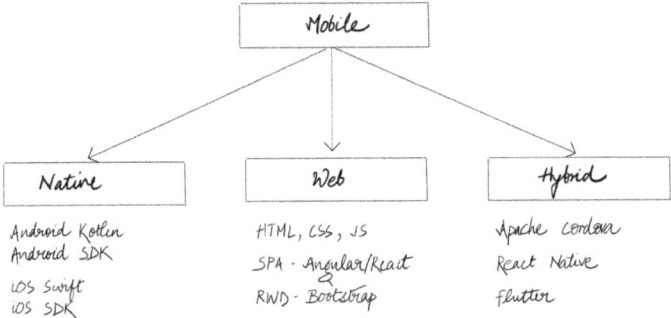

Fig 2.7: Approaches for Building Digital Experiences on Mobile

Wearable devices such as smartwatches and fitness trackers go hand-in-hand with mobile devices and play a key role in augmenting and accelerating the access to digital experiences. Wearable devices have become fairly common and it is quite likely that you have used one. You may already know that you can keep track of your health, hail a taxi, follow social media chatter, make notes, or even control your smart home with the help of these wearable devices.

The approach to build digital experiences for wearables is very similar to building native mobile apps. However, while designing digital experiences for wearables one has to take additional care to design apps that are appropriate to compact screen sizes and limited attention span. From the technology perspective, one has to additionally master platform specific technologies depending on the platform (Apple Watch, Android Wear, etc) that the targeted device(s) support. For example, to develop apps for Apple Watch one has to learn Apple WatchKit[32] along with native app technologies for Apple (Swift & iOS SDK).

You may have noticed here too that there are a wide range of technologies that one has to learn in order to build the mobile/wearable access point for digital experiences. As you zoom in further you will discover that, it all boils down to defining the user interface and processing the user interactions at the access point. The foundational skill to master here is programming which helps describe the logic that goes into designing the interfaces and describing the interactions.

Conversational Interfaces

Digital experience access points evolved from clunky command line interfaces (CLI) where users had to remember the commands, to intuitive graphical user interfaces that mimicked objects in real life; yet, these are far from the natural way humans interact with one another. As Golden Krishna, a renowned designer, aptly put it

"The best interface is no interface"; a new paradigm in the way digital experiences are accessed and consumed evolved in the form of conversational interfaces which can bake conversations and emotions together.

Conversational interfaces are found in various avatars and are primarily classified into two types - voice assistants and chatbots. Voice assistants such as Apple Siri, Amazon Alexa, Google Assistant are general purpose and can be employed for a variety of tasks such as playing music, hailing a taxi, or even controlling a smart home. These are integrated into smart devices such as smartphones, smart speakers, smart TVs, and even new-age cars. Chatbots on the other hand are more specific and focused on delivering digital experiences in areas of e-commerce, customer service, entertainment, etc. and are exposed over websites or messaging apps such as Facebook Messenger, Whatsapp, Slack and Telegram.

29.8% of Internet users aged 16-64 use voice assistants to search for information each week

Source: https://datareportal.com/reports/digital-2024-global-overview-report (Page 73)

Unless you have been living under a rock, you must have heard of OpenAI's ChatGPT[33] which took the world by a storm when it was launched towards the end of 2022. This chatbot which can be accessed as either a web app or a mobile app, uses Artificial Intelligence techniques such as Natural Language Processing (NLP) and Deep Learning (a subclass of Machine Learning), to answer questions, translate text, summarize text content, retrieve information, and engage in conversations. This chatbot can also produce text content using Generative AI techniques which we will discuss in a later section of this chapter.

All digital experiences accessed over conversational interfaces leverage NLP and Machine Learning (ML) techniques. While NLP helps translate the natural language used by humans into instructions that can be understood by the underlying app, ML enables conversational interfaces to become increasingly proficient with time by learning from the conversations that it has with the users. For example, as illustrated in Fig 2.8, while booking a taxi using a voice assistant like Apple Siri, a user speaks out her intent to go from point A to B which is converted to text that is then broken down into a sequence of instructions by the NLP engine in Siri.

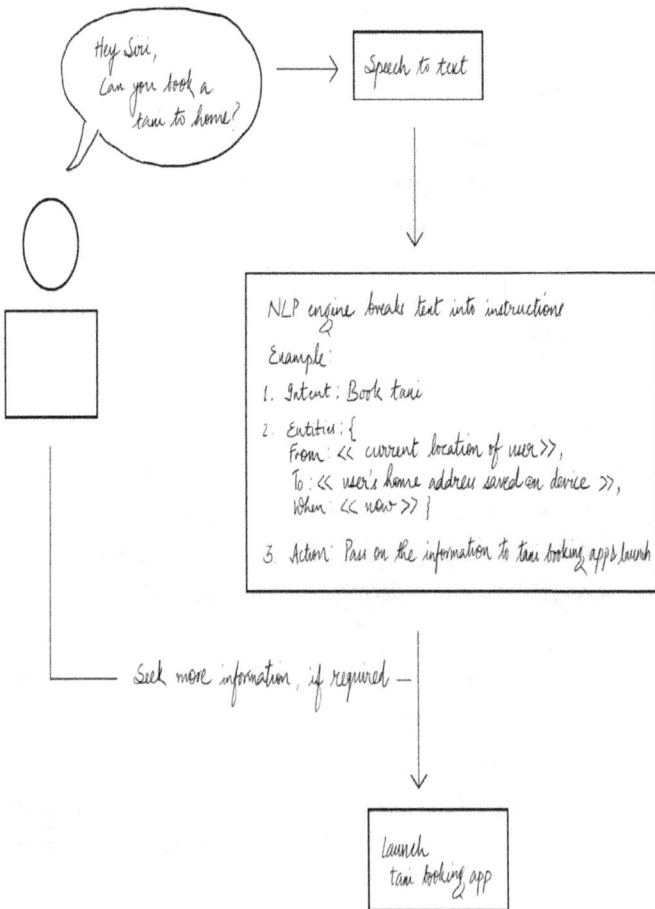

Fig 2.8: Conversational Interface in Action

These instructions are further passed onto the underlying taxi hailing app (such as Uber) which can both seek additional information from the user and convey the status of the booking back to the user via Siri. Over time, Siri also leverages machine learning to learn the user's preferences in order to become more efficient in conversations with her.

To build experiences for voice assistants such as Apple Siri, Amazon Alexa and Google Assistant, one needs to learn SiriKit[34], Alexa Skills kit[35] and Google Assistant SDK[36] respectively. To build chatbots, one can learn chatbot frameworks such as Google DialogFlow[37], Facebook Wit.ai[38], and Microsoft Bot Framework[39]. One can also use OpenAI's APIs to integrate ChatGPT into their web or mobile apps. These SDKs and frameworks abstract the required NLP and ML capabilities and make it easier to rapidly develop digital experiences for conversational interfaces. Above all, the key to baking conversations and emotions together lies in mastering the subtle art of designing engaging and empathetic conversational flows.

Extended Reality Interfaces

Extended reality (XR) interfaces are unique access points which blur the difference between the real and digital worlds. The experiences provided by extended reality interfaces are primarily driven by the user journeys one wants to create - they may be used to digitize the real world, or augment the real world with digital elements, or maybe both. These experiences can be accessed over mobile apps or specialized wearable devices such as AR/VR headsets like Meta (Oculus) Quest, Microsoft Hololens, etc. For example, you need not buy a plane ticket and fly to Paris every time to visit the Louvre Museum but rather choose to experience it digitally by taking a virtual museum tour. On the other hand, if you did visit the Louvre Museum and were curious to learn more about a specific exhibit, the information about it can be contextually delivered through a mobile app or wearable device. While in the first example, the real world is getting digitized; in the second one, the digital elements are being augmented with the real world.

Extended reality is an umbrella term for experiences that encompass various extents of intermixing the real and digital world objects. It includes Virtual Reality (VR), Augmented Reality(AR) and Mixed Reality(MR) as depicted in Fig 2.9. Virtual reality experiences are completely digital but the content that powers these experiences could be based on real world (first example of Louvre museum), or purely synthetic (gaming, simulator, etc.), or both. Augmented reality experiences overlay digital components on real world objects (second example of Louvre museum). Mixed reality experiences remove the boundary between real and digital worlds where digital objects can be embedded in real world spaces. It blurs the distinction between physical and virtual elements further by allowing users to interact with the virtual objects as if they were in the physical world. For example, you could have a holographic projection of an exhibit from the Louvre Museum in your living room, walk around it to inspect it from different angles, and interact with it using various gestures. By using advanced sensors, cameras, and spatial mapping, the MR experience may be able to provide feedback that feels very real - such as if you were touching a sculpture, you may be able to feel its texture and contours, making the experience highly immersive.

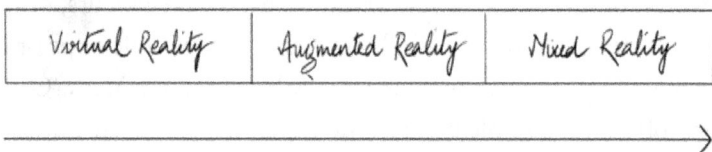

| Virtual Reality | Augmented Reality | Mixed Reality |

$$\longrightarrow$$

Fig 2.9: Extended Reality Spectrum

In the example of the online shopping app, Augmented Reality can be used to allow users to try out dresses or eye wear in the app thus allowing them to experience how it looks on them before making the purchase online. A popular example of this is the "Dress Up" feature on Snapchat which allows users to try out how different products look on them, share it with their friends and get feedback, and eventually buy it on the Snapchat app. This feature has been used more than 5 billion times by close to 250 million users since its launch in Jan 2021.

Building extended reality experiences requires one to master 2 key aspects during the development. The first is to model the objects that are embedded in digital spaces and design their spatial orientation and positioning. The second is to create the interactions that the user can perform on these objects. For modeling the objects one can use tools/platforms such as Unity[40], Unreal[41] and Vuforia[42]. The interaction design would depend on the devices on which the experience is consumed. For example, if the AR experience has to be consumed on a smartphone then one can use ARCore[43] for both Android and iOS, or ARKit[44] for iOS. On the other hand, if the experience has to be consumed on a wearable device such as Meta Quest (Oculus VR), then one has to use device specific SDKs (Oculus SDK[45] in this case) in order to exploit the full range of capabilities provided by the device.

Augmented Reality accounted for more than 55% of all Extended Reality experiences in 2021.

Source: https://www.precedenceresearch.com/extended-reality-market

Note: XR is however still only a small percentage of all digital experiences.

Here again you may have observed that creating access points for digital experiences in the extended reality space requires one to learn a variety of skills, however fundamentally it again boils down to creating the elements of the user experience and coding the interactions with the user. The fundamental skills that one has to master across the wide range of access points is the ability to define the user elements and describe the user interactions effectively.

Digital experience access points will continue to evolve with advancements in technology and offer newer and unique ways to engage with the users. So far we have explored that building these experiences for access points such as Web, Mobile, Conversation Interfaces and Extended Realties requires one to master unique technology skills specific to the access point, as depicted in Fig 2.10. However, one should note that honing skills such as curiosity, problem solving, and empathy, which are pretty much agnostic of any access point, play a crucial role in being able to build desirable, useful, and usable experiences.

Curiosity is the bedrock of observing the world around us and the inherent problems in it. Being curious and engaging deeply with these problems helps one build desirable digital experiences. Problem solving provides guidance to the creators of digital experiences to build solutions that are not just useful to users, but are also optimized to run smoothly on the various access points. Empathy provides the creator with the necessary framework to understand and feel the emotions and needs of the end users, imagine and design for specific accessibility requirements, and thereby create a positive and usable experience for everyone.

Having explored the various access points that end users consume digital experiences over, let us now explore the other aspect of the visible spectrum - Insights. Recall that digital experiences are packed with various insights in order to enrich and elevate the experience of the end users.

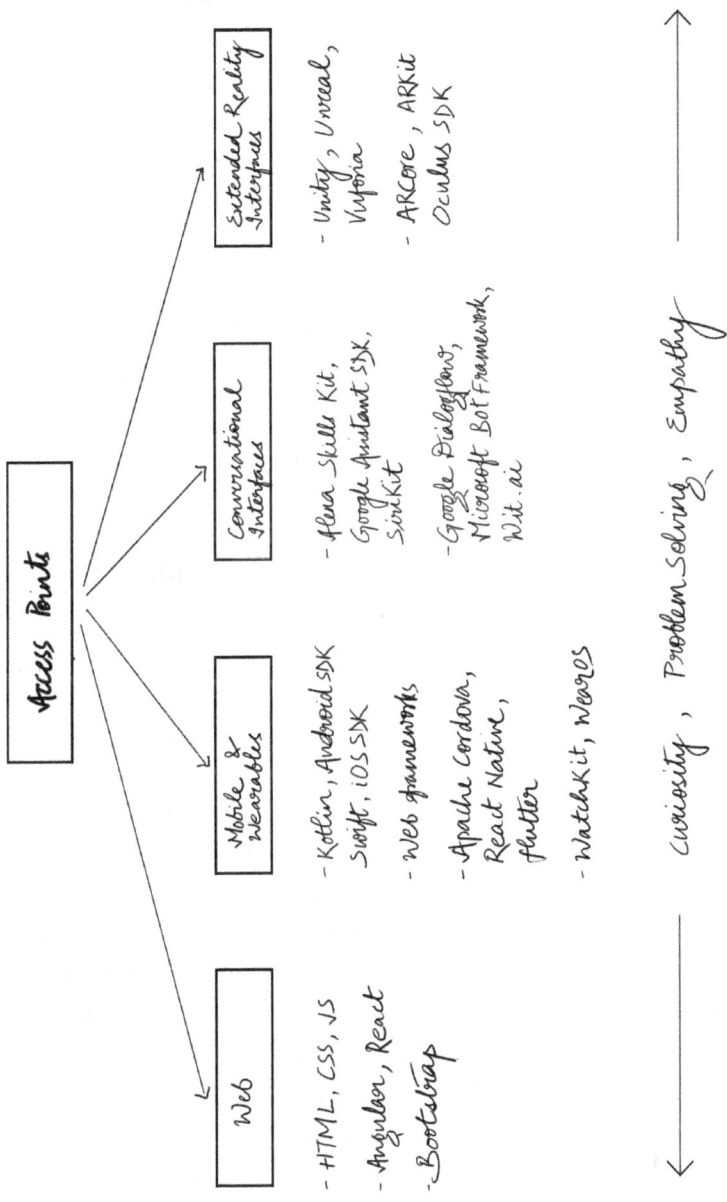

Access Points

Web
- HTML, CSS, JS
- Angular, React
- Bootstrap

Mobile & wearables
- Kotlin, Android SDK
  Swift, iOS SDK
- Web frameworks
- Apache Cordova,
  React Native,
  Flutter
- WatchKit, WearOS

Conversational Interfaces
- Alexa Skills Kit,
  Google Assistant SDK,
  SiriKit
- Google Dialogflow,
  Microsoft Bot Framework,
  Wit.ai

Extended Reality Interfaces
- Unity, Unreal,
  Vuforia
- ARCore, ARKit
  Oculus SDK

Curiosity, Problem Solving, Empathy

Fig 2.10: Building Experiences on Various Access Points

Insights

While diverse access points provide the immediacy, interactivity and immersiveness to digital experiences; the use of insights enriches the experiences and makes them intelligent, insightful, and intuitive. Recall that in the online shopping app example that we discussed earlier, the insightful elements of the app helped create a personalized shopping experience by providing recommendations related to you based on your demographic data, browsing history, wish lists, etc.

A varying degree of insights can be derived from data that is collected as users interact with digital experiences and then used to enhance their overall experience. For example, the health and fitness app on a smartphone or wearable can simply track the number of steps that a user takes in a day and use it to nudge her to achieve her daily moving goal. In a more complex scenario, the app may also be able to track the user's heart rhythm and forecast if she is at a risk of stroke. It can then use this insight to guide the user to adopt a healthier lifestyle. In the first example, the insights are simple and purely statistical; while on the other hand the insights in the second example are complex and almost replicate human intelligence and expertise.

> It is estimated that approximately 328.77 exabytes (328.77 x 10^{18} bytes) of data was created each day in 2022. Of this typically only a small percentage (approximately 2-3%) is saved and retained for later use.
>
> Source: https://www.statista.com/statistics/871513/worldwide-data-created/

Unlike access points which are more discrete and can co-exist independent of one another, insights could be better visualized as a continuum that ranges from simple statistical measures to complex artificial intelligence based outcomes. The insights continuum predominantly has three stages of insights derived from the data viz. Descriptive, Predictive and Cognitive insights, as depicted in Fig 2.11. Descriptive insights are simple and purely statistical; on the other hand predictive and cognitive insights are based on sophisticated machine learning and deep learning techniques.

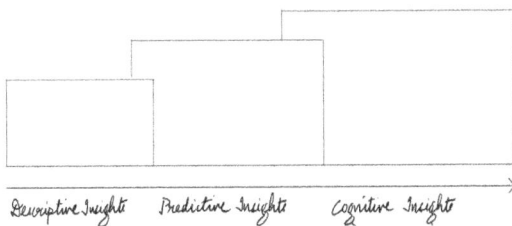

Descriptive Insights   Predictive Insights   Cognitive Insights

Fig 2.11: The Insights Continuum

The complexity of deriving insights increases as one progresses along the continuum, and each degree of insight provides significant value to enrich the user experience. One must note that it is neither necessary nor desirable to implement all degrees of insights. The choice of the level of insight to be derived is solely based on the user journey that one wants to achieve. Let us now explore this half of the visible spectrum.

Descriptive

Descriptive insights are often used to summarize the overall trend in the data and help explore the data at an overview level. For example, a bar chart that shows a user's step count for each day of the current week can help her track if she is poised to meet her daily moving goal. In another example, the online shopping app may record the average spend by a user over a period of time, and eventually incentivise users with relatively higher monthly average spending. Statistical measures such as count, mean, median, and variance are used to describe the data for the user and help them take actions.

In order to enrich digital experiences with descriptive insights, one needs to master fundamental statistical concepts and data visualization techniques. Statistical concepts help understand data at scale and identify behavior/patterns in data. Data visualization helps represent the data trends and glean insights in an intuitive and timely fashion. Deriving common statistical measures can easily be achieved using standard libraries or popular extensions of most programming languages like R[46], Python[47], Java[48], JavaScript, Scala[49], Julia[50], etc. One can also visualize the data using these libraries for analysis and self-consumption using simple charts like bar graphs, line charts, etc. However, to present these descriptive insights to end users over dashboard-like interfaces it is preferable to use sophisticated visualization tools such as Power BI[51], D3.js[52], Tableau[53] and Qlik[54].

Predictive

Predictive insights are used to model and/or replicate human behavior, intelligence or expertise in real world tasks or scenarios. These insights are derived using statistical and machine learning techniques which are applied on historical data pertinent to the relevant task or scenario. For example, you may have noticed how your emails are automatically classified as spam, or how an online shopping app proactively recommends items that you are looking to buy even before you search for them, or when your bank calls you to authorize a transaction when it suspects fraudulent activity on your card or account. In these examples, what you observe is the outcome of machine learning models that are built on historic data to glean the underlying patterns or behavior. In the online shopping app example, machine learning models are trained on historic data of orders, products that users browse, products that users share/recommend to others etc. to learn about users' preferences and predict what you are likely to buy.

Machine Learning(ML) has existed since the 1950s and has captivated scientists, and researchers over the years. It is typically defined as the field of study that gives computers the ability to learn without being explicitly programmed. In contrast to traditional software systems that are explicitly programmed and built on a set of well-defined rules, machine learning based systems use algorithms that discover and learn the underlying rules/patterns from historic data. Machine learning algorithms come in a variety of flavors, as depicted in Fig 2.12, and are chosen depending on the nature of data and the task that needs to be achieved.

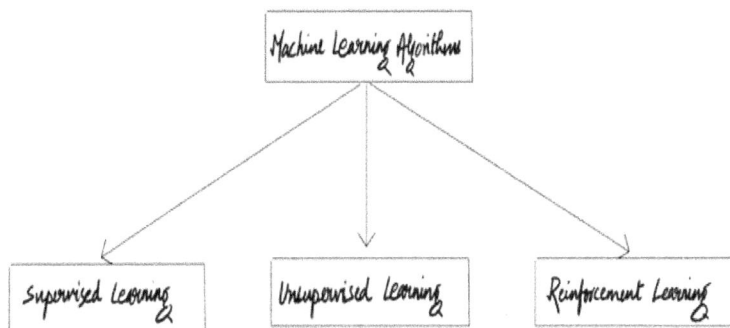

Fig 2.12: Machine Learning Algorithms

Most commercial use-cases of machine learning employ supervised learning[55] algorithms in order to build models on labeled historic data and make predictions. Labeled historic data comprises the inputs provided to a system and the outcome generated by the process. For example, to build an email spam detection model one would need to collect historic emails, label them as spam or not spam, and then use supervised learning algorithms such as Naive Bayes, Logistic Regression or k-Nearest Neighbours to train the model that can automatically predict if a new email is spam or not. Fundamentally, these algorithms are used to learn how to distinguish spam emails from non-spam emails based on various features in the data. For example, spam emails may originate from unfamiliar senders, contain poor spelling and grammar, and even have sensationalized content aimed to grab attention and/or evoke a sense of urgency to trick the user into revealing personal information. Features like these help the algorithms build a model that can distinguish between spam and non-spam emails.

In some cases, where labels to the historic data are not available, unsupervised learning[56] techniques are used to uncover patterns in the data by finding similarities in the data. For example, in an ecommerce app different groups/categories of customers can be identified and clustered together on the basis of data such as their search, browsing and purchase history. Algorithms such as k-Means clustering, hierarchical clustering, or expectation maximization are employed to discover such clusters. Further, these discovered clusters can then be used as labels to a supervised learning algorithm that can be used to provide recommendations to the customers.

While the output of clustering can be used as labels to train a supervised learning model, as discussed in the previous example; unsupervised learning techniques can also be used in a variety of other scenarios. One such scenario is where techniques such as Principal Component Analysis(PCA) are used to explore the various attributes of data, understand the correlation among them, and finally arrive at a smaller and useful set of attributes that can be used as input to supervised learning. For example, PCA can be used to compress large images into smaller sizes while retaining their key features; so that supervised learning tasks such as face recognition can be performed more efficiently up to a reasonable accuracy.

Reinforcement learning[57] addresses those classes of problems that are typically solved through continuous learning and optimization by trial and error. In these classes of algorithms, the learning happens as a result of observing the changes in an environment over a course of actions performed by the learning agent. For example, a reinforcement learning agent that is tasked to play the game of Go, needs to choose among several possible moves (actions) against the opponent at every stage of the game (environment) and finally retrospect on each move given the outcome of the match. These learning techniques can be used in a variety of scenarios which require planning, strategy, and exploration such as supply chain management, automated traffic controllers, trading and finance, resource management in computing clusters and robotics.

In all of the examples described above, predictive insights derived using statistical and machine learning techniques help elevate the overall digital experience for the users. An insightful email app helps the user focus only on the important emails and gets spam out of the way, a customer grouping system helps e-commerce apps deliver personalized experiences to users and is insightful of their needs, and an insightful trading/finance app can help users achieve their financial goals.

In order to build predictive insights and enrich digital experiences, one has to delve into three key topics - fundamental math and statistics, machine learning algorithms, and programming. Learning the fundamentals of math and statistics help understand how data is represented, transformed, and validated in order to be useful for building predictive models. Understanding the various machine learning algorithms helps choose the right kind of modeling technique to derive insights. Finally, programming helps bake these insights into the digital experiences and enrich the user experience.

Programming is a key component to bring these insights to life and it is applied at various stages of the process viz. collecting and process ing data, building machine learning models, and integrating insights with experiences over various access points. Libraries and frameworks such as NumPy[58], Pandas[59], Scikit-learn[60], TensorFlow[61], and PyTorch[62] can be used with programming languages such as Python in order to build machine learning models from the ground up. The popularity of machine learning driven insights and the impact it has on digital experiences has further propelled the need for democratizing the development of machine learning models and gave rise to the availability of several low-code / no-code platforms that anyone can use. Platforms such as Microsoft Azure Machine Learning[63] and Google Cloud Vertex AI[64] which provide abstractions over machine learning algorithms & underlying math, can be comfortably used by non-programmers and business users to quickly build machine learning models.

During the pandemic, Moderna was able to complete the sequence for its mRNA COVID-19 vaccine in just 2 days using machine learning built on AWS. The first clinical batch was released just 25 days later.

Source: https://aws.amazon.com/solutions/case-studies/moderna-machine-learning/

Cognitive

Cognitive insights are typically used to emulate various functions of the human brain such as speech recognition, image processing, language understanding, and knowledge modeling. These insights are derived by employing sophisticated machine learning techniques such as deep learning. Deep learning refers to a class of machine learning methods that use artificial neural networks[65] which mimics the structure of the natural neural network present in the human brain. For example, an effective machine translation system built using deep learning not only encompasses a model that represents elements of language such as words, meanings and grammar, but may also include representations to contextualize statements in situations where idioms and similes used; in order to match up to human level cognition.

Deriving cognitive insights using deep learning typically involves setting up deep neural networks with several thousands of parameters. As we move towards this part of the insights continuum, we observe that these networks are able to derive insights from the data much more effectively even in the absence of well-defined features. In contrast, typically predictive insights perform effectively when data contains well-defined features. For example, in the case of speech recognition, prior to using deep learning techniques, models were built based on data that contained phonetics of various words. These models were not only complex to train because of the high degree of feature engineering required i.e. build the phonetic sounds in various contexts such as accents and noise levels, but also performed poorly in real-time speech recognition systems. Deep learning models on the other hand were able to derive these features implicitly owing to the sophistication represented by deep neural networks and produce highly accurate results. Another example of the usage of deep learning is in generative AI systems (such as ChatGPT) where it currently finds applications in sophisticated cognitive tasks such as having conversations, producing realistic images, simplifying information, and even writing software code.

When you look closely, deep learning techniques also solve problems using supervised, unsupervised or reinforcement learning approaches. For example, a Convolutional Neural Network (CNN), a popular deep learning technique, can be used to train a model that can distinguish between malignant and benign cancers from MRI images. The model is trained using supervised learning by supplying the network with labeled examples of historic MRI images (data). As an example of unsupervised learning, deep learning networks such as auto-encoders may be used to compress the large MRI images and represent them with a handful of encoded features. This new compressed image data can be used to train CNNs faster with a reasonable level of accuracy. Deep learning is also applied in fields such as robotics that learn through reinforcement i.e. trial-and-error. Some of the examples of reinforcement learning applied to robotics include household cleaning robots, and robots in warehouses that pick, pack, carry, and sort delivery goods.

Cognitive insights derived using deep learning are coupled with experiences over access points to deliver rich and intuitive experiences for users. Speech recognition, language understanding and knowledge modeling are used in conjunction with conversational interfaces to make the user interactions insightful and human-like. They can also be used to auto suggest responses to emails or messages that are tuned to the user's style of writing. E-commerce and social media apps can use deep learning techniques for identifying various buyable objects in images and thereby provide insightful and contextual commerce where users can purchase those products anytime, anywhere.

In order to build cognitive insights one has to master various components of deep learning such as neural network architectures, deep learning algorithms, and programming frameworks such as Tensor-Flow, PyTorch, or Keras[66]. These skills need to be built on top of the three key skills required for building predictive insights viz. fundamental math and statistics, machine learning algorithms, and programming. Low-code and no-code platforms such as Azure Machine Learning and Google Cloud Vertex AI that democratize the development of cognitive insights can be used by non-programmers and business users to quickly build deep learning models.

You may have observed by now that when you zoom into any part of the insights continuum, the key theme that repeatedly recurs is the interplay between programming and data. Data is of course the source of truth and therefore central to gleaning insights, however the role of programming here is crucial too as it is used to implement the algorithms which help discover the various patterns in the data and unearth the insights from the data. We will explore more about this interplay in the next chapter. It is also interesting to note that the different kinds of insights are eventually connected together. The journey of deriving higher levels of insights typically begins with first collecting the descriptive measures to explore the data and then eventually progresses towards gleaning more complex insights.

You may also have noticed that you typically associate the various kinds of insights (typically those that fall on the right side of the insights continuum) that you observe in digital experiences with Artificial Intelligence (AI). The insightful behaviors that modern digital experiences exhibit are often strongly correlated with the broad definition of AI i.e. to display/mimic intelligence within a given environment and perform a specific action with some degree of autonomy.

For example, you may have been amazed the first time when an online shopping app recommended something that you may have been wanting to buy, or when a social networking app automatically recognized your face in the photo that you uploaded. AI is not new, it has been there for several decades in some form or the other and continues to evolve with time. OCR (Optical Character Recognition), was one of the successful early commercial applications of AI. When it was first introduced, we were amazed to see machines interpret handwritten texts with human-like ease. Today however, OCR is so commonplace that it is no longer considered AI. AI now manifests itself in more sophisticated applications such as self-driving cars (autonomous vehicles), robotics, understanding human speech, video surveillance, complex planning, and generative AI. The key themes that typically go into building today's AI systems are Machine Learning (and deep learning), Natural Language Processing, Computer Vision, Robotics, Knowledge Representation, Planning and Expert Systems, as depicted in Fig 2.13

We have already seen the potential of Machine Learning and it is not difficult to recognize that it is at the heart of AI. It is both the driver behind the various decisions taken as well as the key component for the continuous improvement of AI systems. Machine Learning is often used in conjunction with the other AI themes like natural language processing or computer vision to create rich and insightful experiences. For example, a self-driving car (autonomous vehicle) leverages computer vision, sensor fusion, planning and machine learning in order to drive passengers safely to their destination.

As conversational interfaces are becoming more commonplace and emerging as the go-to medium to access digital experiences, one can observe here that AI is the "new UI". AI provides end users with the ability to access knowledge repositories using natural languages. Machine learning and natural language processing techniques are usedhere to not only understand the user's intent and respond to them but also to learn the user's conversational style, preferences and environment.

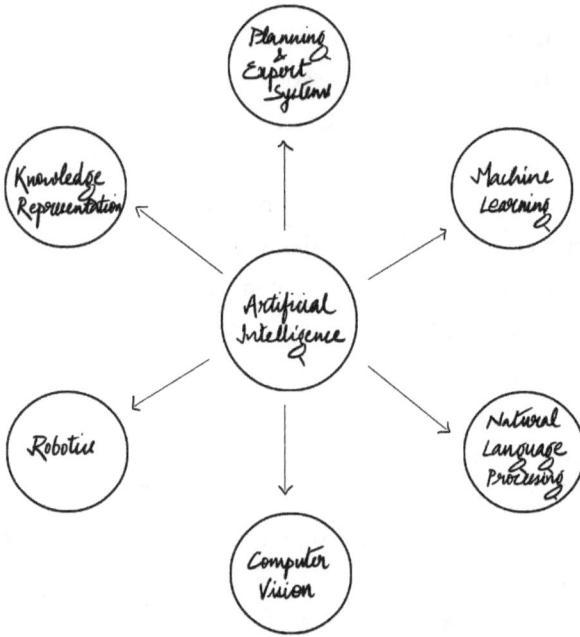

Fig 2.13: AI Themes

Generative AI is another promising trend where deep learning techniques are being applied to generate new data (including text, images, and software code) based on historical data. Popular examples of Generative AI systems include LaMDA[67] (text), GPT-4[68] (text), DALL-E[69] (images), Stable Diffusion[70] (images), OpenAI Codex[71] (software code). Unlike other deep learning systems which are trained to model the relationship between the historical input and historical output and are evaluated based on how close the model's outputs are to historic outcomes, generative AI systems are trained to produce data by learning from historic data and evaluated on how close the generated output is to the desired outcome. For example, DALL-E is a text-to-image generator which accepts a prompt such as "Albert Einstein using a mobile phone in space" and generates images (such as the one in Fig 2.14) that represent the entities in the text (Albert Einstein, mobile phone, space) and the relationships between them (using, in) based on historic data containing these entities and/or relationships either together or separately. To create this image it would mix and match images from the training set containing Albert Einstein, a human being using a mobile phone, and a human being in space to create a unique image that never existed in training; replicating human imagination. Generative AI systems are being used in a variety of applications including music, art, drug design and discovery, material design, and synthetic data generation to protect privacy.

Fig 2.14: Image of "Albert Einstein using a mobile phone in space" generated by DALL-E

By 2026, 75% of businesses will use generative AI to create synthetic customer data, up from less than 5% in 2023.

Source: https://www.gartner.com/en/articles/3-bold-and-actionable-predictions-for-the-future-of-genai

In another example, Generative AI can also help you cull out insights or write code with greater ease and efficiency. For example, GitHub Copilot[72] uses OpenAI's Codex to generate software code based on a programmer's description of what she intends to achieve through the code. This can significantly reduce the time it takes to write code, reduce errors, and allow her to spend more time on imagining how to solve the problems and designing their solutions instead of worrying about the syntax and documentation of the programming language she is using to solve the problem. Similarly, Apache Spark[73] which is a popular framework for data analysis has an English SDK[74] which takes instructions in English and translates them into code instructions for analyzing data, and then produces the desired outcomes.

As all of us are witnessing the evolution of AI, it is normal to observe that with time, some of today's exciting and amazing AI applications may cease to amaze us as they become more commonplace and thus be treated as normal in future. This phenomenon is termed as the AI effect based on Larry Tesler's theorem, that is succinctly expressed as

"AI is whatever hasn't been done yet". AI will continue to evolve into newer themes and technologies which one will need to embrace in order to build even more insightful, relevant and modern digital experiences.

So far, we have seen the various technologies that are used to build insightful digital experiences, as depicted in Fig 2.15. In addition to honing these technical skills, one must also work on building a data mindset, acquiring domain knowledge, delve into the ethical use of data, and empathizing with the users to ensure that the digital experience is desirable, useful and usable.

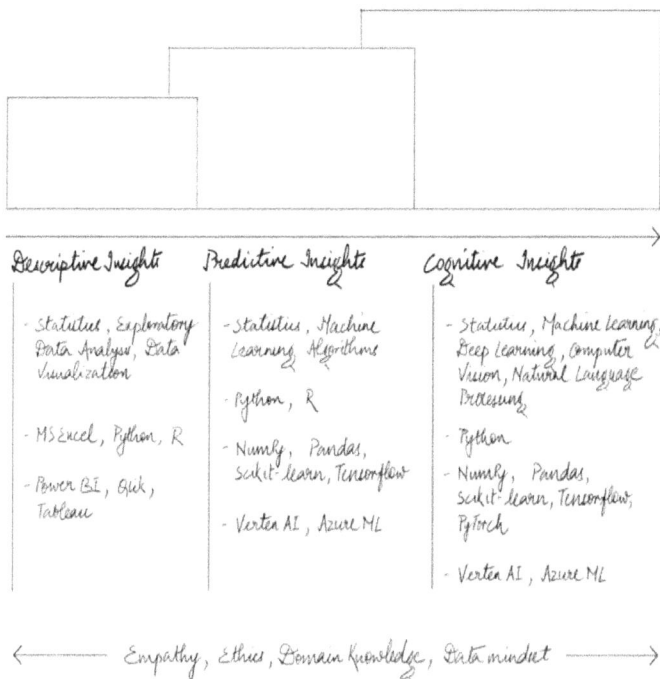

Fig 2.15: Technologies to build Insightful Experiences

Empathizing with users helps one understand the kind of insights that users would love to see and act upon. Empathy combined with understanding the ethical uses of data helps the creator ensure that data is used appropriately so that the privacy of users is respected, and all users are treated fairly. The creator should ensure that when using data about the users, any personally identifiable information (PII) is obscured to protect the privacy of the user. Further, the creator should also ensure that the models do not result in unfair outcomes to any groups of users such as high rejection rate on job applications for people of a specific gender, or high mortgage rates for people from marginalized groups. Ethics play a key role in designing predictive and cognitive systems to ensure that the process of deriving insights and outcomes are accountable, transparent, explainable, and impartial (or unbiased).

Accountability means that the underlying algorithms, data attributes and relationships are auditable and the lineage is preserved. Transparent models allow users to access information about how the model was created/analysis was performed, what kind of data was used, how the model is intended to be used or how the results must be interpreted, how the model performed against different tasks/benchmarks, and what its limitations are/could be. Explainable AI enables users to understand the reason behind the model's output and the creators to troubleshoot the model if and when it produces undesirable outputs. Finally, impartial models are those that are equitable and do not exhibit bias towards one set / group of users.

Domain knowledge plays a crucial role in understanding the business problem that one is trying to solve, the process that generates the data, and the kind of insights that can be derived from the data. To glean insights and work in any area of the insights continuum, one must invest time to hone their domain knowledge and enhance their abilities to effectively work with the data and eventually explain the process and the outcomes to stakeholders and users.

Finally, honing a data mindset would help look at the life cycle of building digital experiences through the lens of data, and identify the potential opportunities of applying insights across various points in the user journey while consuming digital experiences. Building a data mindset is crucial to command expertise over the domain of the data, enhance the imagination of how data should be collected, organized, stored, retrieved and analyzed, and eventually to make better data-driven decisions that benefit businesses and users.

So far, we have seen the visible part of the learning spectrum by exploring the technologies and skills required to build the access points and insights that users see and/or feel. Learning to build compelling digital experiences extends beyond mastering the visible spectrum alone. The invisible spectrum, which we will explore next, is where the rubber meets the road. This part of the learning spectrum deals with those technologies and skills that form the underlying foundation for the visible spectrum.

The Invisible Spectrum

The invisible part of the learning spectrum comprises several layers of intricately connected technologies and skill sets. Although this part of the spectrum is not evidently visible to the end user, the interplay between its technology layers is essential to perform the heavy lifting required to breathe life into the digital experiences; which users eventually consume over access points.

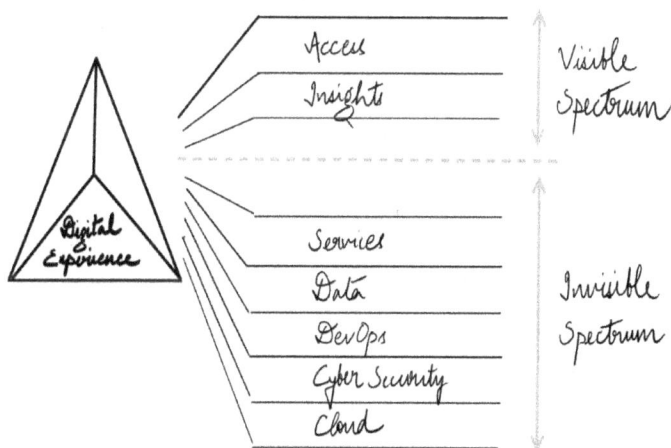

Fig 2.16: The Invisible Spectrum

As depicted in Fig 2.16, exploring the invisible spectrum entails:

1. Understanding the Services that encapsulates the core logic powering the various features and functionalities of the user journeys delivered on access points
2. Delving into the Data infrastructure that enables these functionalities and augments user experiences

3. Learning the DevOps practices and tools that are used to build and deliver these functionalities in a timely and efficient manner

4. Appreciating the Cyber Security pillars used to ensure that the overall experience is trustworthy, and

5. Examining the role of Cloud in scaling these experiences to millions of users in a resilient manner

Services

Services represent the core functionalities of the digital experience and are typically triggered by user actions on various access points. For example, when a user interacts with a taxi hailing app using her favorite access point, the app then hands-off the requests to an array of relevant underlying services. These underlying services perform a variety of related tasks so that the user's request for a taxi is fulfilled.

For instance, a "find taxi" service would determine the set of nearest available taxis and broadcast the user's request for a ride to the different eligible taxis. As the ride comes to a close, and the driver ends it upon reaching the destination, the "payment" service would facilitate the payment of fare from the customer to the driver. In this fairly common scenario, there are several services such as finding the nearest ride, booking, calculating fare, payment and driver feedback operating under the hood to ultimately fulfill the digital experience.

Services could be created using various programming languages, applying various programming paradigms and using different stacks/platforms, and predominantly following one of the three design approaches, as outlined in Fig 2.17.

Programming languages such as Java, C#[75], Solidity[76], and Python are used to build the variety of services which perform the heavy lifting required for digital experiences under the hood. Recall that programming languages were used to build out access points and insights too. For example, we saw that to add interactivity to web applications we could use JavaScript. Similarly, we explored the use of Python or R programming languages to cull out insights from data.

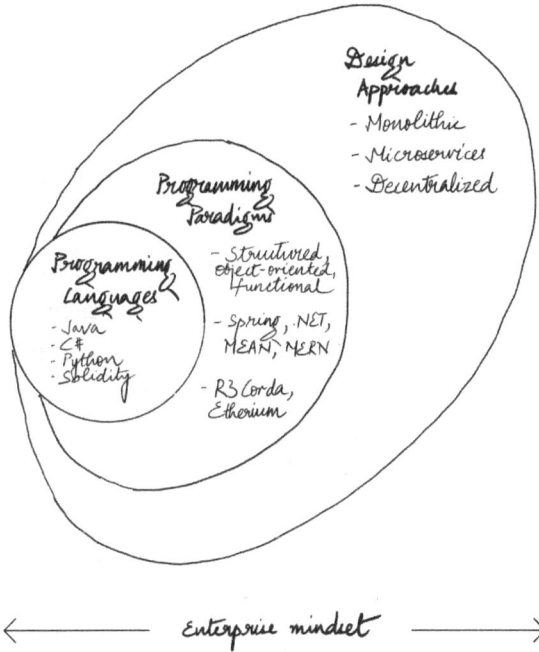

Fig 2.17: Components Required to Build Services

Programming paradigms here broadly refers to the approach that is being used to create services using the programming language. There are several programming paradigms such as object oriented programming, structured programming, and functional programming, and it is important to choose the appropriate approach when building the services. For instance, when working with JavaScript one may typically find themselves using several functional programming aspects to add interactivity to the web application. It is also interesting to note that a programming language may support multiple paradigms, for example, Python and JavaScript support both object oriented and functional programming paradigms.

When using programming languages to create the services, we often encounter repetitive tasks like connecting to a database to store and/or retrieve data, logging, error handling, etc. that need to be implemented across various services and their components. Stacks of frameworks and libraries such as Spring[77], .NET[78], MEAN[79] and MERN[80] can not only help accelerate the creation of services by providing functions/modules to perform repetitive tasks, but also help efficiently structure and define the various components of the services which goes a long way in boosting their maintainability.

Modern digital experiences are composed of several complex services which could benefit from being organized in an efficient manner. The code/program that expresses the functionality of these services increasingly becomes spaghetti code over time as the service evolves, when it is not built with a clear organization but rather built haphazardly. Spaghetti code is often caused by volatile project requirements, lack of using best practices in programming style, and by lack of experience in building code by software engineers. You would be surprised at how common it is to encounter such spaghetti code in modern enterprises! This unorganized code poses challenges such as increased time for development, difficulty with troubleshooting or bug fixing, and has a higher risk of breakdown when new features are introduced. Services therefore can benefit from being organized using various design approaches such as monolithic, microservices, or distributed. These approaches serve as a guide to how the various services are coupled/connected with one another to create the user journeys that form the digital experiences. Using these approaches ensures that services can be scalable, maintainable, optimized for performance, fault-tolerant, secure, cost-effective to develop and maintain, and extensible in future.

Monolithic approach was the primary approach to organize and develop services largely till the turn of the 21st Century. You can observe this approach in a gamut of applications ranging from large mainframes to early web applications, and anything in between. This approach is termed monolithic because the applications package the various functionalities required for the digital experience into a single bundle which is deployed as a whole. Although microservices and decentralized approaches are becoming popular, the monolithic approach still comes handy when the application is not too complex and may not evolve much with time. In order to build or maintain applications using the monolithic approach, one may need to learn specific programming stacks which are composed of an underlying programming language, programming frameworks/libraries, and associated development & testing tools. For example, to learn a Java based stack one might have to master the Java programming language, work with Java libraries and frameworks (such as Spring), and explore Integrated Development Environments (IDEs) such as Eclipse[81] or IntelliJ[82]. Similarly, for .NET based stack one may need to learn C#, .NET Framework and Visual Studio[83].

Microservices is a relatively modern way to organize and develop services where unlike the monolithic approach, each atomic functionality is packaged in its own light weight bundle. These loosely coupled and distributed individual bundles interact with one another to provide the overall digital experience to the user. With the advent of more complex business scenarios that are constantly evolving, this approach wins over the monolithic by bringing in more agility, reusability, and resilience to the development, testing and deployment of applications. However, this approach is not flawless and typically poses challenges when it comes to monitoring and ensuring the security of each bundle and the network of intercommunication, dealing with the technological diversity found across these bundles, and maintaining the rhythm and communication among the development teams delivering these bundles. To develop services using this approach, one must learn the libraries, frameworks, and tools that are unique to the microservices approach and are also available as part of the Java or .NET based stacks. One may also choose to develop microservices using the JavaScript based stacks such as MEAN or MERN, which have become popular with the advent of modern web apps.

Unlike monolithic and microservices approaches which are inherently centralized, the decentralized approach provides a way to bundle functionalities and share them among users over a peer-to-peer network that is not controlled by a central authority. This approach helps in avoiding a single point of control (and eventually single point of failure) by replicating the data/information constantly across the network. One of the most popular examples of how this approach was adopted can be seen in Bitcoin[84]. As you may know, no central organization controls or owns the Bitcoin network, and its transaction ledger is maintained across all of the nodes connected in the network. The decentralized approach is relatively new and is being experimented in a wide variety of other areas such as financial regulation and supervision, collaborative e-commerce, supply chain traceability and many more to build DApps (Decentralized Apps) that benefit from the approach's safer and more transparent way to manage data and transactions. While the apps built using this approach typically leverage open source technologies and inherently have lesser downtime, it is harder to develop and maintain the infrastructure required to run these apps; further, traditional security models and development techniques cannot be applied to apps built using this approach. To build DApps using the decentralized approach one must start by learning the concepts of Blockchain and Distributed Ledger Technologies (DLT) that underpins it. Following which, one has to master blockchain platforms like R3 Corda[85] or Ethereum[86] that use programming languages such as Java, Kotlin or Solidity to build decentralized apps.

As you may imagine, several underlying services usually come together to fulfill various requests that arise from user interactions across access points. These underlying services communicate with each other and access points guided by a set of defined rules codified as APIs[87](Application Programming Interface). In a typical enterprise you may find a heterogeneous mix of access points and services implemented using various approaches and technologies; APIs come handy in such scenarios to provide a structured way for them to interact and hand-off requests. Although APIs have been in existence for several decades, in modern times these are not looked at as just an integration technology but rather as a mindset to build products and services in a consistent, reusable and collaborative way. Developing an API mindset, learning the underlying fundamentals of APIs such as REST[88] and SOAP[89], and becoming proficient with its implementation tools that come bundled with programming stacks is therefore key to building an API driven ecosystem of underlying services that ensures a seamless digital experience.

Overall, 49% of respondents to a survey said most of their organization's development effort was spent working with APIs. That number can vary, depending on the industry.

Source: https://www.postman.com/state-of-api/a-day-week-or-year-in-the-life/#api-development-effort

So far you may have observed when you zoom in further into this part of the spectrum, programming plays a key role in the development of services and APIs. Here, programming helps describe the logic that goes into defining the business objects and processes by virtue of services and APIs. One such example that you may be able to easily relate to is the use of programming languages and frameworks to express the logic of computing the total value of all items in your cart of the online shopping app. Here you may be able to imagine how each item in your cart is a business object with different properties including price, and how programming could be used to represent these business objects, and express business processes such as accumulating the prices of all items in the cart, and computing shipping costs including taxes. Further, the computed total amount may be handed off to APIs which contain the logic of collecting the payment from you, based on your preferred way to pay for your order. Programming is a key skill to master in order to work effectively with services and APIs (and other areas of the visible and invisible spectrum), and we will learn more about how to master it in the next chapter.

Irrespective of the approach and underlying technologies that one chooses to build services and APIs, one must constantly work towards acquiring an enterprise mindset. An enterprise mindset not only demands one to have knowledge of the breadth of the learning spectrum (both visible and invisible), but also requires one to be an excellent communicator, a likable collaborator, an adaptable team player, and an adept problem solver.

Data

"Data is a precious thing and will last longer than the systems themselves", these profound words by Tim Berners Lee, the inventor of the World Wide Web, truly signifies the importance of data. Since ancient times, humans have engaged in the recording and analysis of data. Looking back, we can observe data being documented and exchanged through various artifacts like Cuneiform tablets, Egyptian Hieroglyphs, Clay tokens, and Pictograms, among others. The storage and access of digital data, which is central to digital experiences, has come a long way since the introduction of the binary system by Gottfried Wilhelm Leibniz in the 17th century. As we explore the history of digital data, we can trace its progression from Morse code used in Telegraphs, to punch cards in tabulating machines, followed by vacuum tubes in early electronic computers, and then the emergence of floppy disks, CDs, DVDs, flash drives, solid-state drives, and finally the cloud storage that is predominant today.

You would agree that the proliferation of data that we have seen in recent times is evidence of the increasing adoption of digital technologies in our day-to-day lives. When we closely look at digital experiences, we can observe how data is pivotal across various user journeys and comes into play at every juncture. For example, we can see data flow when users interact with access points and in turn with underlying services, when services communicate among themselves, and when insights are derived from the data which is then baked into the digital experience. For this, digital experiences rely on the underlying data infrastructure which provides the ability to both store and process the data in an effective manner. Let us now delve into the underlying data infrastructure and understand the nuances of how data is stored and processed.

Recall the example of the taxi hailing app where a user transacts with the app to request for a taxi, the data involved here includes the customer details like name, contact number, age, gender, average rating, etc., trip details like time of journey, source, destination, stops, number of passengers, etc., and special requests like wheelchairs, access to a child seat, etc. This data originates at the access point and is passed onto the underlying services for storage and processing. This data can be stored in a structured manner into relational databases (RDBMS) such as Oracle and MySQL. In a relational database, the data is stored in the form of tables containing rows and columns. Each row represents an entity (for example "Customer" and "Trip Details") and the columns indicate the attributes of the entity (for example, name, contact number, age, etc. for Customer; and time of journey, source and destination for Trip Details). Further, these tables can have relationships among them to represent the nuances of how the entities are related to one another. For example, the Trip details table can contain a column named Customer which holds a reference to the customer stored in the Customer table to represent the customer who took the trip. In order to work with structured data, one has to understand the nuances of the relational data model, learn SQL[90] (Structured Query Language) - the lingua franca of such databases, and explore how the services interact with the underlying databases.

SQL and Relational databases have been one of the most popular data stores in enterprises' data infrastructure since their introduction in the 80s. However, around 2010, NoSQL databases started increasing in adoption within enterprises with the rise of newer scenarios that demanded different ways to efficiently store and retrieve data. For example, while the users and drivers interact with the app, the taxi hailing enterprise might be keen to analyze their interactions throughout by collecting clickstream data. Clickstream data may eventually help the app to record events such as time between showing ride options and booking a ride, users switching between different types of rides, users closing and reopening the app after some time, etc. Such data is typically semi-structured/unstructured and is usually stored in NoSQL databases. In this case, clickstream data may be best stored in MongoDB[91] which is a document oriented NoSQL database. NoSQL databases come in different flavors and can be predominantly classified into four types based on the underlying data model as depicted in Fig 2.18.

Document oriented databases such as MongoDB store data in the form of documents typically in JSON[92] (JavaScript Object Notation), BSON[93] (Binary JSON), and XML[94] (Extensible Markup Language) formats. Each document in a document database can have a structure of its own and is identified by a unique id. For example, as shown in Fig 2.18, the taxi hailing app stores clickstream data of the user that opens the app and closes it a few seconds later as one record. Such data collected from several users can help the taxi hailing app unearth insights into customer behavior when they correlate it with other factors.

In graph databases such as Neo4j[95], the emphasis is on easily storing and retrieving the relationship between different data elements. The relationship and its attributes are central to the structure of the data. For example, a social networking site that is primarily keen to connect professionals who worked together may store the data of in dividuals as nodes and form a connection between them if they have worked together; illustrated in Fig 2.18 with 2 people - Peter Thiel and Elon Musk as nodes. Storing data in this format is proven to be easier to navigate several levels of connections based on the relationship between entities.

No SQL databases

Document oriented

example: MongoDB

Sample data (JSON):

```
{
_id : "ccadf32b",
user_id: "abad5462",
app_open: "24/03/2012
1:45:15 PM IST",
app_close: "24/03/2022
1:45:24 PM IST"
}
```

Graph oriented

example: Neo4j

Sample data:

```
(: Person { name :"Peter
Thiel" }) -
[: WORKED_WITH
{ organizations :
[ "PayPal" ] }] →
(: Person { name :"Elon
Musk"})
```

(P/T) —WORKED_WITH→ (M/E)

Key-value pair

example: Redis

Sample data:

preferred_map_type
= "satellite"

Column oriented

example: Cassandra

Sample data:

column 1 (Product name)
iPhone 14, Alchemist,
Kindle paperwhite

column 2 (Price in USD)
800, 25, 125

column 3 (Author)*
, Paulo Coelho,

column 4 (Storage)*
128 GB, , 8GB

* Not all rows have this
column

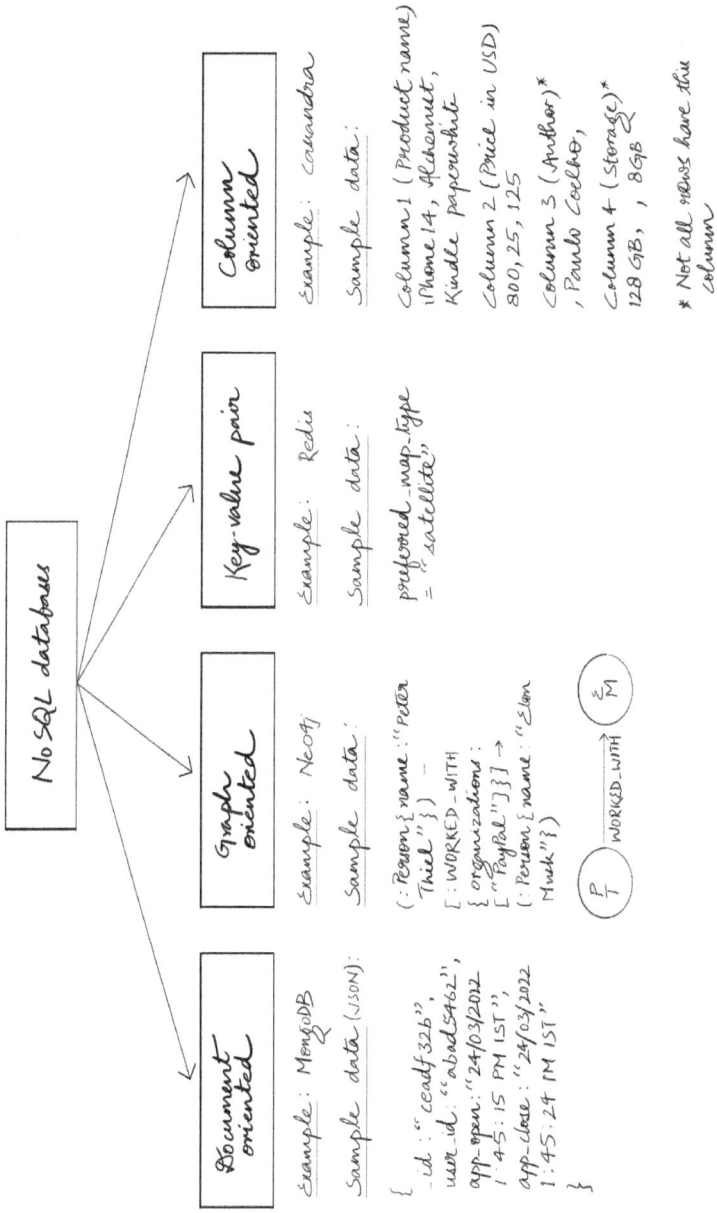

Fig 2.18: Types of NoSQL databases

In a key-value based database such as Redis[96], data is stored in key-value pairs. Each key is unique, every value is associated with a key, and the data is retrieved based on keys. For example, figure 2.18 shows how a maps/navigation app is storing the user's preferred map type.

Another popular type of NoSQL database is the column oriented database which can be observed in Apache Cassandra[97]. These databases store data as columns as opposed to a relational database which stores data as rows. For example, in figure 2.18 we can see that an online shopping app can choose to record its product catalog using a column oriented database such that each attribute of a product forms a column and different products form the rows; and some rows may not have all the columns. Column oriented databases are used mostly for analyzing the data rather than recording regular transactions (like an RDBMS) and they are particularly efficient at aggregating data of a given column.

NoSQL databases form a key part of the data infrastructure of modern digital experiences and in order to work with them, one must learn the nuances of their data model and be able to choose the right NoSQL database for the scenario that is being implemented. One must then learn the intricacies of storing, retrieving and processing this data using services that interact with the selected NoSQL database.

Now consider the scenario where the taxi hailing app has to fulfill the user's request by connecting her to the nearest driver. For this, all drivers connected to the taxi hailing app's network need to periodically (every few seconds) publish their geo-location so that the service can identify which driver can best serve the user's request. The data published here could have a simple structure containing the driver's unique identification, taxi registration number, and the latitude & longitude of the rider's location. Although the size of each data is relatively small, this data is generated at a high velocity i.e. probably every few seconds for each driver, and overall has a sizable volume considering the large number of drivers enrolled into the taxi hailing app. To process such data in real-time, data stream processors such as Apache Kafka[98] can be used. Using these stream processors, the data is processed by the services to identify the most suitable ride for the user by sorting the drivers who are closest to the user; and any other criteria. In order to work with streaming data, one must learn the nuances of stream processors, explore the programming frameworks - typically based on Scala, Python or Java - associated with stream processing, and understand the ways to store such data for subsequent use.

As you may have noticed so far, large volume and variety of data gets generated in modern digital experiences and this data is used for a wide variety of use cases across different user journeys. For example, in the taxi hailing app, data such as user rides and transactions, driver location, user payment information, user/driver and app related feedback, etc. is collected over time and analyzed so that the enterprise can improve the overall experience. Typically the large volume of such heterogeneous data (including structured, semi-structured and unstructured) is collected into data lakes which are built on top of technologies such as Apache Hadoop[99] and NoSQL and can be processed using a variety of frameworks including Apache Spark. Data lakes help consolidate the data that is spread across various siloed systems within an enterprise and eventually serves as the single source of truth for the enterprise data for future analysis. These technologies form the core layer of the data infrastructure and enable distributed storage and processing of large data. Eventually the data from the data lake is consumed by components in the services, insights or access points parts of the spectrum.

In a nutshell, as depicted in Fig 2.19, the data infrastructure provides the storage and processing abilities required to meet the enormous scale, scope and speed demanded by modern digital experiences. To master this component of the invisible spectrum, one has to not only master the variety of data infrastructure technologies, but also work on building a data mindset, developing business acumen, and honing their curiosity.

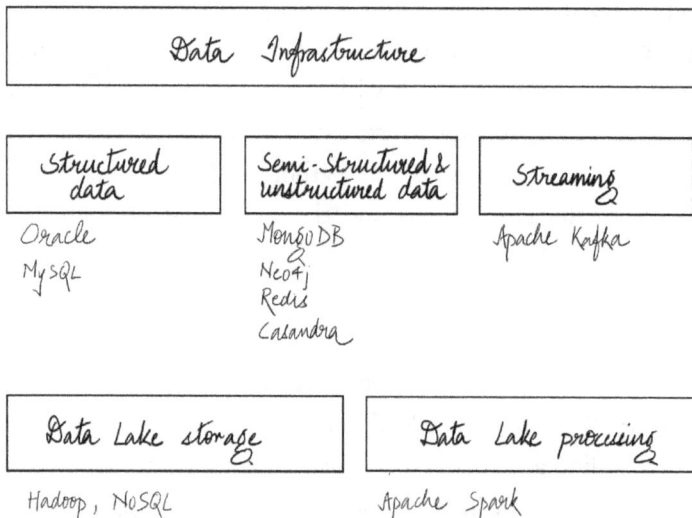

Fig 2.19: Data Storage and Processing

Building a data mindset helps one understand the overall lifecycle of the data and work with varieties of data models and schema. Developing a business acumen helps one understand the overall context of the data and thereby its applicability and relevance to a given problem. Curiosity helps one explore and connect the various aspects of data together, visualize the big picture, and zoom in and out of subsets of data with ease.

DevOps

Digital experiences connect consumers who constantly seek newer and better access points, insights, and services with enterprises that desire to constantly innovate, stay relevant with trends, and distinguish themselves from their competitors. The agility and quality with which the enterprises have to connect their brand and services with their customers is continuously evolving to accommodate the rate of change in technology, business and consumer desires. As a result, the paradigm of how enterprise software is developed and delivered has seen a remarkable shift from slow and painful waterfall based approach to quick and adaptive agile approaches. Software services, features and updates are now released on an hourly to daily basis as opposed to monthly to quarterly releases of the past; as a result of adopting agile approaches.

Although the waterfall based methods to develop software continue to prevail, many enterprises are increasingly adopting Agile methodologies to develop software. The term 'Agile' emerged in the early 2000s[100], and has now become the de-facto approach to building software. Agile is an umbrella term for several methodologies that, even though vary in practice, bear similarities in how they contrast with traditional software development approaches. Fundamentally most agile methodologies are adaptive and people-oriented as compared to traditional approaches which were more predictive and process-oriented. As a result of these fundamental principles, applying agile methodologies promotes practices which lead to iterative and incremental software delivery, increased team collaboration, continuous planning and execution, and sustained learning. Popular agile methodologies used to develop digital experiences include Scrum[101], Kanban[102], Lean[103], SAFe[104] (Scaled Agile Framework), and XP[105] (Extreme Programming).

Scrum is one of the most widely used Agile frameworks that helps teams manage their work through its set of values, principles and practices. A team/pod following scrum (scrum team/pod) is a cross functional team with people playing one or more roles among Scrum Master, Product Owner and Developer (may include Quality Assurance engineers and operations engineers as well). The product owner manages the product backlog which contains work required for a problem, developers select a portion of the work as an increment and build it within a specific period of time (sprint), and the scrum master orchestrates the activities during the sprint and is accountable for the team's effectiveness. The sprint is central to scrum as it turns ideas into value and incrementally generates a viable product. Events such as sprint planning, daily scrum check-ins, sprint review, and sprint retrospective form a part of each sprint and help regulate the progress in each sprint and in the development of the overall product.

Agile methodologies were only a part of the puzzle. These methodologies certainly brought developers much closer to the business, and in turn the end users, and empowered them to create software incrementally and iteratively making it much more customer centric. However, they did not have any significant impact on operations teams which were responsible for deploying/releasing the software and monitoring it in real time. Development teams and operations teams still operated in silos, had different objectives, leadership and performance indicators which sometimes conflicted with each other resulting in poor releases and unhappy end users. DevOps emerged as the crucial piece here. DevOps not only adapted the principles and innovations of agile to operations processes but also extended agile to amplify the efficacy in building and shipping modern digital experiences.

DevOps culture, practices, and tools are pivotal to achieving the desired level of agility in the development and delivery of modern software. DevOps practices streamline and automate the various software development and IT operations practices by inculcating the power of communication, collaboration and innovation which act as a catalyst to develop and deliver high quality software. Eventually this helps shorten the development lifecycle, increase release frequency, reduce the time to market, and enhance the reliability of software systems.

The DevOps tools are key accelerators to enable enterprises to implement and foster the DevOps culture and help apply behavior at scale. In order to adopt this culture, one has to not only adopt various practices and methodologies that lead to improved communication, collaboration and innovation, but also become familiar with a variety of tools across software development (Dev) and delivery (Ops) phases as depicted in Fig 2.20.

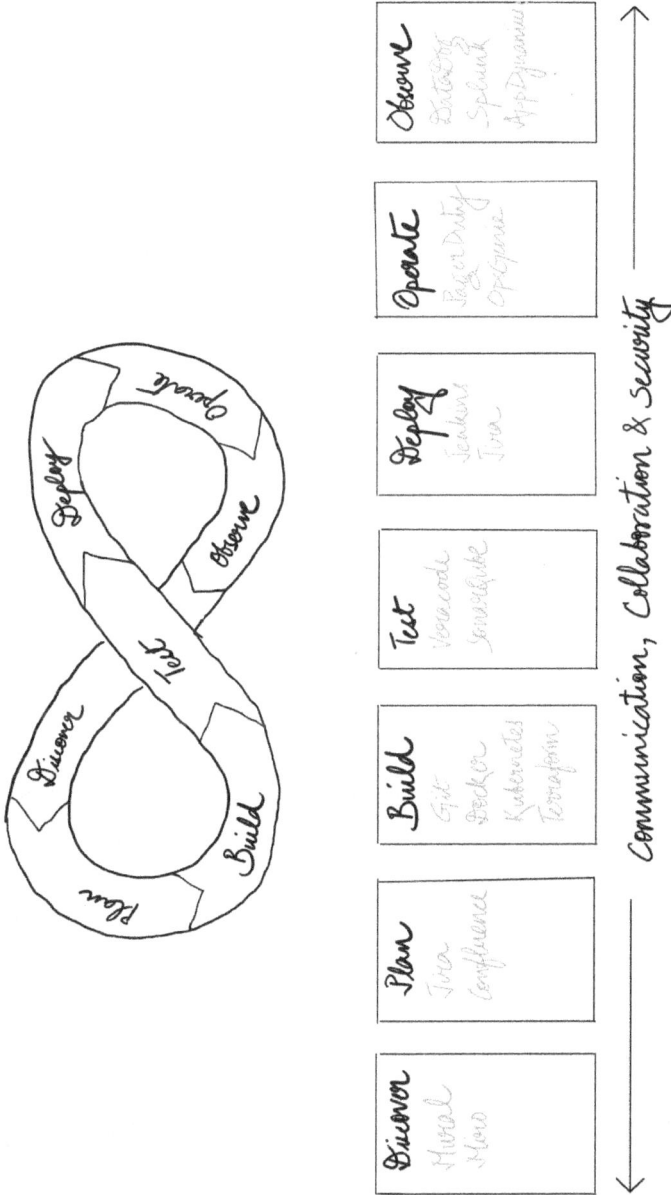

Fig 2.20: DevOps Tools

We can observe that a variety of DevOps tools are employed in each phase of the DevOps lifecycle which is used to deliver the user journeys with agility. In the Discover phase, teams collaborate with one another to ideate and prioritize the deliverables at the end of a short fixed time interval (referred to as a sprint in Scrum). Collaborative tools such as Mural[106] and Miro[107] are used to gather the ideas that are generated based on user research and feedback which eventually become a part of the roadmap of the user journeys.

In the plan phase, tools such as Jira[108] and Confluence[109] are used to break down the work into manageable tasks which can be delivered quickly. If teams are employing Scrum practices, then these tools typically help with sprint planning and creating the roadmap for the product.

In the build phase, the various planned components/modules of user journeys (access points, insights, services, data infrastructure) are created using the appropriate technology and tools. Version control tools such as Git[110], GitHub[111], BitBucket[112], etc. are used to track changes to the code, collaborate among team members and continuously enhance the code quality through peer reviews. Tools such as Docker[113] and Kubernetes[114] are used to provide developers with containers that are identical to the environments to which the application will be deployed. Infrastructure as Code (IaaC) tools such as Ansible[115], Puppet[116] and Chef[117] help provision development and testing environments that are similar to the final production environment so that the software can be tested against different configurations before it is released.

In the test phase, which marks the beginning of the delivering the software, automated testing tools such as Veracode[118] and SonarQube[119] are used to automate the process of testing the software build and identify issues or risks. Typically a delivery pipeline is created using tools such as Jenkins[120] which automatically picks up the latest code from version control tools and then involves the testing tools to validate the software.

In the deploy phase, automation plays a key role to ship the modules to live environments which users can access. Tools such as Jira provide a dashboard for deployment which can provide an integrated view of how the code moves from the source repository to the final deployment infrastructure, and also gives a view on deployment statuses. Tools such as Docker, Kubernetes, Ansible, Chef, Puppet are used here as well to create containers into which the code is deployed, orchestrate the containers at runtime, and automate the provisioning of infrastructure.

In the operate phase, tools such as Pagerduty[121] and OpsGenie[122] help keep track of live incidents that arise as users report them, alert the stakeholders, and help the Dev and Ops teams track and resolve issues. Finally, in the observe phase, tools such as DataDog[123], Splunk[124], AppDynamics[125], and Grafana[126] help automate the monitoring of the infrastructure and application performance. These tools record relevant metrics 24/7 and provide insights into the runtime behavior of the apps and the environments that they are deployed in.

Although the DevOps tool set used may vary among enterprises and may even vary between different teams/pods within an enterprise itself, but at large the overall DevOps culture is all about the Continuous Integration (CI) of incremental updates to the software code, Continuous Delivery (CD) of integrated code which is ready to be released without fear of failure, Continuous Deployment (CD) of new versions of software into production environments through automation, and Continuous Feedback (CF) that flows into discovering and planning subsequent releases of the product.

It is worthy to recognize how Containers (provided using technologies such as Docker and orchestrated using Kubernetes) interplay with DevOps to further propel the agility in developing and delivering modern software. During the software development phase, developers use DevOps tooling to compile, build, test, and package their code into container images. These container images are then funneled into relevant DevOps tooling that are used to deliver the application in test and production. Thereafter, these live containers are constantly monitored using DevOps tooling to record their health and analyze any incidents that may have occurred at runtime. This approach not only enables Dev teams to focus on development of software without worrying about the underlying ecosystem on which the software is going to run, but also isolates Ops teams from the nitty-gritties of the application and enables them to focus on deploying the bundle and manage its scalability and reliability. It is also interesting to note that the DevOps tooling for integration, delivery and monitoring are also available in the form of containers which takes this interplay to the next level. Learning to work with containerization tools that help define container images (such as Docker), and container orchestration tools which help manage the live containers (such as Kubernetes) is a key aspect of delivering modern digital experiences with agility today.

Building a DevOps culture not only includes applying its principles and processes across app development and delivery but it also extends to ensure that security aspects are intertwined with the end-to-end app development lifecycle. Not doing so may deter the agility, and ultimately lead to the failure of DevOps objectives. DevSecOps represents the importance of security aspects being embraced along with DevOps principles. We shall explore security aspects in more detail in the Cyber component of the invisible spectrum.

DevOps principles and practices called DataOps and MLOps have recently made inroads into the agile development and delivery of predictive and cognitive insights via Machine Learning (ML) systems. Unlike apps which are composed largely of code bundles, ML systems are made up of underlying data, data pipelines, machine learning code, models learnt from the data, and the services that expose the insights generated by the models via APIs. DataOps and MLOps practices focus on synchronizing these components in order to ensure that the models stay relevant over time even when changes in data properties (data drift) or changes in the user behavior that generates the data (concept drift) occur. To embrace these principles and practices, one has to become familiar with a variety of tools that primarily deal with the three key ingredients of typical enterprise grade modern ML systems - the data, the model and the services. For data, one has to learn tools such as Pachyderm[127] or DVC[128] which are used for data versioning along with the data infrastructure stack used to build and maintain data pipelines, discussed in the data section of the invisible spectrum. To work with models, one has to master tools such as MLflow[129] or Weights and Biases[130] for experiment tracking in addition to the platforms, frameworks and libraries that were previously discussed in the Insights section of the visible spectrum. For services that expose the insights from these models one has to become familiar with tools such as Kubeflow[131], TensorFlow Serving[132] or Seldon[133] that are used alongside the whole gamut of DevOps tools that deal with continuous integration, continuous delivery and continuous monitoring. This whole ecosystem can also greatly benefit from leveraging the container interplay. It is needless to say that security aspects are also intertwined across the lifecycle of ML systems and hence it may not be uncommon to refer to these principles and practices as DataSecOps and MLSecOps.

As the agility with which access points, services and insights are being delivered is continuously increasing, Ops teams are further challenged to ensure that the overall experience remains reliable and new changes do not break the current experience. To this, organizations are adopting Site Reliability Engineering (SRE) principles and practices in their DevOps teams to keep the software up and running with a great focus on ensuring the availability, scalability, testability, maintainability, and reliability of services. SRE principles and practices emphasize on applying software engineering aspects in the infrastructure and operations space in order to reduce/eliminate toil through automation, implement observability, manage incidents/is sues, forecast and plan for future demand and capacity, and define and measure reliability. In order to master SRE, the most crucial thing is to build the SRE mindset and adopt its principles and practices; on the tooling front one may usually find no or very less difference from the DevOps tooling.

Just like with access points, insights, services, and data, zooming further into DevOps also helps us discover the repeated recurrence of programming and the impact it has on this area of the spectrum. Here we observe that programming has been creatively used in the delivery of software itself to the end users. Programming plays a key role in automating repeated tasks, developing and maintaining the various tools and platforms that boost productivity of teams, and overall contributes to the improvement of software delivery processes and eventually influences the culture of teams.

So far we have seen the various DevOps tools and understood agile practices that are crucial to develop and deliver modern digital experiences that keep pace with evolving customer needs and trends. However, one has to remember that DevOps is not all about tools and practices alone, its key success lies with people and culture. These tools and practices are used to create autonomous teams that share responsibility, communicate openly and collaborate effectively. To thrive with DevOps, one must work towards acquiring and/or enhancing these skills and virtues.

Cyber

The intimacy of digital experiences is founded on the ability of the consumers to trust it to provide safety and security as they engage with it. In the example of the online shopping app, the security, safety and privacy are extremely important for the consumers and the enterprise. For example, end users are typically concerned about the safety of their personal details such as address, phone number, and credit card information that they provide to the online shopping app for making a purchase. Any compromise to the security of the app across different layers poses a threat to the app and its consumers. For instance, a theft of the credit card data exposes the consumers to potential financial loss. Other malicious attacks to extract the consumer's phone number exposes them to potential fraud, identity theft and other crimes. All of this in turn leads to reputation loss, monetary loss and exposes the enterprises to regulatory and compliance risks too. Therefore, it is paramount to protect the underlying networks, systems, hardware and data that enable these digital experiences to ensure the privacy and security of consumers' data and identities.

> The average cost of a data breach to an enterprise in 2023 was USD 4.45 million , and the most common type of data stolen or compromised was customer PII
>
> Source: https://www.ibm.com/reports/data-breach

Cyber security is omnipresent and so are the threats it deals with, for both individuals and society as a whole. Although the landscape of tools and technologies used to ensure cyber security is vast, it can be viewed under 4 key categories viz. Identity and Access Management, Infrastructure Security, Application and Data Security, and the Policies that govern its implementation, as depicted in Fig 2.21.

Identity and Access Management (IAM) is one of the key pillars of cyber security that deals with digital identities of the consumers, the APIs, and the systems, and manages their access and the actions that they can perform on the various components of the experience - access points, services, insights and data. IAM establishes the unique identification of individual users, groups, devices, and applications, and provides a mechanism to authenticate them before granting access to resources. Further, IAM also helps define policies that stipulate what level of access users have to resources and what actions they are authorized to perform. The access management aspect of IAM is responsible for continuously monitoring, controlling and managing

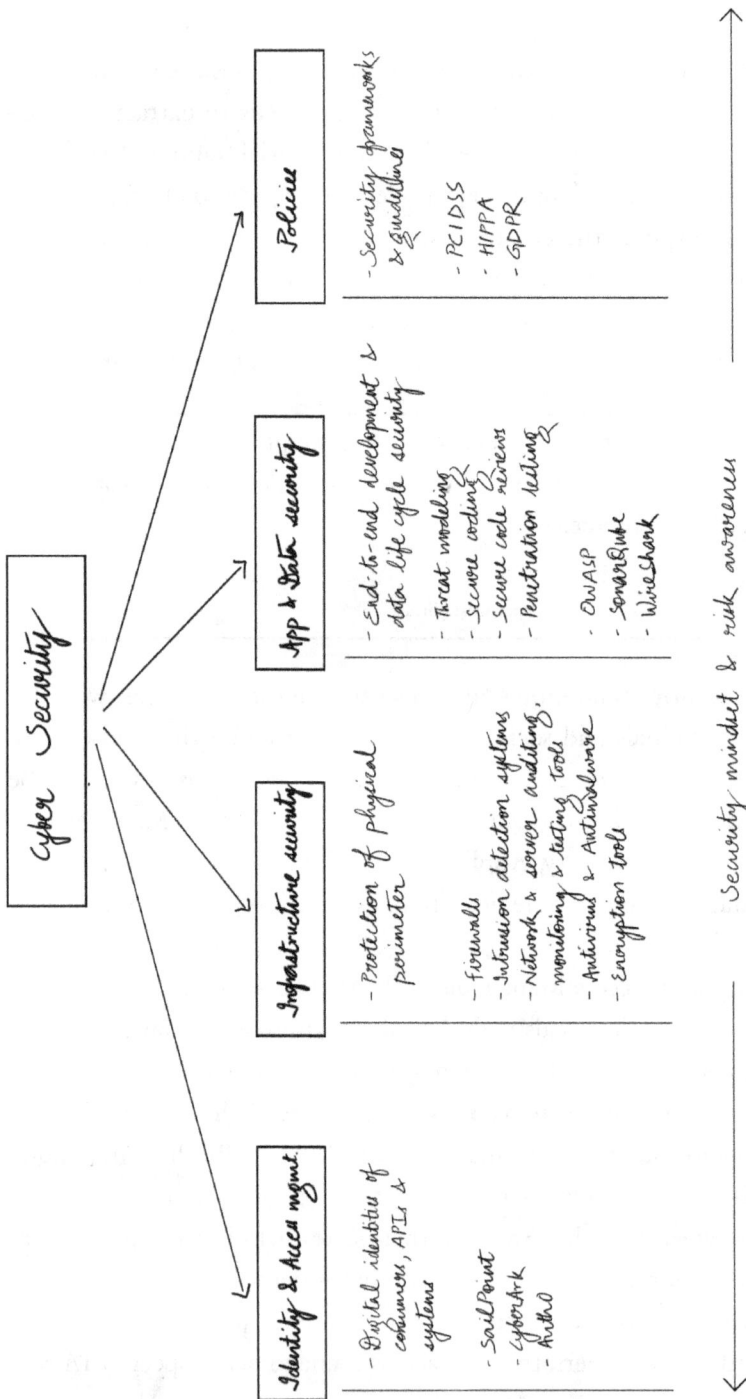

Cyber Security

Identity & Access mgmt.
- Digital identities of consumers, APIs & systems

- SailPoint
- CyberArk
- Auth0

Infrastructure security
- Protection of physical perimeter

- Firewalls
- Intrusion detection systems
- Network & server auditing, monitoring & testing tools
- Antivirus & Antimalware
- Encryption tools

App & Data security
- End-to-end development & data life cycle security

- Threat modeling
- Secure coding
- Secure code reviews
- Penetration testing

- OWASP
- SonarQube
- WireShark

Policies
- Security frameworks & guidelines

- PCIDSS
- HIPPA
- GDPR

Security mindset & risk awareness

Fig 2.21: Key categories of Cyber Security

user access to resources and it involves provisioning and/or revoking access, managing the permissions, and monitoring for security threats. IAM also provides the ability for users to access multiple systems after authenticating them just once through SSO(Single sign-on) capabilities. Above all, IAM provides auditing and reporting capabilities which helps enterprises strengthen their security policies by tracking user activities and monitoring reports. There are numerous IAM platforms/tools that one can choose from to learn. Some of the popular ones are SailPoint[134], CyberArk[135], Autho[136].

Infrastructure Security deals with protecting the physical perimeter of an enterprise which typically encompasses various kinds of hardware, network, servers, and endpoints. A wide spectrum of hardware and software techniques/tools are used to safeguard the physical perimeter. It may include firewalls[137], network and server auditing, monitoring & testing tools, intrusion detection systems[138], antivirus and antimalware systems, and encryption tools. Implementing infrastructure security includes controlling access to the resources, monitoring and securing the networks and the data transmitted over them, periodically applying security patches to address known vulnerabilities and mitigate threats, monitoring the infrastructure to detect unusual activities, implementing robust backup and recovery measures, establishing secure access to the physical perimeter of the resources, enforcing policies and procedures, and regularly conducting security assessments to identify weaknesses and fixing them.

Applications and Data Security deals with providing an omni-present thread of security across the end-to-end app development and data lifecycle. You may recall that this is a key aspect of maintaining a DevSecOps culture in an enterprise. Security is incorporated early on by performing threat modeling and assessment in the early phases of architecting and designing the app/data strategy, followed by adopting secure code practices during the development, doing secure code reviews for individual software modules, assessing vulnerabilities and attack vectors for the application as a whole with penetration testing, and continuously monitoring and revising the application and data security to deal with emerging attack vectors. In order to work with application and data security, one must start by learning OWASP[139] (The Open Web Application Security Project) standards to understand the latest vulnerabilities, attack vectors and their remedies. For example, one of the commonly used attack vectors is security misconfiguration where developers either install unnecessary features or forget to disable default accounts or change default passwords of underlying software. Hackers can use the default information such as passwords to take over the application. In addition to exploring vulnerabilities and attack vectors, one must also get familiar with tools such as SonarQube and Fortify[140] for secure code review, and a combination of tools such as Armitage[141], Nmap[142], Wireshark[143], John the Ripper[144], etc. that help in performing penetration tests.

Cyber security policies govern the implementation of the various key aspects of security and are based on several factors such as demography of the consumers, demography of the enterprise and domain of the business. The implementation of these policies and guidelines aim to ensure the discipline required for the safety and security of consumers and enterprises' data, and in turn builds trust among the various stakeholders. One must familiarize themselves with the various data security frameworks and guidelines such as GDPR[145], HIPPA[146], and PCI DSS[147] on a need basis.

When we zoom further into the various areas of Cyber Security we will observe that here too programming and data play a key role. Their role becomes more apparent as we learn to effectively design and describe policies and procedures to establish the identity of users and software, analyze threats such as malware and automatically intercept or mitigate them, and scan the various components of the spectrum for vulnerabilities to eventually help secure them. We will explore the interplay between programming and data in the next chapter and understand how learning these areas are fundamental to mastering the cyber security area of the learning spectrum.

Cyber Security is a broad area within the invisible spectrum and its technology landscape and techniques rapidly evolve to keep pace with emerging threats. In addition to honing the technology skills, one must cultivate a security mindset which involves being vigilant to threats, being aware of risks, and constantly considering security implications of decisions and actions. One must also foster a collaborative mindset, proactively share information and communicate effectively by recognizing that cyber security is a shared responsibility within an enterprise.

Cloud

So far, we have seen the various technologies that come together to make the awesome digital experiences that we enjoy everyday. In terms of the online shopping app we now have an idea of the diverse access points through which we can shop, the spectrum of insights which enrich our online shopping experience, the myriad services that work under the hood to fulfill the different user journeys that we experience, the data infrastructure that houses the massive volume and variety of relevant data, the various software development practices and tools that are at the helm of the release of newer features with increased agility, and the cyber security principles practices, and tools that ensure the privacy, security and safety of our shopping experience.

If you zoom further deep into each of these areas, you will eventually discover that all of this is supported by a combination of hardware, software and networks which run round the clock to provide reliable, scalable and secure computing resources required for modern digital experiences. Today, Cloud virtually encompasses all of the massive infrastructure comprising computing servers, storage systems, networking hardware, operating systems, software for virtualization, middleware that help different applications/software integrate and interoperate with the speed, scale, and resilience required for modern digital experiences. Here, virtualization refers to technology that enables the creation of several isolated virtual environments that can share physical resources and in turn utilize the hardware more efficiently. Cloud computing not only offers the underlying infrastructure as services, but also provides several services which can be used across the different components of the visible and invisible spectrum.

It is often humorously remarked that "There is no cloud, it's just someone else's computer", to imply that at core the Cloud is nothing but a collection of distributed and interconnected compute and storage systems. Amazon Web Services[148] (AWS), Google Cloud Platform[149] (GCP) and Microsoft Azure[150] are some of the well known Cloud Service Providers(CSPs).

The cloud has evolved (and is continuously evolving) from providing just compute and storage infrastructure to offering a spectrum of specialized and sophisticated services that provide a flexible, reliable and scalable way to develop and deliver modern digital experiences, as depicted in Fig 2.22.

As end users, we consume digital experiences over the cloud day-in, day-out in almost all realms of life - be it communicating with each other through instant messaging or video conferencing tools like Zoom, staying connected on social media using apps like Instagram, entertaining ourselves with apps like YouTube, learning on demand using apps like Coursera, and many more. The cloud enables these software/apps to effectively scale to millions of users while ensuring their availability and resilience in a cost efficient manner. These software/apps are typically hosted on cloud and delivered to consumers in an on-demand manner; this delivery model is referred to as SaaS (Software as a Service). From a developer's lens, when we zoom in on these software/apps they are composed of various services and insights which themselves can be independently hosted as SaaS, and can be consumed across other services/software/apps to bring in more agility while building digital experiences. For example, to enable email and text notifications for friend requests, shipping updates or sign-up

Software services
Google Docs, GMail, Zoom

Serverless computing (FaaS)
Google Cloud Functions, AWS Lambda

Access dev services Google Dialogflow Amazon Lex	**Insights services** Google Vertex AI AWS Sagemaker

App/API dev services Google App Engine AWS Elastic Beanstalk	**Data services** Google DataProc AWS Elastic Mapreduce

Cloud DevOps services
Google Cloud Build, AWS Code Build

Cloud cyber services
Google IAM

Cloud container services (CaaS)
GKE, Amazon EKS & ECS

Cloud store and compute services
GCE, GCS, AWS EC2, AWS S3

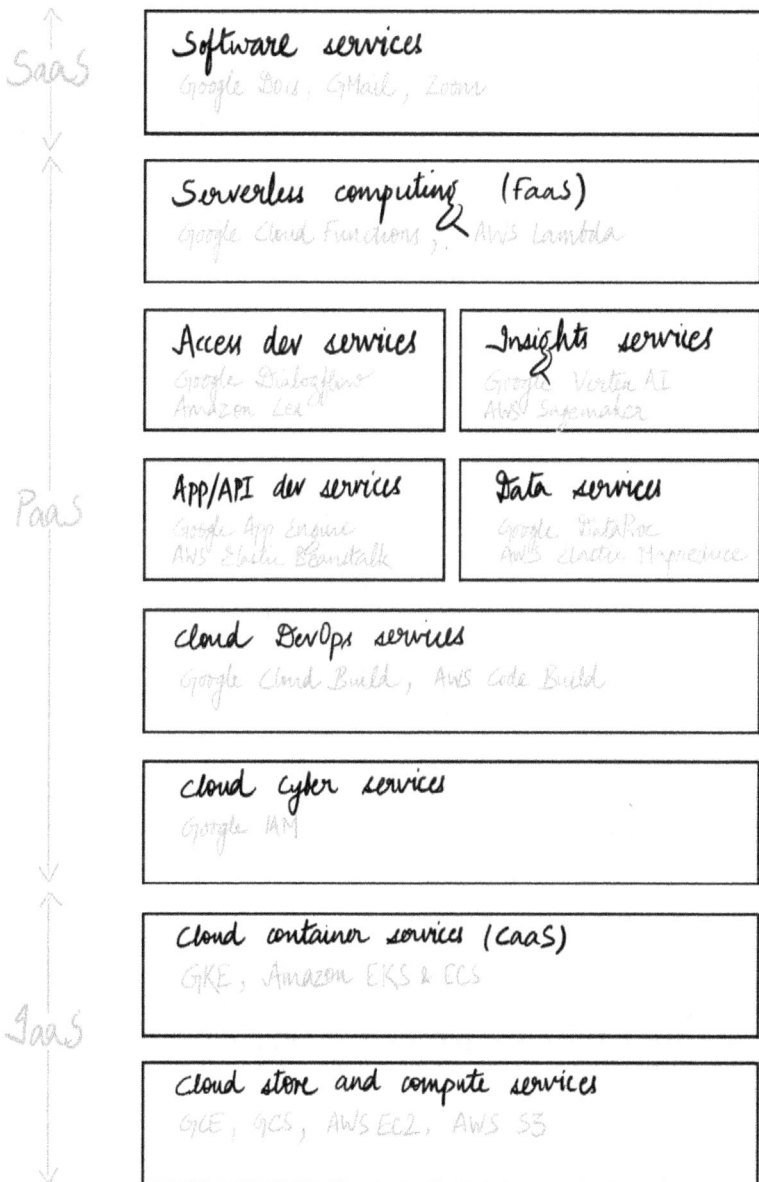

Fig 2.22: Spectrum of Cloud Services

confirmations, developers may leverage pre-built SaaS services such as Twilio SendGrid[151] to speed up the development and delivery of digital experiences instead of building such functionality ground-up.

In 2023, the global spending on public IT cloud services amounted to approximately 669 billion U.S. dollars in total. Software as a service (SaaS) spending is the largest segment with revenues of around nearly 413 billion U.S. dollars.

Source: https://www.statista.com/statistics/370305/global-public-it-cloud-services-spending-by-segment/

Underneath the services and insights provided as SaaS, there exists a range of tooling, platforms, and various kinds of software servers viz. Database servers, Web servers, App servers, Middleware, etc. which help create and host these services/software/apps on the cloud. The tooling, platform and software servers are provisioned as PaaS (Platform as a Service) for developers to leverage while developing and/or deploying their services/software/apps on the cloud. For example:

- To build access points such as conversational interfaces you can use platforms like Google DialogFlow, Amazon Lex[152] or Azure Bot Service[153].

- To build machine learning models you can use Google Ver-tex AI, AWS SageMaker[154] or Azure Machine Learning.

- To develop the underlying Java or .NET services you can use GCP App Engine[155], AWS Elastic Beanstalk[156] or Azure App Service[157].

- To perform data analytics on large volumes of data you can use GCP DataProc[158], AWS EMR[159], or Azure Data Lake Analytics[160].

- To build DevOps CI/CD pipelines you can use Google Cloud Build[161], AWS CodeBuild[162], AWS CodeDeploy[163], AWS CodePipeline[164], or Azure DevOps[165].

- To enforce security and identity you can use Google Identity and Access Management (IAM)[166], AWS IAM[167], or Azure Active Directory[168].

It may be interesting to note that as PaaS continues to evolve into several abstractions to provide more flexibility and agility to developers, some of the services mentioned previously may not slot into the pure definition of PaaS but for our understanding we shall treat these services and other abstractions broadly as PaaS. One such abstraction is FaaS (Function as a Service), popularly known as serverless computing, where developers need to focus only on the application code and the cloud caters to everything else including the provisioning and scaling of the underlying platform required to run it. Google Cloud Function[169], AWS Lambda[170], and Azure Functions[171] are some of the well known FaaS offerings and are used by developers to implement use-cases that are processed by light weight code.

All of these services/software/apps that are created and hosted on cloud are powered by the underlying infrastructure of distributed and interconnected computation and storage systems. Since the beginning of the cloud, the cloud service providers have been offering these building blocks as Infrastructure as a Service (IaaS) that you can use to compose services/software/apps from the ground up. For example, Google Compute Engine[172](GCE) , AWS EC2[173], and Azure Virtual Machines[174] can be used to provision raw compute instances in the form of virtual machines. In order to store large volumes of data on cloud, you can use Google Cloud Storage[175] (GCS), AWS S3[176] and Azure Blob Storage[177].

The cloud not only provides raw compute instances but also provides Containers as a Service (CaaS) to manage and orchestrate containers, which is key to building modern software. You can leverage Google Kubernetes Engine[178] (GKE), Amazon Elastic Kubernetes Service[179] (EKS), Amazon Elastic Container Service[180] (ECS) , and Azure Kubernetes Service[181] (AKS) to automatically scale, deploy and manage containers using Kubernetes.

In 2023, enterprise spending on cloud infrastructure services amounted to 270 billion U.S. dollars, a growth of 45 billion U.S. dollars compared to the previous year. The growing market for cloud infrastructure services is driven by organizations' demand for modern networking, storage, and databases solutions.

Source: https://www.statista.com/statistics/1114926/enterprise-spending-cloud-and-data-centers/

In order to work with the cloud, one must get an overview of the various core services offered, learn the nuances of the services they are interested in using, and understand how the various services interplay with each other to provide a holistic environment for creating and hosting scalable, resilient and cost-effective modern digital experiences; a bit of Linux and networking knowledge will also be helpful to efficiently navigate the various services provided within the CSP platforms.

When we revisit the spectrum of services offered on Cloud (as shown earlier in Fig 2.22) and zoom out of the individual services to observe the entire suite of offerings, we can see that it resembles the overall learning spectrum almost in entirety. This is akin to how when we zoom in on a Romanesco broccoli and look at one of its buds, the part we are looking at resembles the whole. We can observe that the offerings of cloud spans across Access points, Insights, Services, Data infrastructure, DevOps, Cyber and even Cloud itself (yes, you can build your own cloud using the services from cloud service providers!). It is also interesting to note how the continuous adoption of the cloud within modern enterprises is progressing in an eternal, self organized and connected fashion. We can observe that within enterprises the range of cloud offerings being included are continuously growing (eternal), all these services are getting cohesively linked (connected), and overall the cloud landscape resembles the entire spectrum (self-organized). The cloud reflects the beauty of our learning fractal - the learning spectrum, and zooming into it offers us a way to appreciate how the learning spectrum truly embodies fractal nature.

The Learning Spectrum

The Kaibab Squirrel is considered a special and beloved animal by many people who inhabit the area around the Grand Canyon. This species of squirrel is unique from other squirrels and is found mostly in the Kaibab Plateau of North Arizona, which includes part of the Grand Canyon. According to Native American folklore, the squirrel braved several challenges such as harsh weather, difficult terrain, and dangerous predators, to travel the vast expanse of the Canyon and reach its heights to meet with the Creator. Impressed with the squirrel's perseverance and bravery, the Creator gave it a new coat - one that had all the colors of the Canyon, and the ability to glide from tree to tree with ease. The Kaibab squirrel is seen as a symbol of resilience and bravery in the face of challenges, and its unique appearance is considered a reminder of the natural beauty and diversity of the Grand Canyon region.

Enterprises and individuals are like the Kaibab squirrel, for they too have to brave several challenges as they navigate their digital journeys in the ever changing and continuously evolving world of modern digital experiences. To travel to the top, they have to master the learning spectrum by inculcating the virtues of the learning fractal viz. perseverance, discipline and curiosity. And eventually, their mastery of the learning spectrum and their ability to effortlessly glide from one area of the spectrum to another is reflected in the beauty of the modern digital experiences that they craft.

So far, in this chapter, we have explored the breadth and depth of the visible and invisible parts of the learning spectrum and become familiar with the various digital skills that are used to craft modern digital experiences. Using real life examples such as online shopping, taxi hailing, etc., we not only articulated the various attributes of modern digital experiences but also associated them with the different areas of the learning spectrum. For the most part of this chapter we zoomed into the different areas of the spectrum and understood the different digital skills that one has to acquire to master that area of the spectrum.

Let us now zoom out and appreciate the beauty of our learning fractal - the learning spectrum as a whole as depicted in Fig 2.23. The figure depicts the overall learning spectrum in totality where you can see both the visible and the invisible parts and also note some of the digital skills (only few are shown for the sake of brevity) that one has to master in each area of the spectrum.

Zooming into our learning fractal, you may have noticed that just like any other fractal, our learning fractal too is eternal. We can continue to zoom into each area infinitely, be intrigued every time, and acquire new skills as we go deeper. However we must remember that like in a true fractal pattern, the whole is much more than the parts, and we must acquire the ability to see how everything connects together to reach the whole.

Zooming out of the fractal helps you understand how the different parts of the learning spectrum are connected with one another. We can observe interconnections across the different areas of the spectrum such as end users consume digital experiences through access points which are enriched with insights; access points and insights are powered by services and data infrastructure under the hood; the agility required to deliver the different features which end users experience in modern digital experiences comes from a healthy DevOps culture which is supported by a variety of tools; all parts of the software stack that powers digital experiences are secured using components related to Cyber Security; and overall the complete stack benefits from the various services offered in the Cloud.

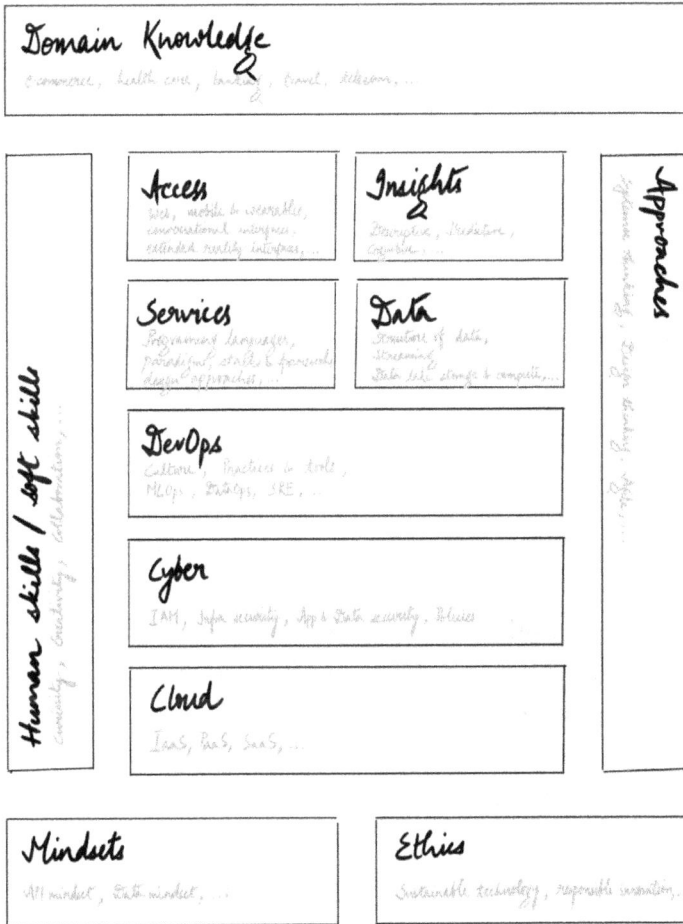

Domain Knowledge
e-commerce, health care, banking, travel, telecom, ...

Access
web, mobile & wearable, conversational interfaces, extended reality interfaces, ...

Insights
Descriptive, Predictive, Cognitive, ...

Services
Programming languages, paradigms, stacks & frameworks, design approaches, ...

Data
structure of data, streaming, Data life, storage & compute, ...

DevOps
Culture, Practices & tools, MLOps, DataOps, SRE, ...

Cyber
IAM, Infra security, App & Data security, Policies

Cloud
IaaS, PaaS, SaaS, ...

Approaches
Systems thinking, Design thinking, Agile, ...

Human skills / soft skills
Curiosity, Creativity, Collaboration, ...

Mindsets
AI mindset, Data mindset, ...

Ethics
Sustainable technology, responsible innovation,

Fig 2.23: The Learning Spectrum

Across the entire spectrum, enterprises and individuals have to acquire a wide variety of digital skills that not only include technology skills such as programming languages, frameworks, platforms and tools, but also include human skills such as curiosity, problem solving communication, collaboration, and many more. Further, enterprises and individuals have to also acquire a deep understanding of the domain that the modern digital experiences they build operate in. For example, enterprises and individuals working to build digital experiences for financial institutions such as banks should have an understanding of the concepts of banking, financial instruments, and various financial services. Similarly, when creating digital experiences such as the online shopping app, one must learn concepts such as product catalog, e-commerce business models, pricing strategies and applicable tax laws.

In our learning fractal - The Learning Spectrum (shown in Fig 2.23), you can also observe that inculcating ethics and honing various mindsets such as enterprise mindset, API mindset, and data mindset plays a key role in mastering the learning spectrum. Ethics plays a key role in building sustainable technology that delivers fair outcomes to all the users, and the communities that enterprises serve and operate in. Enterprises and individuals must inculcate ethics to innovate responsibly, protect privacy and ensure security, and design technology which is unbiased and transparent to its users. Honing the various mindsets help enterprises and individuals to approach the problems with the required perspective and eventually make better and informed decisions towards success in the long term.

The zoomed out learning spectrum, like any complex fractal pattern, may seem daunting and overwhelming. Its eternal nature serves as a constant reminder that there is always more to discover as we zoom in to focus on any one part of the spectrum. Simultaneously, the spectrum as a whole too is ever changing and continuously evolving. Not just the individual areas, but the connections between them also continue to grow with time. Small changes to even a part of the spectrum cause a snowball effect and results in dramatic changes to the spectrum as a whole. Mastering the learning spectrum may seem impossible, just like comprehending a complex fractal pattern, however leveraging the self-organized nature of fractals can help bring order to the chaos.

As you look at the overall spectrum now, you may be able to identify where you are at and which parts of it you are comfortable with currently. You may also be able to visualize a path that serves as your personalized learning map to achieve your own learning goals. For example, if you are currently learning or working with digital skills in the insights part of the spectrum, you may now know the range of skills that you can delve deeper into to become more proficient at gleaning insights. Further, you may also be able to better understand how insights are connected to other areas of the spectrum and perhaps identify your next learning areas as Data Infrastructure, DataOps/MLOps (along with DevOps), and Cloud services. On the other hand, if you are currently learning or working with digital skills in the web access point, perhaps your next learning goals may be in the Services, DevOps, Cyber and Cloud areas.

In the next chapter, The Learning Foundations, we will distill down the learning spectrum to its fundamental learning blocks and discover the self-organized fundamental fractal which is at the heart of our learning fractal - the learning spectrum. These foundations coupled with the virtues of the learning fractal viz. perseverance, discipline and curiosity, not only helps beginners build a solid foundation to design their own learning map to acquire digital skills, but also bolsters the learning agility of digital practitioners who can trace their learning journey so far and help them charter the next steps on their learning map.

Chapter-3
The Learning Foundations

Jackson Pollock, the American artist, is regarded as one of the most influential artists of the 20th century. Known for his unique style of drip painting in which he would pour paint onto a canvas that was laid on the floor and later using hardened brushes, sticks, and basters, he would squirt, splash and drip paint onto the canvas. If you visited the National Gallery of Art in Washington DC, you may be able to see Pollock's seminal painting titled "Lavender Mist" (a.k.a Number 1, 1950). Lavender Mist is described as an abstract horizontal painting with densely spaced lines and splatters in black, white, pale salmon pink, teal, and steel gray criss crossing on a rectangular cream-colored canvas[182].

The painting at first seems like total chaos, the lines move in every direction, the colors blend and bleed into each other, the drips and splatters are layered on top of each other, and it all suggests a chaotic and frenzied creative process. However, upon closer examination at various levels of magnification, art historians and scientists have discovered that the painting reveals fractal-like patterns[183], particularly characterized by the presence of self-similar structures in terms of shapes and forms that repeat at different scales.

Our learning fractal - the learning spectrum, which we discussed in the previous chapter, too may seem like total chaos. You may feel dizzy when contemplating the variety of digital skills, some layered on top of others too, that not only crop up in different parts of the spectrum but also seem to grow out in different directions. Observing the spectrum as it continuously evolves is perhaps like watching Pollock's painting come to life. However, here too, if we closely examine the learning spectrum, we will discover the presence of a self-similar structure which repeats itself at different scales. We will be able to observe that like a typical fractal pattern, our learning spectrum too is self-organized where-in a fundamental fractal repeats across the entire spectrum, contributing to its beauty, creativity and surprise.

It is also interesting to note that when Richard Taylor[184] used an eye tracking machine to measure where people's pupils focussed on when looking at images of Pollock's paintings, he found that the search pattern used by the pupil was itself a fractal[185] (we use fractals to comprehend fractals!). He further observed that looking at fractals (both natural and stimulated) is soothing because when the fractal structure of eye matches with the fractal structure of the image, it causes a physiological resonance that eventually leads to reduced stress[186]. In a similar vein, using the fundamental fractal (of the learning spectrum) makes it easier to comprehend our learning fractal - the learning spectrum, and resonating with it optimizes our learning and bolsters our ability to assimilate the nuances of the learning spectrum.

In the previous chapter, we explored the breadth and the depth of the learning spectrum by zooming into its different areas and discovering the variety of digital skills that one has to acquire in each area of the learning spectrum. You may also recall that after exploring the individual parts we further zoomed out to view the entire learning spectrum as a whole, and observed the interconnections between the different areas of the spectrum. Having experienced the eternal and connected nature of our learning fractal, it is typical to be overwhelmed by the complexity of the spectrum which may seem unapproachable and impossible to master.

In this chapter, we will draw inspiration from the self-organized nature of fractals and zoom into the learning spectrum to discover its underlying fundamentals. We will distill down the learning spectrum to its fundamental fractal which enables us to tackle the daunting complexity of the spectrum and sets us up for success on our learning journey. Here again, like in chapter 2, we will use digital experiences as the pivot to discover the fundamental fractal and then observe how this fractal repeats across the breadth and depth of the learning spectrum. We will further dive into the different components that make up the fundamental fractal and explore how mastering these components becomes key to mastering the learning spectrum across its breadth and depth.

The Learning Triad

Recall the example of online shopping, which we discussed in chapter 2, in order to demystify the various areas of the learning spectrum. We saw that various access points such as web, mobile and conversational interfaces help consume this digital experience, anytime, anywhere. We also observed how the insights part of the learning spectrum enriches the digital experience by personalizing and contextualizing it for the end users. Under the hood, access points and insights interact with a variety of services and the underlying data infrastructure which perform most of the heavy lifting required to facilitate the user journeys. We also understood the role of DevOps, Cyber security and Cloud in delivering these user journeys in a secure, reliable and flexible manner with agility.

If you further contemplate the online shopping experience, you will see that it is composed of several user journeys such as finding the product in the catalog, adding it to your shopping cart, paying for it at check-out, tracking your shipment along its way, letting others know that you liked it, or even dealing with a change of mind to return it. As you may recall, these user journeys have made way into online shopping over a period of time, and the earliest online shopping experiences only displayed the product catalog and allowed users to place orders over a telephone call. As you continue to ruminate, you will realize that all these user journeys came to being as a result of the continuous changes created by consumer demands and technology advancements. You will further realize that this flux evoked the power of imagination (and vice-versa), which lies at the heart of this evolution; and of every user journey of every digital experience. **Imagination** being the source of creativity and innovation, acts as the driver for progress of digital experiences. It underpins every aspect of digital experiences - both the visible ones that users see and feel, and the invisible ones that aren't immediately apparent.

If we take a closer look at the online shopping experience, we will see that as end users navigate through the various user journeys using the access points, they consume and/or generate **data**. Further, under the hood, the various components of the learning spectrum also engage with this data and we can observe that any user journey can be described based on how the data gets consumed, generated, transformed and exchanged. One of the ways to bring imagination to fruition is to understand the data and how it is consumed, generated, transformed or exchanged across the user journey. For example, if we were to visualize the journey of 'finding the product', where a user searches for a product that she is interested to buy, we need to start by understanding the product catalog data which is consumed to generate a list of products that match the user's search. Similarly, to visualize the user journey of 'adding the product to a shopping cart', we need to understand how the product data of the selected product gets transformed into order line item data which is used to create an order for the user. And to visualize the 'tracking a shipment' user journey, we need to understand the order details data that gets exchanged with a shipment tracking provider system so that the user can see where each item of her shipment is in real-time and track their arrival. As you can see from these examples, understanding the data and how it gets consumed, generated, transformed or exchanged is crucial to designing and concretizing the imagined user journeys.

While imagination reflects the purpose and inspiration of a user journey, and data represents the nuances of what happens in the user journey, **logic** provides the framework to implement the user journey and the whole digital experience. In order to implement any user journey, one has to formulate the logic that is required to achieve it. For example, if you were to implement the 'finding a product' user journey, you would have to dabble with various scenarios that could arise from the search. You would have to think about - how you want to display various products that are related to the user's search i.e. if 100 products matched the search would you display them all at once or fetch them in batches?. Similarly, you would also want to factor for a situation where the product that the user is looking for is unavailable. In this case, maybe you would like to show them some alternate products or inform them of when the product they are looking for will be available. Similarly, to implement the 'return an item' user journey you may have to decide whether the product is returnable, and if so what would you do if the user is trying to return it after the return period elapses, or what if the product is damaged beyond repair - could it be destroyed by the user instead of being returned to the seller?

As you look at any digital experience you can see that these three elements viz. imagination, data and logic, are central to conceiving and implementing it. Imagination is the seed for the continuous evolution of the user journeys, data is representation of the various objects that are part of the user journeys, and logic represents the actions on the objects and eventually leads to realizing the imagined experience. These three elements are fundamental to digital experiences, and by virtue of it to the learning spectrum as well. When we zoom into any part of the learning spectrum, we discover the presence of these three elements. For example, in the web app (access point) of online shopping, imagination helps us conceive the layout of the web pages presented to the users, logic helps describe the sequence of actions that the user can perform and their responses, and data is consumed to display the products and generated when user interacts with the web app. As we zoom into different parts of the learning spectrum, we observe that this triad of Imagination, Data and Logic constantly recurs across the breadth and depth of the spectrum at various scales and sizes. This triad is the self-organized fundamental fractal which is the key to mastering the learning spectrum, and therefore is referred to as the learning triad, as depicted in Fig 3.1.

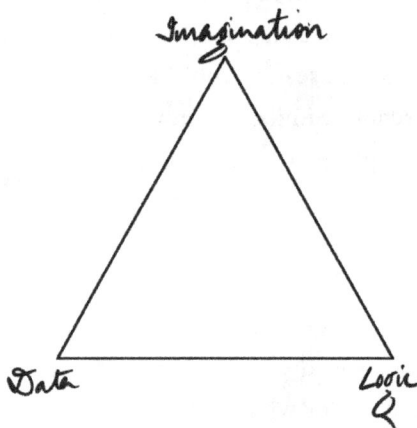

Fig 3.1: The Learning Triad

Just like in a fractal pattern such as the Romanesco Broccoli, where we see the pattern of cones of cones repeating in a logarithmic spiral at various scales, the learning triad too repeats at various scales within the learning spectrum. We may observe that as we progress on the journey to master the learning spectrum, some individual elements may be more apparent than the others. For example, typically when we are thoroughly zoomed into the services part of the learning spectrum, the role of the logic element of the triad may be more apparent and visible than the data and imagination elements which stay in the background. However, understanding the interplay between these three elements in all parts of the learning spectrum is crucial to producing the overall digital experience and mastering the entire spectrum.

It is also interesting to note that any of these three elements can take the center stage in the origin of the experience. So far, we have observed the role of imagination as the pivotal element in the origin of the online shopping experience example, however it is not always the case. For example, observing the patterns in clickstream data generated by user behavior on the online shopping app could ignite the imagination of newer/enhanced user journeys such as 'recommending alternate products for up-selling/cross-selling'. In this scenario, the data element takes the center stage to help imagine user journeys and eventually realize them using logic. In a similar manner, logic may also become the pivotal element where keenly observing and analyzing the implementation of the existing user journeys, and the data that supports it, could fuel the reimagination of these user journeys and yield more desirable experiences.

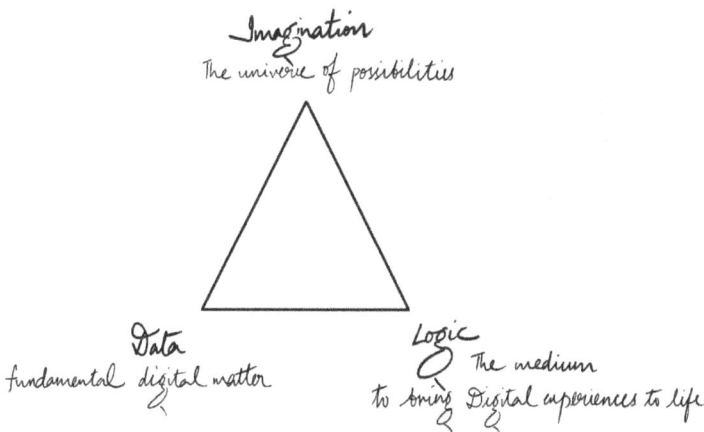

Imagination
The universe of possibilities

Data
fundamental digital matter

Logic
The medium to bring Digital experiences to life

Fig 3.2: Essence of the elements of the Learning Triad

Fig 3.2 depicts the essence of each element of the triad in a nutshell. Imagination is the seed to creating compelling user journeys and digital experiences and represents the **universe of possibilities**; data is the key element in every user journey as it gets consumed, generated, transformed and exchanged across the digital experience making it the **fundamental digital matter**; and logic helps realize the digital experiences thus becoming the **medium through which digital experiences are brought to life.**

This learning triad is the fundamental fractal (or the seed fractal) of our vast and expansive learning spectrum. The interplay between its elements is at the heart of all digital experiences that exist today, and will come to being in the future. You may recall that in Chapter 2, we discussed the prism of digital experiences, and explored the seven key attributes viz. intimacy, interactivity, immediacy, intelligence, insightfulness, intuition and immersiveness, that we can observe in modern digital experiences. Having understood the learning triad, you may now be able to appreciate that these seven attributes that lend color to modern digital experiences are a result of the varying degrees of interplay between the elements of our learning triad. For example, you may recall that when we described interactivity, we highlighted the range of user inputs, across a variety of user interfaces, that modern digital experiences are expected to swiftly respond to. When you look at this through the lens of the learning triad, you should now be able to see that this is fulfilled through the interplay between imagination and logic, where-in imagination helps visualize the range of inputs, and logic helps describe how the user interface is supposed to respond to these inputs; and of course data gets consumed, generated, transformed or exchanged along the process.

By now you may have realized that any user journey of a modern digital experience, irrespective of the degree of intimacy, interactivity, immediacy, intelligence, insightfulness, intuition, or immersiveness that it exhibits, is fundamentally crafted by interplaying the three elements of our learning triad. Therefore, learning to master this fundamental fractal by studying each of its individual elements and exploring the interplay among them, is key to mastering the learning spectrum and successfully navigating your digital journey.

Logic

Logic provides the framework to implement the various user journeys and is the medium through which digital experiences are brought to life. It helps organize ideas and relevant information into a sequence of steps to form tangible digital experiences which end users consume. Unlike common sense which is an informal and intuitive tool to understand the real world, logic is a more formal and structured way of looking at problems and their solutions. Although informal forms of logic do exist and are used in everyday communication, reasoning, and making judgements based on past experiences, formal logic is a structured approach to solving problems in a precise and systematic way. The development of symbolic logic, which is a form of formal logic that employs the use of symbols to represent statements, has been key to the development of a variety of fields such as mathematics, philosophy, and computer science. In the learning spectrum, formal logic takes the form of programming and is widely prevalent and can be seen across access points, insights, services, data infrastructure, cyber security and cloud areas. Logic is therefore an appropriate starting point that one must learn in order to break down the real world (physical and digital) problems, build digital experiences, and overall to master the learning spectrum.

Across the learning spectrum, logic manifests itself through programming which as you may know by now is fundamental to creating digital experiences. Programming helps express the logic in a way that can be interpreted and followed by the various devices and underlying infrastructure that enable the digital experiences. It is the lingua franca of digital systems and helps thoroughly detail the various sequence of steps and instructions that the devices and underlying infrastructure must process and execute to realize the desired digital experience. For example, referring back to the online shopping app, if we take the task of computing the total value of all the items in a customer's cart, the logic would probably be like this:

1. Input:
   a. The items in the cart of the user. Let's assume there are three items for now - coffee, cheese and chips
   b. The entire shopping catalog and the prices for each item. Let's assume there are 5 items - apple, coffee, cheese, chips and carrot with respective prices
2. Process:
   a. Look up the price of each item in the user's cart from the shopping catalog
   b. Accumulate the individual prices and compute the total value of the cart
3. Output:
   a. Display the total value of the cart to the user

Here we have expressed the logic to complete the task at hand as a sequence of steps, which is typically referred to as an algorithm. At the foundational level, the logic for accomplishing any task essentially comprises three blocks - input, process and output. The process block describes the steps that are performed on the input to yield the output. Although this logic is quite structured, it cannot be understood/executed by a device directly. This is where the logic needs to be translated into a program/code (using a programming language) which can be executed by the device.

In the below code snippets, we can observe how the logic of computing the total value of a user's cart is being implemented using Python, Java and JavaScript. If you aren't familiar with programming, the code snippets may seem alien at first. However, you may find it easy to interpret it as you read along and correlate it with the algorithm described earlier.

```python
# Code Snippet 1 - Language: Python

# Note: '#' represents comments/notes in the code.

# Input

# The shopping catalog along with the prices for
each item

shopping_catalog = {"apple": 12,
                    "coffee": 15,
                    "cheese": 20,
                    "chips": 10,
                    "carrot": 30}

# In Python, the above data structure is called a
dictionary. Here it contains the name of the item
as a key and its price as value. E.g. 'apple' is
the key and 12 is its value

# The cart containing the items added by the user

cart = ["coffee", "cheese", "chips"]

# In Python, the above data structure is called
a list. Here it contains the three items that the
user has added to her cart.

# Process

# To calculate the total value of the cart we de-
fine a function which accepts the input and returns
the output.

def get_total(cart, shopping_catalog):
    total = 0

    # Check if the cart is empty
    if not cart:
      print("Cart is empty. Add items to the
            cart")
      return 0
    else:
```

```python
        # Use a loop to iterate over the cart and
fetch each item in it
        for item in cart:
        # Fetch the price of each item from the
shopping catalog and add it to the total
            total = total + shopping_catalog[item]
        return total

# Output

# Invoke the function using the inputs to get the
output. The print function can display the output
returned by the get_total function on the screen.

total_price = get_total(cart, shopping_catalog)

if total_price > 0:
        print(f"Your total is ${total_price}.")
```

Code Snippet 1: Finding the total value of items in a shopping cart using Python

```java
// Code Snippet 2 - Language: Java

// Note: '//' represents comments/notes in the
code.

import java.util.HashMap;
import java.util.Map;
import java.util.List;
import java.util.ArrayList;

public class ShoppingCart {

// Input

        // The shopping catalog along with the pric-
es for each item

static Map<String, Integer> shoppingCatalog = new
HashMap<String, Integer>() {
    {
            put("apple", 12);
```

```
                put("coffee", 15);
                put("cheese", 20);
                put("chips", 10);
                put("carrot", 30);
        }
    };
```

// In Java we use a HashMap. It stores data as key value pairs. For example, here apple is the key and 12 is the value

// The cart containing the items added by the user

```
    static List<String> cart = new Array-
List<String>() {
        {
            add("coffee");
            add("cheese");
            add("chips");
        }
    };
```
// In Java, we use an ArrayList. Here it contains the three items that the user has added to her cart.

// Process

// To calculate the total value of the cart we define a function which accepts the input and returns the output.

```
    public static int getTotal(List<String>
cart, Map<String, Integer> shoppingCatalog) {
    int total = 0;

    // Check if the cart is empty
    if (cart.isEmpty()) {
        System.out.println("Cart is empty. Add
items to the cart");
        return 0;
    } else {
        // Use a loop to iterate over the cart
and fetch each item in it
```

```java
                for (String item : cart) {
            // Fetch the price of each item from
the shopping catalog and add it to the total
                total = total + shoppingCatalog.
get(item);
        }
        return total;
    }
}
```

// Output

// Invoke the function using the inputs to
get the output. The System.out.println function
can display the output returned by the getTotal
function on the screen.

```java
    public static void main(String[] args) {
        int total_price = getTotal(cart, shop-
pingCatalog);
        if(total_price > 0){
        System.out.printf("Your total is $%d.%n",
total_price);
        }
    }
}
```

Code Snippet 2: Finding the total value of items in a shopping cart using Java

```javascript
// Code Snippet 3 - Language: JavaScript

// Note:'//'represents comments/notes in the code.

// Input

// The shopping catalog containing along with the
prices for each item

const shoppingCatalog = {
        'apple': 12,
        'coffee': 15,
        'cheese': 20,
        'chips': 10,
        'carrot': 30
};
```

```javascript
// The cart containing the items added by the user
const cart = ['coffee', 'cheese', 'chips'];

// Process

// To calculate the total value of the cart we de-
fine a function which accepts the input and returns
the output.

function getTotal(cart, shoppingCatalog) {
    let total = 0;

        // Check if the cart is empty
        if (cart.length === 0) {
           console.log("Cart is empty. Add items to
the cart");
           return 0;
        }
        else {
        // Use a loop to iterate over the cart and
fetch each item in it
           for (let i = 0; i < cart.length; i++) {
               const item = cart[i];
                 // Fetch the price of each item
from the shopping catalog and add it to the total
               total = total + shoppingCatalog[item];
           }
           return total;
        }
}

// Output

// Invoke the function using the inputs to get
the output. The console.log function can display
the output returned by the getTotal function on
screen.

let total_price = getTotal(cart, shoppingCatalog);
if (total_price > 0) {
      console.log(`Your total is $${total_
price}.`);
}
```

Code Snippet 3: Finding the total value of items in a shopping cart using JavaScript

We have implemented the logic to compute the cart in three different programming languages viz. Python, Java and JavaScript, to not only give you a glimpse of how the logic looks when it is translated into code, but also demonstrate the similarity in how the logic is expressed across different languages. You may have noticed, though these code snippets are written in different languages they achieve the same task at hand and fundamentally use similar constructs. Across different languages the code contains similar constructs such as data structures to store the data (cart and shopping catalog), a function that does the processing (to get the total cart value), a conditional statement (to check if the cart is empty), and a loop that is used to repeat the same action several times (adding the price of each element to the total). Fundamental constructs such as variables, operators, control structures that conditionally execute code and/or repeatedly execute the code, functions or methods, and input/output are the building blocks of any programming language and are heavily employed when we translate the logic into code.

If you zoom out of the online shopping experience and mull over the code and its building blocks, you will see that a similar set of building blocks (and code) can be used in several other digital experiences. For example, in an online ticket reservation system, the code would have to take the list of selected seats (like the cart in an online shopping app), and look up the prices of all the seats (like the shopping catalog), then compute the total cost of all tickets selected and finally display the cost to the user. In another example, a similar code can be used for a restaurant's bill calculator, with some modification to add a tip at the end. Programming is used to implement the logic across different user journeys and across them, the logic is always constructed using the fundamental constructs. These simple constructs form the foundational lego blocks used to create the complex and intricate logic that powers modern digital experiences.

You may have now realized that learning the nuances of programming is key to mastering the learning spectrum because as you may have seen, programming is omnipresent across the breadth and depth of the spectrum. Programming is essential to building user interfaces on access points; creating, orchestrating and monitoring services; storing, processing and gleaning insights from data; provisioning, managing and scaling infrastructure; and securing the full stack from threats and vulnerabilities, as depicted in Fig 3.3.

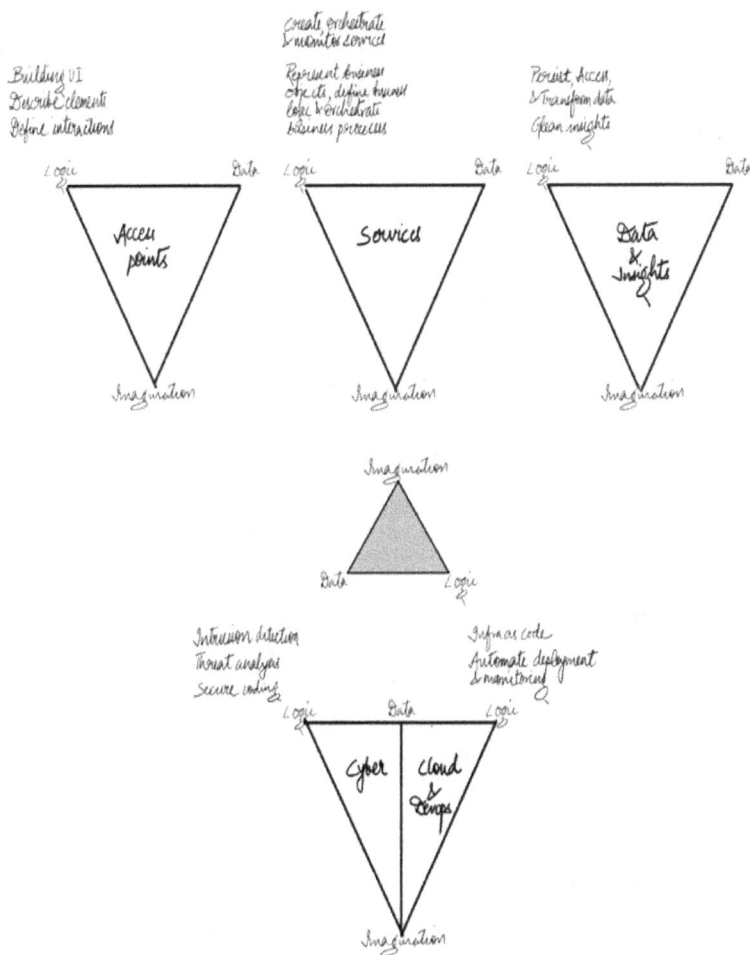

Fig 3.3: The omnipresence of Programming/Logic across the components of the Learning Spectrum

Recall that in Chapter 2, we discussed the various access points on which digital experiences are consumed by end users. We also discussed the various digital skills that one has to learn in order to build the access point components of the digital experiences. Programming plays a key role in building user interfaces on access points across two key aspects - defining the elements that the users interact with, and describing the response of the interface for each user interaction. For example, on web access points we use HTML to define the various interactive elements such as text fields, buttons, radio buttons, check boxes, navigation bars and images that the users see on the web page and CSS is used to define how these elements must be organized and styled. We use JavaScript to describe the behavior associated with various actions such as click, touch and drag on these elements. JavaScript is also used to alter the properties of the various elements making the webapps more interactive to further enhance the overall experience. You may also recall that modern JavaScript frameworks such as Angular or React help create Single Page Applications(SPAs) which give web apps a rich and native mobile app-like feel. These frameworks provide a structured and friendly way to organize the logic associated with the behavior of webapp. Similarly, for building native mobile apps on Android or iOS, we declare and define the user interface elements such as buttons, toggle switches, sliders and lists using XML for Android and SwiftUI for iOS and use programming languages such as Java/Kotlin for Android and Swift for iOS to describe and detail the various logical steps that must be performed, in line with the users' interactions with the app.

In the realm of Services, programming plays a key role in describing the logic that does most of the heavy lifting required to fulfill the various user journeys of digital experiences. These services encapsulate the business objects, business logic that talks with the underlying business objects, and describe the business processes which orchestrate the business logic required to fulfill these user journeys. Programming is vital to creating and orchestrating these services irrespective of the approach (monolith, microservices, etc.) that is used to develop them. Recall that to create these services we use stacks based on programming languages such as Java, .NET or JavaScript; and to orchestrate the communication among them (and with access points) over APIs we use XML or JSON.

Programming also plays a key role in the storage and processing of data that is consumed, generated, transformed and exchanged across multiple user journeys. In terms of storage, programming is used to interact with structured, semi-structured or unstructured data stores (or databases) to persist the data. Recall that we use SQL and NoSQL programming to interact with a variety of databases. In terms of processing, programming is used to describe the various operation that are to be performed on the data - be it simply accessing or exchanging the data, or transforming it to fulfill various user journeys. Programming is also essential to analyze the data in order to glean descriptive, predictive or cognitive insights from it. Recall that we use various frameworks or libraries based on programming languages such as Python, Java, Scala or Julia to process and analyze the data.

Both on-prem and cloud infrastructure required to run modern digital experiences are typically provisioned and managed using programming. Programming enables the automation of various tasks such as creating new virtual machines or containers, configuring the networks and servers, installing software libraries, load balancing various resources, and monitoring and scaling the environments at runtime. Programming also helps reduce/eliminate toil through automation, implement observability, forecast and plan for future demand and capacity, and ensure the overall reliability of the infrastructure. Programming is heavily employed across enterprise infrastructure to bring in reusability, consistency and transparency in implementing and managing the infrastructure; and is popularly referred to as Infrastructure as Code. Python, Go[187] and Perl[188] are some of the popular programming languages used in this space.

Programming plays a pivotal role in protecting the full stack of access points, services, data, and the underlying infrastructure from various malicious attacks that aim to compromise the safety, privacy and security of digital experiences. It is very interesting to note the dual play of programming here, while on one hand we use programming to inherently implement security in every aspect of the experience, on the other we also use programming to orchestrate various attacks on the system in order to unearth the various vulnerabilities that it might be susceptible to; and eventually make it foolproof. Secure programming practices are baked into the development of digital experiences using the various features available in almost all the programming languages, software libraries and programming frameworks to ensure that the system is inherently secure. On the other hand, specialized software tools and libraries are used to automate the identification and resolution of vulnerabilities in the system with the help of programming.

By now you may be able to appreciate and fathom the omnipresence of programming across the entire learning spectrum. Having seen a glimpse of the different programming languages that are used in various parts of the learning spectrum, you may have noticed that there is a wide variety of programming languages, each employed to do a range of tasks. While this variety may seem overwhelming at first, it is important to remember that across these various programming languages what still remains constant is the fundamental building blocks of programming such as the constructs for accepting input, producing output, storing data, performing various operations, conditionally and/or repeatedly executing code using control structures, and functions/methods for modularizing the logic so that it can also be reused in different parts (wherever applicable).

When using programming across any area of the learning spectrum, what matters the most is three key aspects - identifying a programming language fit for the task, choosing the programming paradigm (approach) to construct the logic, and optimizing the program to get the best performance out of it, as depicted in Fig 3.4.

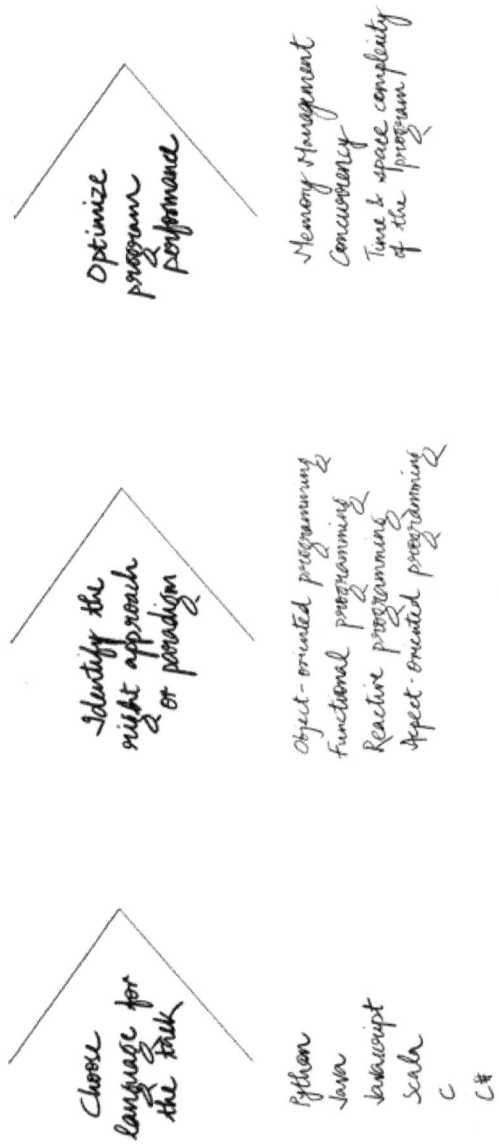

Choose language for the task

Python
Java
Javascript
Scala
C
C#

Identify the right approach or paradigm

Object-oriented programming
Functional programming
Reactive programming
Aspect-oriented programming

Optimize program performance

Memory Management
Concurrency
Time & space complexity of the program

Fig 3.4: Key Aspects of Programming

Let us take the example of adding interactivity in the online shopping web app. Here, we describe the logic using JavaScript as it is the best suited language to add dynamic behavior to a web app. In JavaScript, we represent the various elements of the page and the browser as objects, and hence follow the object oriented paradigm to construct the logic for interactivity. Further to this, understanding how JavaScript interacts with the browser, based on its specifications, helps build more performant, elegant and secure web apps.

In another example, to analyze the user data of the online shopping app and build machine learning models to recommend products to the user, we typically use Python. This is because in addition to being a powerful general purpose programming language, Python also boasts an extensive ecosystem of libraries that are well suited for such numerical and scientific computing. Here, we use the functional programming paradigm to frame the logic of the various transformations that can be applied on the data in the form of functions that accept the data as input and produce transformed data in the output. Finally, appreciating the nuances of the Python specification and how the program runs on the machine enables us to reduce the time to analysis, and build optimized models that offer greater performance on the underlying machines.

Irrespective of the programming language or paradigm that one chooses to work with for a given task, the learning journey to becoming a programmer typically progresses incrementally (and often iteratively) along the following stages, as depicted in Fig 3.5.

One must first learn to develop a programming mindset that helps them break down any problem and visualize its solution logically in a way that a computing device understands and executes it to provide the desired outcome. This stage is often the most challenging and at the same time most rewarding where the learner breaks the inertia associated with adapting to the programming mindset. The idea is to gradually build the skills that help break down complex logic as

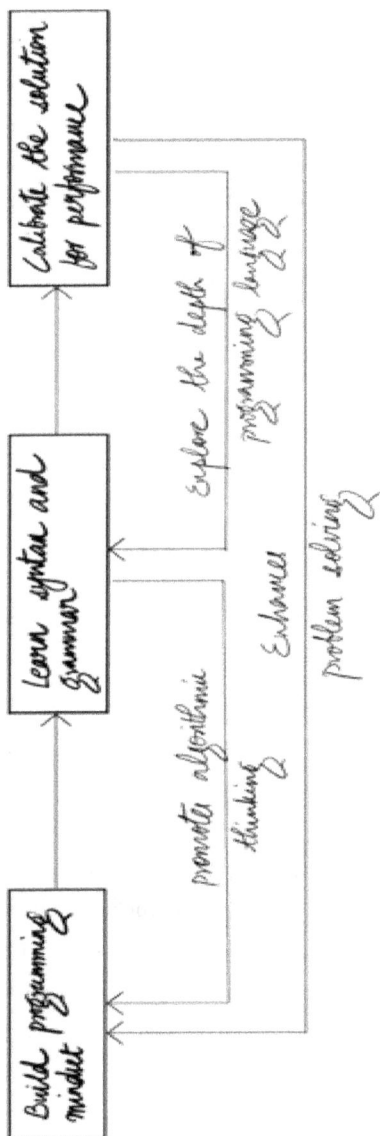

Fig 3.5: Learning Journey for Programming

Build programming mindset

promotes algorithmic thinking

Learn syntax and grammar

Explore the depth of programming language

Enhances

Calibrate the solution for performance

problem solving

a set of simpler and connected blocks which a machine understands. Pseudocodes and flowcharts are some of the helpful tools that come handy along this journey. Pseudocode expresses the logic in simple (natural) language and describes the steps required to achieve a task at a high level. A flowchart on the other hand is a visual representation of the logic structured as the steps of an algorithm. Unlike pseudocode which may be written without any fixed structure or standards, flowcharts specify standard symbols to represent the various fundamental constructs that are used in logic. For example, referring back to the code snippets (1, 2, and 3) we saw earlier where we computed the total value of a customer's cart, the code was written after visualizing the logic using pseudocode and/or flowchart. The pseudocode and its equivalent flowchart for the task of computing the total value of the customer's cart is depicted in Fig 3.6.

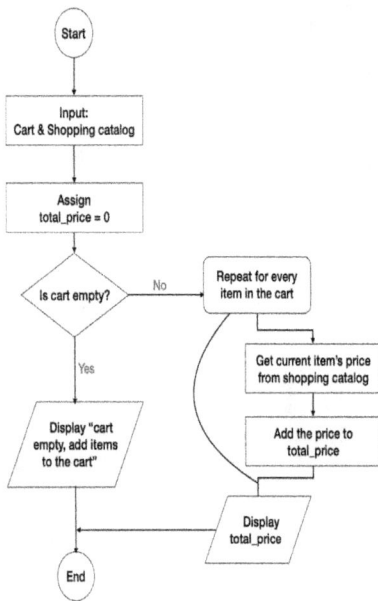

```
Input: User's cart and shop-
ping catalog
Set total_price = 0
if cart is empty:
    Display "Cart empty, add
items
    to the cart"
else if cart is not empty:
    Repeat for each item in the
    cart:
Pick the item from the cart
and look up its price from the
shopping catalog
Add the price to the total_
price                  .
    Display total_price to user
```

Fig 3.6: Pseudocode and Flowchart

The next step after beginning to acquire a programming mindset by experimenting with pseudocodes and flowcharts is to get familiar with the vocabulary and grammar of the programming language. This typically implies becoming comfortable with the basic constructs and algorithms that are commonly used across a variety of tasks. For this, one must learn the language specific keywords, understanding the fundamental constructs available such as sequence, selection, iteration and recursion, and learning the key modules/libraries available to deal with repeated tasks such as string manipulation, mathematical calculations, and access to underlying system resources like file system, memory, etc.

Recall that we saw the various constructs such as if condition (selection), for loop (iteration) and arithmetic operators (mathematical calculations) in the code snippets that demonstrated writing the logic of computing the total value of a customer's cart. To practice this, one should start with tackling simpler problems - by visualizing their solution using pseudocodes and flowcharts and then implementing it using the various programming constructs; eventually combining it all to realize more complex problems along the learning journey. IDEs (integrated Development Environments) such as Visual Studio [189], Visual Studio Code (VS Code)[190], Eclipse[191], and PyCharm[192] are some of the popular tools that come handy along this journey. These IDEs provide an environment to write and execute code, contain features such as highlighting, autocomplete and debugging which enhances productivity, and also offer features to enhance the code quality and implement best practices which help learn programming more effectively. As one progresses on their journey to learn the syntax and grammar of a programming language, it further enhances their programming mindset by promoting algorithmic thinking which boosts their ability to break down a problem into multiple sub problems and devise algorithms for solving them.

Finally, learners must continuously look towards calibrating their solutions to ensure that their programs are more precise, complete, elegant, secure and optimized. To do this, one should start by understanding the nuances of how the programs are executed by the underlying machine and what resources (time, memory, etc.) are consumed by it during the execution. One may have to experiment with various possible solutions and evaluate their efficacy of execution in the given environment to arrive at an optimal solution. Mastering this skill enables one to become a proficient programmer and differentiates them from amateurs. Tools such as SonarQube[193] are used to evaluate the efficacy of the programs against various parameters such as code quality, code coverage, security and performance. This continuous learning stage of calibrating the solutions feeds back into the other stages of learning programming. It not only helps delve deeper into any programming language's syntax and grammar to help identify optimal ways to write code, but also enhances the problem solving abilities of the learners and contributes to a well developed programming mindset.

Building modern digital experiences within enterprises requires a huge deal of collaboration among individuals and teams, as they dish out new features periodically to keep pace with growing consumer demands and technology advancements. This means that there is a huge deal of emphasis on the code (programming/logic) to be both functional and efficient. Ignoring problems during the software development process and deferring them for a later time in the need for quicker releases often leads to technical debt[194] which compounds over the lifetime of the software. Technical debt increases the likelihood of bugs, vulnerabilities and eventually system failures. Therefore, in addition to building out a programming mindset, we should also cultivate a DevOps mindset which means taking responsibility for the code we write, sharing knowledge on the code and test cases, continuously improving the quality of code while also building out newer features, and using logic and programming for automation to enhance the delivery of digital experiences.

Referring back to the example of building the online shopping web app, we have to cultivate a programming mindset as we start learning JavaScript which is the lingua franca of modern web apps. We also need to familiarize ourselves with the vocabulary and grammar of JavaScript that enables us to represent the various HTML elements such as text fields, buttons, radio buttons, check boxes, navigation bars and images on the web page as objects and construct the interaction and logic using the object oriented paradigm. As we continue to learn and develop modern web apps we must also explore the nuances of the environment that the apps run in. We must understand how JavaScript is interpreted by the web browsers, how the browser exchanges information while making API calls to various services that we may want to interact with, and how all of this should be done in an efficient, secure and accessible manner over the Internet. Along this journey we also need to learn the various IDEs, tools and frameworks that enable us to become proficient modern web app developers. JavaScript frameworks like Angular or React provide modules that encapsulate the functionality associated with several common tasks such as dynamically rendering page elements, making secure API calls, and synchronizing the data between the access point and the backend services. CSS Frameworks such as Bootstrap provide the functionality required to make the web app responsive so that the experience across various access points with diverse screen sizes and types is seamless and delightful. The various IDEs and tooling enable us to work with agility by adopting DevOps practices, create secure and performant apps by providing automated analysis of security and performance challenges and help fix them, and deploy the apps to the underlying on-prem or cloud infrastructure in order to make it scalable and resilient.

Similarly, referring back to the example of analyzing data from the online shopping app and building machine learning models using Python, we must start by cultivating a programming mindset as we learn Python for data analysis. We must also understand the domain of the data that is being analyzed, explore the various data transformations and their outcomes, and visualize the several possible solutions to the problem at hand. Getting familiar with the vocabulary and grammar of Python enables us to implement the logic to operate on the data by defining the functions that perform various transformations on the data. We should further strengthen our prowess by leveraging various Python packages or modules like Numpy, Pandas, Scikit-Learn, Matplotlib, etc. that provide the functionality for several common tasks such as reading data from disparate sources, representing data efficiently to perform large computations, and plotting or visualizing data to glean insights. Getting to know the nuances of how data is stored at source, how it is extracted and read, how it is processed in large volumes across distributed systems, how the various underlying algorithms are used to build machine learning models, and how the various resources such as memory can be efficiently used to process the data will enable us to become proficient data analysts. Mastering the various tools and IDEs will enable us to work collaboratively in agile teams, build and maintain large data pipelines on both on-prem and cloud by following DataOps/MLOps practices, ensure data privacy and security is maintained across systems, and enable the outcomes to be fair, accountable, and explainable.

By now, you may be able to appreciate the role of logic across the learning spectrum and understand the importance of programming in crafting modern digital experiences. You may also have noticed that across the learning spectrum, different programming languages are employed based on the task at hand. As a learner, it would be prudent to learn to write code in more than one programming language. Learning multiple programming languages further boosts one's ability to cultivate a programming mindset and sets them up to become a versatilist; recall that we discussed this as one of the growing expectations on talent archetypes today in Chapter 1 of this book.

Although programming is key to implementing logic across the entire learning spectrum, it usually has a steep learning curve which deters the agility required for modern enterprises while crafting digital experiences. The introduction of several LCNC (low-code no-code platforms) such as Microsoft Power Platform[195], Appian[196], Mendix[197], Webflow[198], Glide[199] and Makerpad[200] has lowered the barrier to entry and democratized logic such that business users can build solutions without learning the nuances of programming. These platforms help the users express their logic through simple and intuitive visual building blocks, reuse pre-built templates for common tasks, integrate with external systems such as databases and APIs easily, and deploy their applications effortlessly. Using these platforms reduces the steep curve required to learn programming, nevertheless cultivating a programming mindset is essential to mastering the logic element of the learning triad.

So far, we have seen how logic - one of the elements of the learning triad - manifests itself in the form of programming and prevails across the length and breadth of the learning spectrum. We have also explored how we can approach learning logic by cultivating a programming mindset, learning the vocabulary and grammar of programming languages, and understanding the nuances of how the underlying machine plays the programs. When we zoom out of the logic and look at the learning triad and its elements - logic, data and imagination - as a whole, we observe that the interplay of logic with data and imagination becomes even more prominent in the context of an enterprise. Most of the time in the enterprise context, we may not compose the logic for a greenfield situation, but rather learn from the underlying data or existing user journeys and reimagine the existing logic to create enhanced or newer digital experiences. On the other hand, in greenfield situations, logic is iteratively applied to rapidly prototype the imagined experience, and validate the data flows to create new digital experiences.

Data

We have so far seen how logic manifests itself through programming and plays a vital role in the development of digital experiences. Data, the second element of the triad, serves as the fundamental digital matter around which the digital experiences are orchestrated. As Martin Kleppmann writes in his book Designing Data-Intensive

Applications[201] "Data models are perhaps the most important part of developing software because they have such a profound effect: not only on how the software is written, but also on how we think about the problem we are solving". As we delve deeper to understand the data element of the triad we will see how it not only interplays with logic to get consumed, generated, transformed or exchanged across various user journeys, but also helps fuel the imagination of newer/improved digital experiences.

Data is omnipresent across all digital experiences. It may transform into different forms or structures as it gets exchanged across various stages of underlying user journeys. Along these stages, data that is either historic or instantaneously generated gets eventually consumed to fulfill the overall digital experience. Across these user journeys as data is consumed, generated, transformed or exchanged, it may need to be stored in relevant spaces based on its structure. If you closely examine the data, it can be distilled down to 3 dimensions - structure, time, and space. The structure dimension enables us to understand the shape, size, and type of the data; the time dimension helps trace its origin, lineage, and its applicability in the current context; and the space dimension helps identify the appropriate data storage and retrieval mechanisms, as depicted in Fig 3.7.

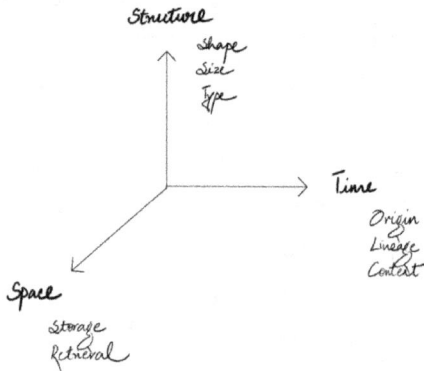

Fig 3.7: Three Dimensions of Data

Consider the example of the 'add to cart' user journey of the online shopping app. When the customer adds an item to her cart from the web app, data is generated and exchanged with the underlying services to update her cart and to compute the total value. This data is transformed to JSON format and then exchanged between the access point and underlying services over API calls. Services process the data and further store the relevant parts in a NoSQL database such as MongoDB in the data infrastructure. Here, in terms of the structure dimension, the data is represented in JSON (the shape of data) for both the data at the access point as well as the data in the underlying data infrastructure. In terms of the time dimension, the data at the web access point is instantaneous, whereas at the data infrastructure-several items could have been accumulated into their cart over a period of days. Finally as for the space dimension, the cart data could be stored on both the web browser's local storage and on the data infrastructure in a document database such as MongoDB. Code snippets 4 and 5 represent the JSON data generated upon adding an item to the cart on the web app access point, and the JSON data stored in the data infrastructure after processing by services respectively.

Code Snippet 4 Data generated when an item is added to the cart	Code snippet 5 Data stored in data infrastructure after processing by services
| ```json
{
"user_id": 8530271929374,

"items[uniq_id]":
"1784162124",

"merchantID":
"Z1GY732584PF08",

"session-id": "138-
1328164-9277034",

"timestamp": "2022-08-21
19:47:07 GMT + 5:30",

"quantity": "1",
}
``` | ```json
{
"user_id": 8530271929374,
"items": [
{
"product_id":
1784162124,
"name": "coffee",
"price": 15,
"quantity": 1,
"merchantID":
"Z1GY732584PF08"
},
{
"merchantID": "R9BX-
U562931LKN2"
},
{
"product_id":
99087654321,
"name": "chips",
"price": 10,
"quantity": 1,
"merchantID": "H7MTF-
415267BXCA"
}
],
"total_price": 45.0
}

"product_id":
79123456789,
"name": "cheese",
"price": 20,
"quantity": 1,
``` |

Code snippet 4 and 5: Data at access point and data infrastructure

If you zoom out of the shopping cart user journey and ruminate over the several other user journeys in the online shopping app, you can observe that the app deals with a variety of data with different properties along its structure, time and space dimensions. For example, the user data contains the user's personal details as well as transaction history of several thousand users, the product catalog contains data including name, category(ies), subcategory(ies), price, merchant(s), product description, product images, product videos, etc. about perhaps a million products, the order data contains the order details including the user's information and the information about the products that the user ordered for millions of orders. A typical online shopping app may consume, generate, transform and exchange well over a few terabytes of data across different components of the learning spectrum. The data may be in different structures such as text files, JSON, XML, images, videos, relational data, data in NoSQL databases, log files, and configuration files. It may be collected well over a period of a few years while at the same time new data gets generated every second; and the origin and lineage of the data may also be recorded as metadata. The online shopping app's data infrastructure may use a variety of ways to store the data (either on cloud or on-prem) such as flat files, SQL and NoSQL databases, data warehouses, and data lakes; based on how often it is intended to be accessed and how it should be processed.

Although data takes different forms across the spectrum, if you zoom into the most foundational level, under the hood all data is stored as bits. Each bit is a binary digit which has a value of either 1 or 0. The binary system is fundamental to most computing devices today and the processing units (processors) that are at heart of these devices essentially execute instructions to manipulate data in binary form. The process of converting any data to binary is called encoding, and the process of translating back from bits to the data which humans and applications interact with is called decoding. There are several encoding systems, each employed based on the data that needs to be represented. For example, when storing and transmitting videos, the popular encoding techniques are MPEG-4, H.264, and AV1. Similarly when storing and transmitting text the ASCII encoding, which converts each text character into a 7-bit binary code, is commonly used. If you look up the ASCII chart, you can see that the letter 'F' in 'Fractal' is represented as the number 70, which gets encoded to '1000110' (7 bits with each digit either 1 or 0) in binary. At the foundational level, all data is binary i.e the input data, the instructions to process it, and the output of processing are all represented in binary. Just like atoms make up the physical world and are considered its fundamental matter, data makes up the digital world (and digital experiences by extension) and therefore it is the fundamental digital matter.

Although atoms are the fundamental matter of the physical world, the beauty and variety in the world comes through the different physical or chemical processes through which atoms interact with one another. In a similar vein, beauty of digital experiences come from how logic (the processes) interplays with data (the fundamental digital matter) across the entire learning spectrum. Therefore, mastering the learning spectrum to build modern digital experiences requires one to embrace learning the nuances of data alongside logic/programming. Understanding this interplay not only helps us visualize the shifts along the structure, time and space dimensions of data, but also enables us to appreciate the full context in which the data gets generated, transformed, exchanged and consumed.

To understand this interplay, we need to further expand Fig 3.3 (represented earlier to describe how programming is omnipresent across the learning spectrum) and visualize the role of data in each area of the spectrum. As we observe the core of this interplay, we understand that data is typically consumed and/or generated by users across the user interfaces on various access points; transformed and exchanged with/across underlying services; transformed and analyzed to glean insights; used to define and automate the provisioning and management of scalable infrastructure; and analyzed to strengthen the security of the full stack and defend it from vulnerabilities and threats, as depicted in Fig 3.8.

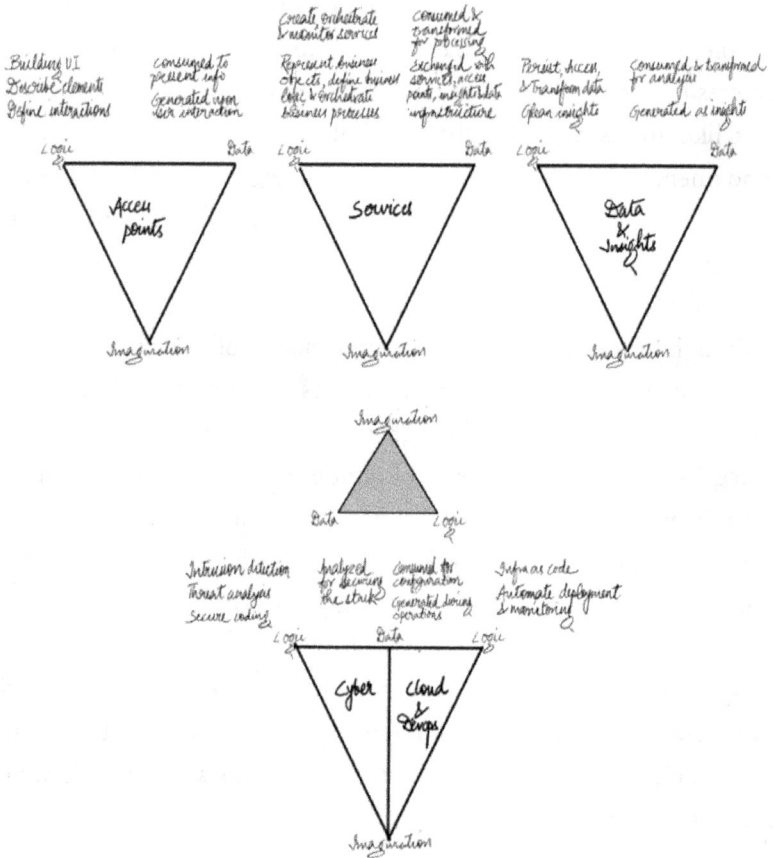

Fig 3.8: Interplay of Data with
Logic/Programming across the Learning Spectrum

Data typically gets consumed and generated across user interfaces on access points when users interact with digital experiences. It gets consumed within the logic defined in the access points to present users with relevant information and insights that they can act upon. For example, in the case of the online shopping app, data about the various products available for purchase is consumed to be displayed to the users so that they can browse the products they are looking for and add them to the cart. Data also gets generated by the users as they interact with digital experiences. In the example of the online shopping app, the logic at the access points can generate data about how the users navigate the experience - what products they browse, how long they spend looking at a product, etc. Here if you dissect the data into its time, space and structure dimensions, you will see that along the time dimension, the data generated at the access point is instantaneous vis-a-vis the one that is consumed is probably historic and is sourced from the underlying data infrastructure. In terms of the structure dimension, the data that gets consumed or generated at access points such as web and mobile is typically semi-structured and represented in JSON or XML. On conversational access points such as voice assistants, data that gets generated when users speak in natural language to the interface is unstructured. In terms of the space dimension, the data handled by the logic at access points is typically light-weight in comparison to that handled by other parts of the spectrum. And since most of the consumed data is required only for a short duration of time at the access point, it is typically only stored temporarily at the access point. However, the data that is generated by the user's interactions is usually passed on to underlying services for further processing and longer-term storage.

The core logic of digital experiences is encapsulated within services and it is entirely orchestrated around the data. Services communicate with one another and with access points through the exchange of relevant data. During this process, the data may also get transformed to adapt to the needs of the services and access points that consume it. For example, in the online shopping app, after a user adds an item to her cart on the access point, the cart data may get transformed and exchanged with the underlying shopping cart service that records the user's intent to purchase. Here, when we dissect the data into its time, space and structure dimensions, we see that the data is not only changing its structure from a semi-structured format such as JSON to maybe a structured format support by a SQL database (RDBMS) but also changing along the time dimension from transient and instantaneous to persistent and historic. In terms of the space dimension we can observe that this data is also typically stored into (and retrieved from) data stores such as SQL or NoSQL databases depending on its structure.

Data is central to gleaning various kinds of pertinent insights that delight end users over digital experiences. Data is primarily consumed and transformed in order to analyze various underlying patterns that aid in providing an enhanced overall experience. For example, in the online shopping app, clickstream data pertaining to how the user navigates the app collected at access points can help derive insights on what products users are more likely to browse and purchase together. Similarly, aggregating purchase data collected from multiple users can help forecast the seasonal demand for products and accordingly ensure that the inventory is refreshed. In another user journey - searching for products - a user may be able to upload an image of a product that she is interested in and search for products in the online shopping app that look similar to it. The logic to derive these insights from data may reside either on access points or underlying services. In these scenarios, when we observe the time dimension of data that is being analyzed we usually see that the data is historic. Of course, the historic data here has a more recent lineage given the context, wherein you may want to associate more importance to data from the user's most recent browsing history rather than something she browsed several days or months ago. On access points, the logic is typically used to derive light-weight descriptive insights that can be displayed to the user. Most of the heavy lifting for predictive and cognitive insights is typically handled by the logic in underlying dat services. Here, when we observe the structure dimension we see that a the data could be either structured, semi-structured, or unstructured. On the other hand, the insights that are gleaned from the data that is being analyzed may have a different composition in the structure, time and space dimensions. In the time dimension, they could be transient in nature or may also get persisted to underlying data stores in order to be consumed at a later point of time. In structure dimension they could be either structured or semi-structured depending on how they would be accessed, and correspondingly in space dimension, they would be stored in a relevant data store that allows for easy access and retrieval based on the use case.

The logic that orchestrates the automation and provisioning of both on-prem and cloud infrastructure heavily relies on data. Data is used to specify the configurations of how the infrastructure must be provisioned. In real-time, data pertaining to the live environments where the digital experiences are hosted gets collected and analyzed in order to observe, scale, and optimize the infrastructure. For example, seasonal patterns about the number of users of the online shopping app extracted from the real-time monitoring data of the infrastructure helps scale and optimize the number of servers, load balancers, network routers, etc. during peak and off-peak loads. Looking at the structure, space and time dimensions, the data pertaining to the definition and configuration of infrastructure is typically lightweight and semi-structured and stored in data stores which are suited for lightweight storage and frequent retrieval. The data probably undergoes sporadic changes and that happens typically when new infrastructure is designed for provisioning. On the other hand, the real-time data collected from live environments is typically large in volume, may either be structured or semi-structured, and frequently changes.

Data also plays a crucial role in protecting the full stack of access points, services, and infrastructure from cyber attacks that aim to exploit vulnerabilities and compromise the safety, privacy and security of digital experiences. By sifting through the data generated from monitoring systems, predictive and cognitive insights about potential attacks and suspicious behavior can be derived. These insights can help secure the full stack from similar malicious attacks in the future. Data analysis also helps in detecting intrusion in real-time and classifying the vulnerability of the various components of the full stack. Most often, the data collected and analyzed to identify threats and vulnerabilities is either structured or semi-structured. It is typically persisted in relevant data stores for various reasons such as further analysis, auditing, governance and regulatory compliance.

So far we have seen how Data interplays with Logic in various areas of the learning spectrum. We have learnt that data gets consumed, generated, transformed and exchanged across the user journeys of the digital experiences. We have also understood the nuances of how logic operates on the data across its three dimensions of structure, time and space. To appreciate the relevance of data across any part of the learning spectrum, a learner must focus on broadly three key aspects - understanding the interplay of data and logic in a particular area of learning spectrum to specialize in that area; understanding the data flow across the components of the learning spectrum to visualize the bigger picture; and understanding the nuances of structure, time and space dimensions of the data, as depicted in Fig 3.9.

Fig 3.9: Key aspects to learn Data

Recall the example of building web apps using JavaScript that we discussed earlier in the logic section. We saw that JavaScript was used to represent the various elements of the page and the browser as objects. Data is used to define the structure of the various UI elements on the page which the logic in turn processes to render the desired user interface of the web app. The logic also interplays with the data that gets consumed by the web app from various underlying services to provide relevant information and insights to the user. User actions on the web app generate data which is transformed by the logic and in turn exchanged with services via APIs. While one may begin by delving deep into the relevance of data in the context of JavaScript (at the web app's access point), in order to fully understand the relevance and overall context of data one must be able to visualize the bigger picture of how the data flows across the breadth of the full stack that makes up the web app. Eventually, visualizing the bigger picture of data flow across the full stack helps arouse empathy and accentuates imagination. Irrespective of whether the logic is interplaying with the data at the access point or the underlying full stack, understanding the dimensions of the data viz. structure, time and space, helps build performant, elegant and secure web apps.

In the other example of using Python to build machine learning models we noted that Python was used to frame the logic to transform and analyze data and learn patterns or glean insights from it. Here, we can fully appreciate the interplay of data and logic by understanding how logic is used to access data from a variety of sources, to apply relevant transformations on the data and prepare it for analysis, and to unearth patterns and build machine learning models. Further, in this scenario, learning to visualize the bigger picture of the data flow across the full stack enables us to select the right data for analysis, define appropriate transformations on the data, eliminate bias to create models that are fair and accountable, bake in privacy, security and transparency, and overall imagine newer/improved digital experiences for the users. In this scenario also, we need to deeply understand the nuances of data along its structure, time and space dimensions in order to be able to build relevant, accurate and ethical models.

The learning journey to understand the interplay of data with logic, visualize the data flow across the full stack, and understand its nuances along the structure, time and space dimensions typically progresses (iteratively) along the following stages - developing data mindset, exploring the data tooling, and optimizing solutions for performance, as depicted in Fig 3.10

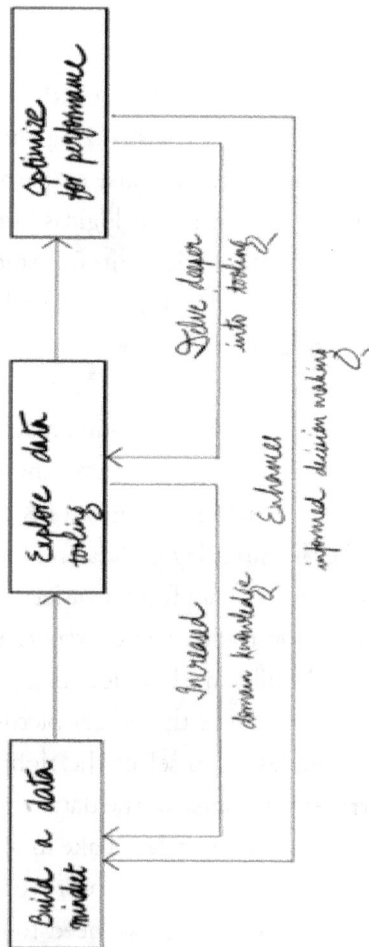

Fig 3.10: Learning Journey for Data

The learning journey typically begins with developing a data mindset which eventually leads to appreciating data as the fundamental digital matter that prevails across the entire learning spectrum in a variety of forms/structures. This is an ongoing process that often begins with familiarizing oneself with fundamental concepts such as understanding the different types of data, and how data is collected/stored. For example, recall that in Chapter 2, we discussed the taxi hailing app which stored the Customer and Trip related information in a relational database (RDBMS) such as Oracle or MySQL. In RDBMS, the data is stored in the form of relation/table (e.g. Customer table and Trip Details table), where each row represents an entity (e.g. a single customer in the Customer table or a single trip in the Trip Details table), and the columns represents the attributes of the entity (e.g. name, address, phone number for Customer, and source, destination, start time for Trip Details).

Like pseudocode and flowcharts which aided our ability to express the logic in a structured manner to solve a problem, in the parlance of relational data we can use an Entity-Relationship (ER) diagram to model the structure and organization of the data. The ER diagram is a visual representation of the various entities, their attributes, and the relationships among different entities in a database.

Fig 3.11 depicts the relationship between the Customer and the Trip Details entities using an Entity-Relationship(ER) diagram, and shows a few sample entries in both tables. The diagram represents the relationship between Customer and Trip details as "books" to indicate that a customer books a trip, and further it shows a 1 to many relationship (1,N) between customer and trip to indicate that a customer can book multiple trips, and a trip is booked only by one customer. In addition to understanding the ER diagram one has to also learn fundamental concepts such as:

1. data type of each column (e.g. name and address of customer is a string, contact number is a number, etc.)

2. constraints on any column (e.g. the contact number of a customer is unique to each customer and cannot be same for more than one customer) and

3. how the relationship is recorded between the tables (e.g. each row of the trip details table contains the unique customer id to identify which customer booked the trip).

Entity-Relationship (ER) Diagram

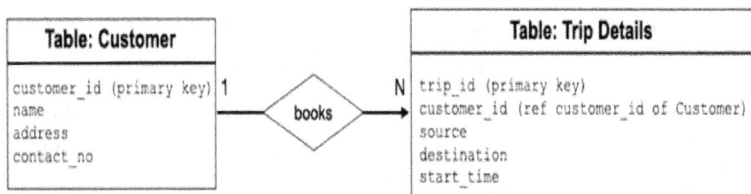

Table: Customer		Table: Trip Details
customer_id (primary key) 1 name address contact_no	books → N	trip_id (primary key) customer_id (ref customer_id of Customer) source destination start_time

Sample data in both tables

Table: Customer

customer_id	name	address	contact_no
9HbG4K7	Mei Chen	654 Birch Street	29876 54329
2eVnY5R	Juan Garcia	987 Elmwood Avenue	91234 56784
Px8X6E9	Maya Gupta	321 Pine Lane	22876 54317

Table: Trip Details

trip_id	customer_id	source	dest	start_time
392874	9HbG4K7	123 Main Street	456 Elm Avenue	2021-03-19 10:20
578921	9HbG4K7	135 Willow Lane	543 Cedar Road	2021-08-20 13:10
643912	Px8X6E9	567 Pine Avenue	321 Maple Street	2022-11-17 14:45
106543	2eVnY5R	678 Oakwood Drive	890 Cedar Lane	2023-01-16 09:30

Fig 3.11: Sample data and ER Diagram from Database of the Taxi Hailing App

Similarly in the example of the customer's cart data of the online shopping app (discussed earlier in the logic section of this chapter), we observed how the data was stored in a NoSQL database such as MongoDB. Referring back to Code Snippet 5, we see the sample data contains attributes such as user_id, multiple items (each containing product_id, quantity, merchant_id, and price), and the total_price of the cart. Here too, one has to familiarize themselves with the fundamentals of the structure and organization of the data. One must explore the different data types of each field, and look for references in the data across different MongoDB documents to explore the connections within the data. In general, it is difficult to say which data model (relational, document, key-value, graph, etc.) is best suited and leads to a simpler logic for storage and retrieval. The choice of the data model always depends on the relationships within the data. For example, if the data is highly interconnected such as to model a social network scenario, then rather than choosing a document database, it might be prudent to select a graph oriented database that can capture the relationship extremely well. Learning to identify the appropriate data model happens over time as one works with several applications and delves into the interplay of the logic and data.

As you may have noticed, looking at the data and exploring its structure and organization enables one with the confidence to explore the data across the learning spectrum and in turn helps towards building a data mindset. This stage establishes the comfort that is required to break free from the inertia towards learning data. This stage is also crucial to help one navigate the emotional cycle of data that may typically begin with a feeling of disbelief about the world of possibilities that arise from harnessing data and eventually ends with mastery of data across the learning spectrum. As one navigates the emotional cycle of data, one may come across several intermediary stages between disbelief and mastery such as curiosity, engagement, and ownership as depicted in Fig 3.12.

As you may observe from the emotional cycle of data, when it comes to building a data mindset it is not always love at first sight. One typically feels overwhelmed by the vast expanse and variety of data, and the endless possibilities that arise from harnessing it. To overcome this inertia and disbelief, one must start by curiously exploring the world of possibilities and imagining the probable problems/scenarios that could be catered to using the data. Curiosity leads one to subsequently empathize with the end users who consume/generate the data, and then helps delve deep into the services that consume, generate, transform and exchange it. As one engages with the data from the point of view of the end users and underlying services they not only get a perspective of the domain that the data operates in and how it interplays with logic currently; but also start to imagine newer or improved use cases with data. Experimenting and refining these newer or improved use cases leads one to take ownership of data across the entire spectrum which eventually leads to developing mastery over the data and its interplay with the logic. Navigating this emotional cycle of data iteratively across several user journeys equips one with the necessary skills required to hone the data mindset and sustain a data-driven culture.

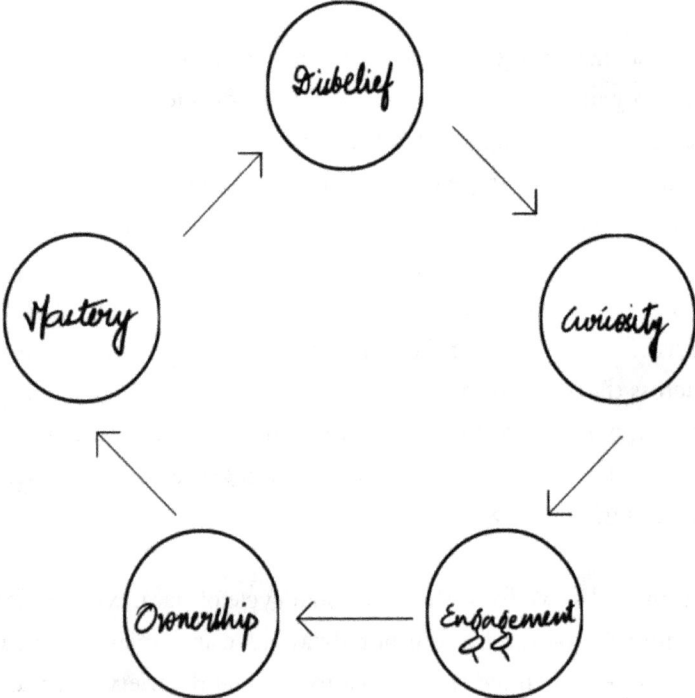

Fig 3.12: Emotional Cycle of Data

Getting familiar with the various data related tools, frameworks and libraries alongside navigating the emotional cycle of data is key to succeeding in the data learning journey. This stage typically starts with the exploration of data in order to reduce the inertia and build curiosity in and around the domain and related data that one is dealing with. Exploratory data analysis techniques are used on data that resides in SQL and NoSQL databases with the help of libraries or frameworks such as Hadoop and Spark, and programming languages such as Python, Scala, Java and R to familiarize oneself with the domain and the related data. Depending on the area that one chooses to further engage with the data (and how it interplays with the logic) such as data pipelines, data visualization or data analytics, one must become familiar with the gamut of tools, frameworks and libraries suited for the purpose. For example, if one is interested in data visualization, then one should further explore tools such as Tableau, PowerBI or Qlik. This stage further expands one's data mindset as they begin to explore data using tools to progressively enhance their domain knowledge by deriving various insights from the exploration.

Finally, in the data learning journey, one has to learn the nuances of processing the data to build more performant solutions. For this, one has to not only dive deeper into how the data is stored, retrieved, exchanged, processed and visualized; but also explore how to effectively calibrate its interplay with the logic so that it is consumed, generated, transformed and exchanged in a secure, performant, and optimized manner. For example, when working with services that interact with underlying data infrastructure composed of relational databases one must not only learn to write optimized queries in SQL but also learn to choose appropriate SQL drivers and libraries required to interface with the logic element. In another example, while designing real-time data visualization dashboards one must not only learn the nuances of how the data is efficiently streamed and consumed in real-time but also learn to select the appropriate libraries that contain the logic to optimize the user experience at the access point. As learners progress along this stage they not only become more proficient with the data tools but also apply a data driven approach to solving problems which eventually enhances their data mindset.

It is important to acknowledge the role of domain knowledge in mastering the data element of the learning triad. Delving into the domain of the data provides the overall context of the data and you understand the big picture of how data takes various shapes and forms across the learning spectrum. Referring back to the example of the online shopping app, we need to delve into understanding the domain and the underlying data i.e. e-commerce domain. In this scenario, we must understand how the data regarding the various categories, products, orders, etc. is represented and used across the full stack of the web app. We must cultivate the data mindset by exploring the various properties of the data in its structure, time and space dimensions as it gets consumed, generated, transformed and exchanged across the web app.

By now, you may have realized that exploring the interplay between data and logic is key to navigating the learning spectrum. For example, in the web access point of the online shopping app we must not only understand how the logic at the access point consumes the data in order to display the various user interface elements to the user, how the access point transforms or generates data based on various actions performed by the user, how it exchanges the data with underlying services through APIs, but also dive into how the logic at the underlying services consume, transform, and exchange the data, how the data gets stored in the underlying data infrastructure and how it is made available to other services, etc. As we explore this interplay at various stages we also need to become familiar with the various tools, libraries and frameworks used. For instance, if the data is stored in relational databases, then we must not only develop a good understanding of the schema of the data but also become familiar with SQL and frameworks such as Spring framework used by various services to store and retrieve relational data in an efficient manner. We must continuously seek to enhance the effectiveness of the interplay between the data and the logic across the full stack so as to ensure that the app is secure, performant and optimized. To do this, we must not only explore the nuances of the underlying data infrastructure and learn to optimize both the storage and retrieval of the data but also seek to optimize the logic at services and access points so that the interplay is accentuated across the full stack. Ultimately, understanding the nuances of the interplay between data and logic when data is both at rest and in motion across cloud and on-prem infrastructure, and leveraging the right DevOps practices, processes, and tools will enable us to become proficient at effectively leveraging the interplay between data and logic across the learning spectrum.

Similarly, in the example of analyzing data and building machine learning models using Python for the online shopping app, cultivating a data mindset is extremely crucial to analyzing the data, and building accurate and reliable models. We must seek to understand the domain of the data while also exploring its characteristics along the structure, time and space dimensions. As we explore the data we may discover several anomalies or atypical values which may lead us to unearth patterns in data that correspond to deviations in the processes that generated it. Tracking the lineage and understanding how the data interplays with the logic across various layers of the full stack will equip us with information required to build accurate and reliable models. Along the journey of exploring the data we must build expertise in relevant Python libraries, frameworks and tools such as Numpy and Pandas for exploratory data analysis, Matplotlib and Seaborn for data visualization and Scikit-Learn or Tensorflow for building machine learning models. While working with these tools, libraries and frameworks, we must delve deep into their nuances to exploit the interplay between the logic and data in a performant and optimized manner. We must leverage DevOps/DataOps/MLOps practices, processes, and tools so that the various components such as underlying data, data pipelines, machine learning code, models learnt from the data, relevant services, and APIs are synchronized. We must further ensure data privacy and security is maintained across systems, and enable the outcomes to be fair, accountable, and explainable.

Data is also witnessing democratization just like programming with the introduction of several LCNC (low-code no-code platforms) such as AWS SageMaker, Azure Machine Learning, and Google Cloud Vertex AI. These platforms are enabling business users who have strong domain knowledge to become citizen data scientists. These platforms make it easier for the users to express the logic of consuming, transforming, exchanging data and generating relevant insights easier using intuitive visual elements and pre-built templates for common tasks. Although these platforms help reduce the steep learning curve required to get used to the data world, cultivating a data mindset is nevertheless essential and forms the foundation of mastering the data element of the learning triad.

So far, we have seen how data - the second element of the learning triad - interplays with logic across the length and breadth of the learning spectrum. Data is consumed, generated, transformed, and exchanged across the full stack and used in various contexts such as visualizing trends, synergizing APIs, automating routine activities, and building predictive analytical models to create modern digital experiences. We have also explored how we can approach mastering this element by cultivating a data mindset, exploring data related tooling, and understanding the nuances of how data is stored, retrieved, exchanged, processed and visualized while interplaying with the logic.

When we zoom out of the data element and look at the learning triad as a whole from the larger context of an enterprise, we can further understand how data interplays with logic and imagination at large. Data not only interplays with the logic across various user journeys, but also fuels the imagination that brings newer and enhanced business cases to life. Digital experiences will continue to evolve with time, and data (the fundamental digital matter) will always be the necessary substance that propels logic and imagination along this continuous journey.

Imagination

So far we have seen how logic and data - two key elements of the learning triad - interplay with one another across the learning spectrum to bring digital experiences to life. While data represents the fundamental digital matter, and logic is the medium through which digital experiences are realized; Imagination, the third element of the learning triad, represents the world of possibilities in which the other two elements operate and continuously evolve. Imagination plays a quintessential role in not only refreshing the digital user journeys as trends change but also plays a vital role in creating a breed of new experiences that disrupt the world altogether.

Imagination is key to facilitating the creation of products, platforms and services that keep pace with the ever changing world where digital and physical experiences are continuously converging. The interplay between imagination, data and logic is not only fundamental to producing desired digital experiences but also key to staying abreast with emerging technology trends, adapting to changing customer behavior, competing with challenger businesses, navigating regulatory and compliance requirements, and succeeding in new operating models/markets. Newer and enhanced experiences may also find their origins in imagination being ignited from logic and/or data. Keenly observing the various forces that influence digital experiences, analyzing data and gleaning insights, and continuously striving to optimize logic in order to improve products, platforms and services are typically some of the triggers that lead to imagination of newer or enhanced digital experiences.

Imagination, alongside logic and data, prevails across the learning spectrum. Mastering the learning spectrum requires one to not only comprehend the role that imagination plays in both the visible and invisible parts of the spectrum but also continuously find ways to exploit its power to the maximum potential.

Fig 3.13 further expands on Fig 3.8 to illustrate the interplay of imagination with the data and logic elements across the various areas of the learning spectrum.

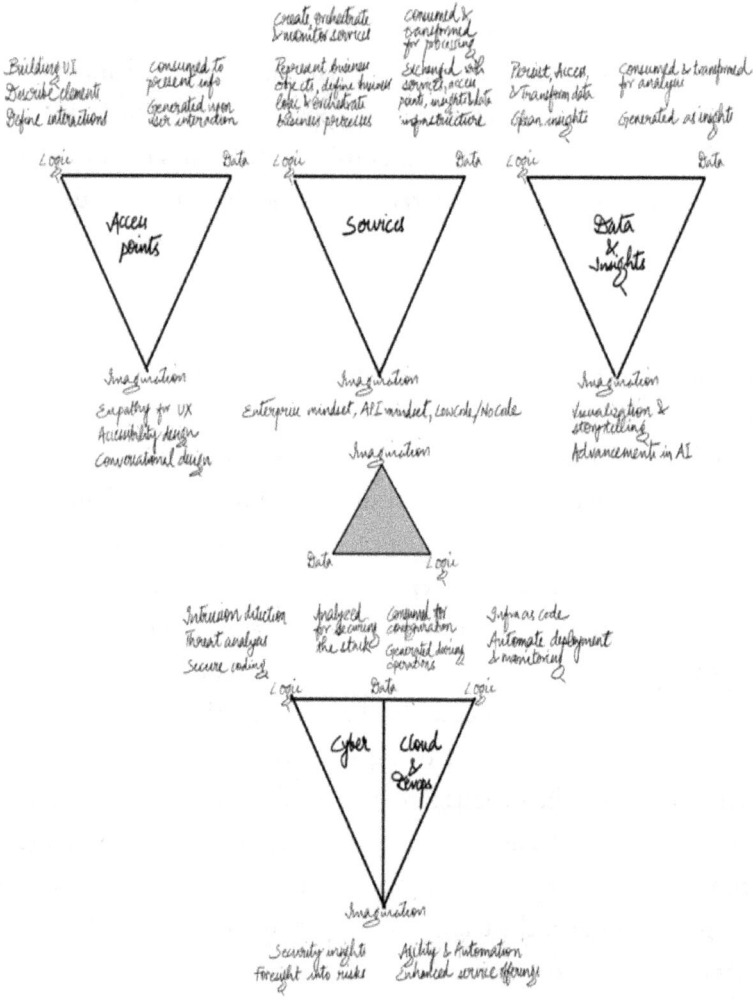

Fig 3.13: Interplay of Imagination, Data and Logic across The Learning Spectrum

Imagination is key to building new access points and continuously enhancing the user experiences delivered over access points. It plays a crucial role in designing the architecture of services and in the development of various tools and processes that support the creation of services. Imagination is not only an essential component for gleaning insights and storytelling with the data, but also crucial to the advancement of technologies such as Artificial Intelligence. In the realm of Cloud and DevOps, imagination is used to not only enhance the agility with which teams deliver software using automation and collaborative ways of working, but it is also key to enhancing cloud based offerings by providing new services and operating different service models. Imagination is also a key factor that helps strengthen the security mindset within an organization and enables baking security into every aspect of the enterprise by helping foresee risks, identify vulnerabilities and defend against cyber attacks.

Imagination is essential in identifying and designing appropriate interfaces across different access points, unifying the user experience across the various access points to provide seamless user journeys, and accommodating to newer kinds of user engagement models that brands strive to achieve with changing trends; which boosts the advocacy among consumers. For example, in the online shopping app, in terms of access points, imagination guides the design of the user experience of web and mobile apps, and the design of the conversations between a voice assistant/chatbot and consumers. It is also pivotal in creating a coherent digital experience where users can start a user journey on one access point and finish it on another, wherein she can add an item to her cart in the morning using a voice assistant and pay for it using a mobile app later in the day. In another example, imagination is key to enhancing customer experience over access points using Augmented Reality, as seen in the "Dress up" feature of Snapchat which allows users to try out products like dresses and eyewear before they order them through the app. Imagination is also key to ensuring that the experience on these access points make consumers from different walks of life feel included and the experiences are curated by considering the accessibility needs of various user groups. Some of the ways to implement this is by offering users the ability to personalize and customize the experience, providing clear and consistent naviga tion, considering accessibility aids such as keyboard/screen readers, using appropriate color contrasts, and following accessibility standards such as WCAG[202] (Web Content Accessibility Guidelines).

When we look at services, imagination interplays with the data and logic elements to not only support the creation of newer/enhanced user journeys but also forms the force that bolsters the adoption of an enterprise mindset. Recall that earlier in this chapter, we discussed the role of imagination as the central theme to envisioning the various features and user journeys such as a digital cart, online payments and personalized recommendations in the online shopping app. Imagination also plays a key role in the design of various APIs that help integrate these services with a suite of services hosted both within and outside the enterprise so as to create a robust ecosystem. For example, you may recall that although Snapchat (a social networking app) has the Dress Up feature using which users can try out different apparel and accessories, the actual product(s) may be owned by a different enterprise which provides an online shopping app. The purchase of the product from the online shopping enterprise through social networking apps like Snapchat is possible due to integration of APIs between the two enterprises. Imagination is the key driver to creating such an ecosystem between different enterprises.

Imagination plays an extremely crucial role in the world of data and insights. It is the differentiating factor between just generating insights (which comes from the interplay between logic and data alone) and crafting engaging stories using data. For example, in his book "The Visual Display of Quantitative Information", Edward Tufte, a notable data visualization expert, discusses the map of Napoleon's march to conquer Russia in 1812[203]. The chart was designed by Charles Joseph Minard, a French civil engineer, in 1869 to illustrate Napoleon's disastrous campaign. It is a stellar example of presenting several variables that play a part in the story of the conquest using a single map. The chart effectively combines multiple variables such as geography, time, temperature, size of the army, and the direction and casualties suffered by the army, and presents a large amount of complex information effectively with a clear narrative. In the world of digital experiences too, imagination is key to creating impactful representations of data and presenting compelling narratives. For example, in the online shopping app, imagination can help present a narrative about customer preferences and behaviors through compelling charts and lead to enhanced decision making which uplifts the overall experience for both end users and the enterprise. Imagination is also key to continuously expanding the capabilities of the insights spectrum (descriptive --> predictive --> cognitive) and fuelling the advancement of technologies such as Generative AI.

The interplay of imagination with data and logic in Cloud and DevOps areas of the learning spectrum can be observed when we look into the agility with which digital experiences are continuously developed and delivered. Imagination helps usher in innovative practices that foster increased collaboration between development and operations teams so as to accelerate the delivery of software. It not only leads to discovering more creative ways of working, enhanced processes, and robust automation practices but also enables the design of products, platforms and services that are secure, scalable, resilient, and account for failures. For example, in the online shopping app, imagination is a key factor right from the beginning in planning the user stories and their releases/deployments, to later setting up load balancing and failover infrastructure to boost resilience of the app, and adopting a multi-cloud strategy to promote flexibility and foster innovation during the development and deployment of the app.

In the area of cyber security, imagination interplays with data and logic to help foster a security mindset that is essential in securing the full stack of technologies which make up the digital experience. Imagination helps gain an enhanced awareness of the risks, threats and vulnerabilities that may compromise the security of digital experiences. It supports the development of a proactive and defensive security strategy and helps build a robust incident response required to contain and recover from attacks.

So far, we have seen the interplay between imagination, data and logic elements across the different areas of the learning spectrum. In the previous sections we also discussed the learning journey that one can undertake to master logic and data. However, unlike data and logic elements of the learning triad which can typically be mastered as a science, mastering imagination is more of an art. Some people may have an innate inclination to imagination; while others may acquire it over a period of time. In either case, one should aim to continuously strengthen their imagination by tapping into the brain's adaptable mechanisms.

For example, imagine your daily commute to work, where you rely on public transportation, like a metro train. During this journey from home to your workplace, you encounter various instances of human imagination. You might start by considering the town planner who imagined the location of your home, the neighborhood, and all the conveniences it offers. You may then relate to the vision of highway engineers and town planners who brought the road you take to reach the metro station to life. The metro station itself was created by talented architects, the train's route was envisioned by the rail company, and the software you interact with to purchase tickets or recharge your metro card was crafted by engineers and designers. As you step into the train, you may notice the fabric on the seats, the work of textile engineers, and so on. When pondering this entire experience, you will be amazed to realize how science and imagination have united over centuries to enable this everyday convenience. Exploring the world around you and witnessing the collaboration of countless minds can truly inspire you, ignite fresh possibilities, and motivate you to embark on your own creative ventures.

As you may have observed from the above example, strengthening one's imagination typically follows three stages - being curious about the world and the various experiences it offers, visualizing the connections among various components of the experiences, and drawing inspiration to express your own creativity to envisage new/renewed experiences. To hone imagination, one can adopt the infinite imagination spiral comprising three key stages - being curious, exploring connections, and unlocking creativity, as depicted in Fig 3.14.

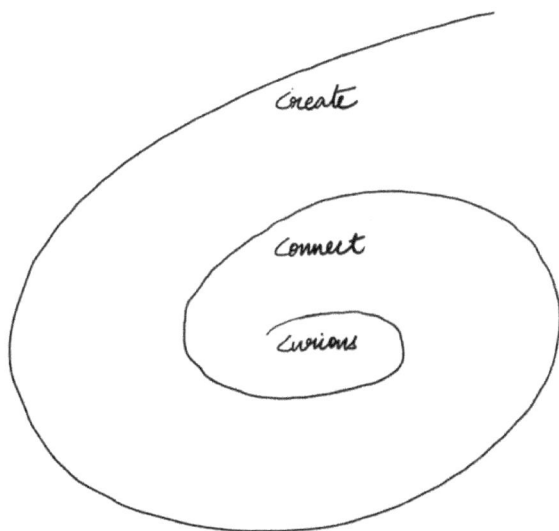

Fig. 3.14: The Imagination Spiral

Being curious is the first ability that one has to embrace along the learning curve of the imagination spiral. Curiosity enables the discovery of newer trends, technologies, ideas and is the oil that lubricates the lifelong learning journey. Next, one has to connect what they discover with what they already know to build a more comprehensive view of the world of possibilities. Connecting the dots bridges the gaps in learning and provides guidance on how to progress in the learning journey. Finally, in order to translate imagination into some thing substantial, one has to apply the learning to create something; be it a throwaway prototype or a multi-billion dollar product. It is important to note that creation not only converges the imagination, but also diverges one's outlook further leading to more curiosity and connectivity which in turn helps continuously navigate the imagination spiral for lifelong learning.

Once we start imagining the new world of possibilities, the journey of getting from the status quo to there may involve different paths depending on how we learn to imagine. There is no one size fits all learning path or approach to developing the skills required to hone imagination. One can start by choosing an approach from a variety of formal and informal approaches, and then subsequently explore others along their learning journey. Systemic Thinking and Design Thinking are some of the formal approaches that one can adopt to hone imagination in the context of digital experiences. One also greatly benefits from informal and social approaches to honing imagination. Drawing inspiration from the people and the world around us is a key aspect of this learning journey.

Systemic Thinking is an experiential learning approach that involves understanding how different parts of a system interact and influence each other, and come together as whole. This approach involves two key stages - deconstruction of the system that you wish to understand into its components, and (re)construction of the components to the whole. Deconstruction helps arouse curiosity and further helps connect the dots, and construction enables the creation of the newer/enhanced components/system, leading to another iteration of the imagination spiral. In the context of digital experiences, one starts by deconstructing the user journeys into its various components/subsystems to understand how they are integrated and interact with each other. For example, in the online shopping app we can deconstruct the user journey of finding/searching for a product into its various components across access points, services, data infrastructure and insights. This helps one to not only imagine enhancements to the indi

-vidual components but also imagine how to enhance the connections between the various components and thus improve the overall user journey as a whole. One then begins to construct newer/refreshed user journeys using the various components by exploiting the interplay of imagination with logic and data. This stage not only helps one to hone the skills required to create compelling digital experiences but also further enhances their imagination.

Design Thinking is a non-linear innovative problem solving approach that promotes 'learning by doing' while keeping the users at the center of the overall experience that one is designing. It iteratively progresses along various stages such as empathizing with users to understand the crux of the problem one is trying to solve, defining the problem formally by analyzing the observations from user research, ideating various solutions that may help solve the problem, rapidly prototyping the solutions to evaluate which of the ideas are feasible, and testing with end users to seek their feedback and evolve further. This approach is not only useful for developing customer-centric products and services but also beneficial to hone the various skills that help accentuate imagination along the journey. Empathizing with users helps hone one's curiosity as they discover the problems faced by the users, defining the problem and ideating various solutions further enhances one's ability to connect the dots, and rapidly prototyping and testing solutions enriches one's creative abilities and helps navigate the continuous learning curve. In the context of digital experiences, as one empathizes with users and defines the problem they are able to imagine newer/refreshed user journeys. For example, in the online shopping app, connecting with users and listening to their feedback helps one empathize with users' needs and leads to the imagination of new features. Ideating the various solutions and toying with prototypes helps them better understand the interplay between logic, data and imagination. Iteratively seeking user feedback and continuously applying the design thinking process enables one to enrich the overall digital experience over time and stay abreast with changing trends in user preferences, technologies and market forces.

Referring back to the example of your daily commute via a metro train, you can see that you could draw inspiration by observing the world around you more deeply and intentionally. Drawing inspiration from people and the world around is an essential aspect of honing one's imagination. Informal and social learning techniques such as reading, networking, discussions, observation and visualization play a key role in enriching the skills required to hone imagination. These techniques not only help naturally enrich one's curiosity, connectivity and creativity but also form the bedrock of formal learning approaches such as systemic thinking and design thinking. Drawing inspiration from people and the world around us is a key aspect to navigating one's continuous learning journey and supports the fundamental tenet that **the more we learn, the better we can imagine.**

As Albert Einstein has rightly said "Imagination is more important than knowledge. For knowledge is limited to all we now know and understand, while imagination embraces the entire world, and all there ever will be to know and understand." Imagination truly unlocks the potential of individuals and enterprises to continuously evolve with changing technology and customer trends and keep innovating to deal with the emergence of new operating models, rise of challenger business, and enforcement of newer rules and regulations. Imagination is at the heart of any digital experience and underpins every aspect of it that users see and feel. Honing the skills of curiosity, connectivity and creativity helps foster imagination transforming one from a problem solver to a problem finder. It helps them orchestrate their thoughts, skills, and learning to create compelling digital experiences.

The Learning Foundations

In a radio interview in 1951, Jackson Pollock compared modern painters (of his time) to their predecessors, noting that today's painters do not have to rely on subject matter outside of themselves. He expressed, "The thing that interests me is that today painters do not have to go to a subject-matter outside themselves. Modern painters work in a different way. They work from within." In another interview, he further elaborated on the role of the modern artist in a mechanical age, stating, "The modern artist is living in a mechanical age and we have a mechanical means of representing objects in nature such as the camera and photograph. The modern artist, it seems to me, is working and expressing an inner world – in other words – expressing the energy, the motion, and the other inner forces... the modern artist is working with space and time, and expressing his feelings rather than illustrating." Interestingly, Pollock's paintings were initially studied in relation to fractal expressionism, which distinguishes fractal art generated by human artists from those created using mathematics or computers. His paintings were often described as natural and organic, and further studies revealed their fractal nature, supporting the idea that his paintings contain "the fingerprint of nature".

The concept of "working from within" in the context of modern digital experiences holds special significance for enterprises and individuals on their digital journeys. On one hand, they draw inspiration from the constantly evolving digital experiences around them. On the other hand, they must tap into their inner resources, imagination, and creativity to craft compelling digital experiences. In this case, the manifestation of the learning triad becomes even more crucial, as it enables them to express their energy, work with their inner forces, and bring their envisioned modern digital experiences to life. Applying the learning triad across every area of the learning spectrum unlocks the potential to master the underlying digital skills required to build compelling digital experiences.

In this chapter, we have zoomed into the eternal and connected learning spectrum to discover the self-organized fundamental fractal - the learning triad- that prevails across it. We have demystified the learning triad and explored the importance of the interplay among its elements - logic, data and imagination across the learning spectrum. Further, we not only observed how the elements of the triad are crucial to building modern digital experiences, but also delved into the fundamentals of each element and the various approaches to learning them.

Fig 3.15 depicts how the entire learning spectrum can be distilled down to the fundamental fractal i.e. the learning triad. We have already seen how the elements of the triad interplay with one another across all areas of the learning spectrum. Further, if we ruminate more about this depiction of the triad across various areas of the spectrum, we can observe a few more key takeaways for every learner. First, we can see that services are intentionally positioned among the access points and data & insights areas. This is to highlight the role of services in bridging these areas - where they act as the conduit for the movement of data between these areas, and encapsulate the logic that both processes and exchanges the data. Second, recall that we discussed the growing expectations on talent archetypes where enterprises seek individuals to be versatilists. To achieve success in this endeavor, individuals should first specialize in any one of the areas depicted in the upper section viz. Access points, Services, and Data & Insights. And simultaneously, it is crucial for them to embrace and apply the power of Cloud, DevOps and Cyber security (represented in the bottom section) irrespective of whichever area they specialize in.

It is also interesting to note how closely digital skills of the learning spectrum such as Human skills/soft skills, mindsets, ethics and approaches relate to imagination. Imagination is central to enhancing these skills, is a key differentiator between specialists and versatilists, and overall a crucial factor in how individuals reach their highest potential along their digital journeys.

Having understood the fundamental fractal that beats across the spectrum you must feel more confident to delve into your journey to master the learning spectrum. All individuals, beginners and experts alike, are already somewhere on this learning map. We encourage you

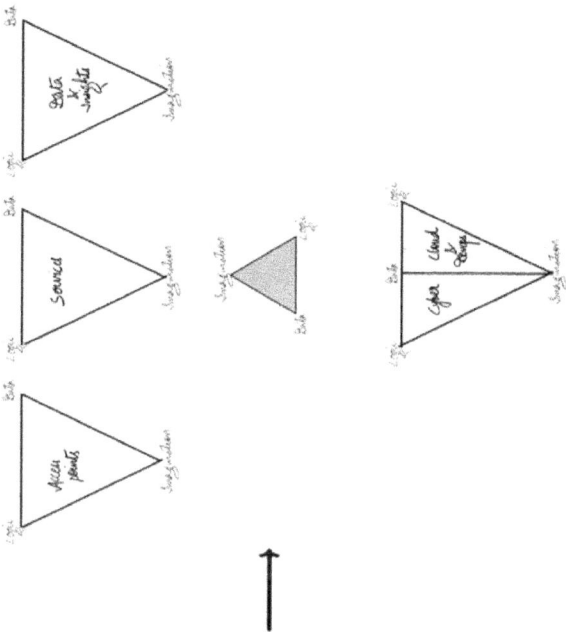

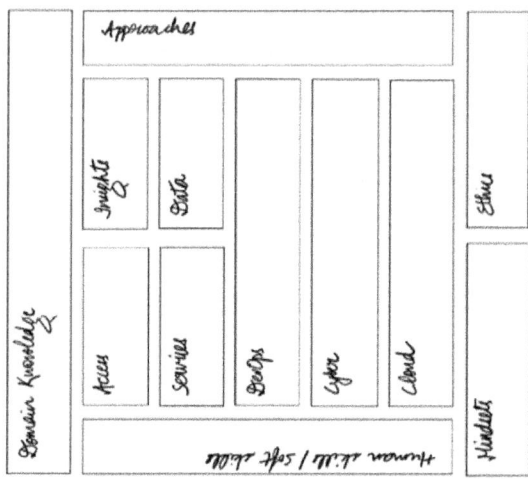

Fig 3.15: The Learning Foundations

to discover where you are on the map and chart your journey accordingly by relying on the learning triad. For example, if you are aiming to become a data infrastructure engineer, you should focus on how the elements of the triad interplay in the Data & Insights areas while also grasping an overall understanding of the spectrum, simultaneously exploring the areas of Cloud, DevOps and Cyber, and nurturing your imagination to enhance your complementary skills data mindset, enterprise mindset, ethics, empathy, systemic thinking, and design thinking approaches. Similarly, if you are aiming to become a cyber security engineer, then you should focus on thoroughly understanding the interplay between the elements of the triad in the Cyber Security area. Further you should explore how Cloud, DevOps, and the other parts of the spectrum are connected with the Cyber security area, and nurture complementary skills such as cyber mindset, enterprise mindset, systemic thinking and design thinking approaches. It is worthwhile to note that there is no prescribed starting point, you have to discover your own journey, and realize that all roads eventually channel into the learning spectrum.

Finally, if we recall the essence of each of element of the triad, we should fully understand that Imagination represents the world of possibilities and is the seed for creating compelling digital experiences, Data is the fundamental digital matter which gets consumed, generated, exchanged and transformed along the various user journeys of digital experiences, and Logic helps realize the digital experiences and is the medium through which they are brought to life. Ultimately, we would like you to assimilate the interplay between the three elements of the learning triad as described in the following sestet:

" Logic without Imagination is Impaired,
Logic without Data is Arid,
Data without Logic is Inert,
Data without Imagination is Dead,
Imagination without Data is Ignorance, &
Imagination without Logic is Impractical "

Chapter-4
The Learning Ecosystem

In Aristotle's Nicomachean Ethics, he wrote "For the things we have to learn before we can do them, we learn by doing them. e.g. men become builders by building and lyre-players by playing the lyre; so too we become just by doing just acts, temperate by doing temperate acts, brave by doing brave acts." This classic written more than 2,000 years ago, provides many valuable insights into how virtues are acquired by practice.

We all "learn by doing". Learning by doing is a great way to inculcate the three virtues of the learning fractal viz. perseverance, discipline and curiosity. For example, imagine the experience of you learning to drive a car, which you of course learn to do by doing. You may often start by being curious about vehicles, how they work, and also begin to observe and understand the traffic laws, road signs and markings. You may have done these for several years before you even begin learning to drive a car. The next phase of your learning typically involves you to adhere to a discipline to practice driving regularly. To do this, you study diligently for the learner's permit test, and once you have the permit, you set aside time to practice driving everyday, diligently follow the instructions of your driving instructor, and cautiously adhere to all the rules and regulations. Finally, as you learn you understand that perseverance is a key attribute to success. The initial phase of learning to drive could be quite overwhelming where you have to overcome several challenges including coordinating multiple tasks, becoming more spatially aware, managing the speed and controlling the vehicle, obeying traffic rules and driving alongside other vehicles, and dealing with distractions. You have to continue to practice and learn to adapt to the different scenarios that happen as you learn to drive and often your learning continues even after you qualify the driving test and receive a license.

As you may have noticed, in the above scenario, and many other learning experiences, learning by doing promotes the adoption of experiential learning techniques which helps learners like you nurture the virtues of the learning fractal. This approach boosts your curiosity as you begin to apply your learning to real world scenarios, ensures that you cultivate discipline as you act autonomously to take control of your learning, and enables you to persevere as you observe the incremental progress that you make all along the learning process. From taking first steps to gracefully ballet dancing, from scribbling on paper to painting on a canvas, from uttering a sound to singing a tune, and many more, experiential learning is fundamental to how we all master various skills.

In the context of mastering digital skills, learning by doing holds particular relevance for enterprises and individuals. When individuals and teams acquire digital skills through experiential learning, it bolsters their ability to craft compelling digital experiences. Naturally, enterprises should promote these learning techniques in the learning avenues that they offer for individuals to engage with. To quote John Dewey, a prominent American philosopher, psychologist and education reformer, "Give the students something to do, not something to learn; and the doing is of such a nature as to demand thinking; learning naturally results". Enterprises should nurture a **learning ecosystem** which encourages individual learners to learn through experimentation, make incremental progress, and cultivate a growth mindset. Such a learning ecosystem not only enhances the learning agility of individuals but also aids in creating and sustaining a future-ready workforce capable of thriving in challenging environments.

Learning ecosystems have existed since time immemorial. Ancient Indian texts such as the Vedas reference the Gurukul system which emphasize the relationship between a Guru (Teacher) and Shishya (Student). In this system, the students would live in the ashram (hermitage) of the teacher and receive education in a variety of subjects such as martial arts and warfare, politics and governance, literature and philosophy, ethics and morality, and spirituality. One of the highlights of the Gurukul system was that it promoted a personalized learning approach for each student where the Guru would tailor the education for each student by assessing their unique strengths and aspirations. You may recall that the shloka, *"Kaak Cheshta, Bako Dhyanam, Shwan Nidra Tathaiwa Cha | Alpahari, Grihtyaagi, Vidyarthi Panch Lakshnam | |"*, which we discussed towards the end of the first chapter, not only emanated from the Gurukul system itself, but also succinctly summarized the attributes expected of a student during their learning in the Gurukul (and of course remains relevant even today).

Over time learning ecosystems of the society evolved to become the formal education systems comprising schools and universities that we see today. Ancient Indian universities such as Takshashila (estimated to be founded around 5th Century BCE) and Nalanda (founded in 5th century CE) were renowned seats of learning, and scholars from around the world traveled here to pursue their education across a broad range of subjects such as theology, philosophy, law, astronomy, mathematics, medicine, and languages. During the medieval period in Europe, universities emerged as centers of learning and initially promoted the trivium (grammar, rhetoric, and logic) and quadrivium (arithmetic, geometry, music and astronomy). Over time the curriculum expanded to include other subjects such as law, medicine, philosophy, and theology. These universities played a crucial role in the Renaissance and scientific revolution of Europe. Throughout history, one can observe the role that education and learning has played in transforming society. To quote Nelson Mandela here, "Education is the most powerful weapon which you can use to change the world."

You may recall that in Chapter 1 of this book, we discussed the three main challenges that enterprises and individuals face on their journey to becoming a learning organization. So far we have addressed two out of those three main challenges. In chapter 2, we tackled the first challenge of coming to terms with the vast expanse of ever changing digital skills by exploring the eternity of our learning fractal - the learning spectrum, and piecing together the connections between its various areas. And subsequently, in chapter 3, we addressed the second challenge of how one can adapt to the growing expectation of talent archetypes and become a versatilist, by distilling down the learning spectrum to its fundamental fractal - the learning triad, and exploring how to master each element of the triad; and the interplay among them.

In this chapter, we will turn our attention towards the third challenge of creating a learning ecosystem which provides an environment conducive for learning and in turn bolsters an organization's learning agility. We will start by discussing the archetype of a holistic learning ecosystem, and then explore the nuances of how to build one that promotes learning by doing. We will also discuss how such a learning ecosystem can benefit individuals and enterprises in the acquisition of the digital skills that span our learning fractal - the learning spectrum, and in accentuating their understanding of the learning triad. Finally, we will explore how learners can inculcate the virtues of perseverance, discipline and curiosity to foster a sustainable and progressive learning culture which leads to the success of the learning ecosystem.

Archetype of a Learning Ecosystem

The modern learning ecosystems that you interact with today are widely accessible to everyone, digitally - anytime and anywhere. We now live in a time where knowledge is getting increasingly democratized and we can leverage digital technologies to learn from various individuals, communities, and cultures across the globe, at our fingertips. Although the learning ecosystems in various organizations may have different look and feel depending upon the learning maturity of the enterprise; a holistic learning ecosystem should largely cater to the following five aspects, as depicted in Fig 4.1.

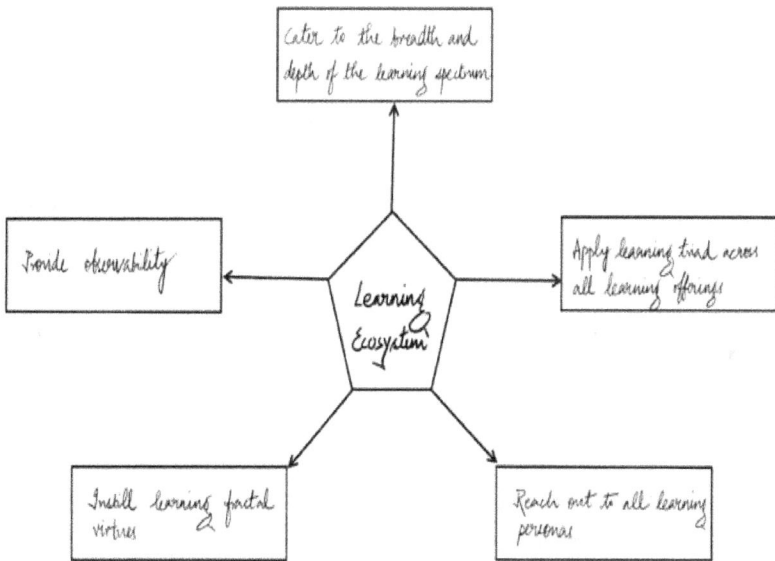

Fig 4.1: Key Aspects of a Learning Ecosystem

A holistic learning ecosystem should cater to both the **breadth and depth** of the learning spectrum. It should be able to fulfill the learning needs of individuals across learning areas such as Technology,

Domain Processes, Tools and Leadership & Behavioral skills. Individuals must not only be exposed to the breadth of these learning areas to arouse their curiosity, but also be able to delve into their depth with experiential learning so that they can connect and create.

A holistic learning ecosystem's components such as learning pathways, learning campaigns, and learning programs should contain a desired mix of the **elements of the learning triad**. The right mix of logic, data and imagination in these learning components in a collectively exhaustive way should help individuals to reflect on the interplay of these elements as they navigate the learning spectrum. For example, learning resources or learning pathways that help an individual become a data scientist should not only cover aspects of data but also help them appreciate the role of logic (programming) in data science and the role of imagination in exploring different use cases and representing insights with pertinent visualizations.

A holistic learning ecosystem should cater to the learning needs of the **various personas** in an enterprise. Although organizations may typically be composed of individuals in a plethora of roles, titles and structures; but in a simplified view from a learning perspective, we can represent their personas broadly in three categories - decision makers, influencers and implementers. Decision makers such as CEOs, directors and senior executives, typically represent the top echelon of an enterprise in business and technology. They are often primarily responsible for strategy, investments, and sponsorships. Implementers such as engineers do most of the heavy lifting in terms of designing, developing and maintaining the technology, processes and systems that power the business of the enterprise. Influencers such as mid-senior level managers help steer the enterprise internally and aid in achieving the end goals by not only forming a bridge between decision makers and implementers, but also being the leading voice in the implementation of strategy and central to the action of realizing it. Here, it is also important to note that individuals may perform activities across one or more of these roles within an enterprise and the persona described here is not correlated to the title that an individual holds.

A holistic learning ecosystem should drive the agenda of a continuous learning culture by taking a cue from the three underlying characteristics of fractals - eternal, self-organizing and connected. The learning ecosystem should ensure that it **instills perseverance, discipline and curiosity** among individuals and teams across the enterprise as they continuously navigate their learning journey. Perseverance encourages learners to constantly acquire knowledge and fathom the eternal nature of learning, discipline enables them to organize their learning and continuously hone their skills through practice, and curiosity elevates their comprehension of the connected nature of the learning spectrum and propels them further.

A holistic learning ecosystem should be **observable** so that it can be nurtured for growth. Enterprises should be able to measure the learning done by individuals and teams to not only determine the current skill set in the organization, but also channelize the learning efforts towards the development of future skills.

Overall, enterprises should build a holistic learning ecosystem with various components that promote these key aspects. A holistic learning ecosystem is brought to life using two key tenets - **a learning architecture**, and a **learning culture**. Enterprises should work towards implementing a learning architecture that supports learning across the breadth and depth of the learning spectrum, emphasizes the interplay between the elements of the learning triad, and encompasses learning for the various personas within the enterprise. As they build out the learning architecture, they must also understand that it is only a part of the puzzle; the key ingredient to sustaining the learning in the long term comes from fostering a continuous learning culture. The learning culture enables enterprises to become continuous learning organizations, and individuals to become perpetual learners, by instilling the three virtues of the learning fractal to support them on their life-long learning journey and stay relevant to the times while also preparing them for the future.

Learning Architecture

The learning architecture is the collection of related components or structures that coexist in the enterprise to help individuals and teams navigate their continuous learning journey. It serves as the master blueprint for guiding enterprises and learning teams towards building and sustaining a skilled workforce that is fit to meet the enterprise goals.

The learning architecture could be described using various viewpoints or perspectives. Irrespective of the several viewpoints, the common goal that any learning architecture strives to meet is to support a holistic learning ecosystem that not only caters to the adequate breadth and depth of learning with appropriate learning components for all personas but also instills perseverance, discipline and curiosity to promote a progressive learning culture. Fig 4.2 describes a reference learning architecture organized in 5 layers, which can be used to guide enterprises and learning teams to lay the foundations for a holistic learning ecosystem which helps them on their journey to becoming a learning organization. The architecture is built using several components that progressively bolster an organization's learning agility - starting with learning platforms that help with the acquisition of knowledge and skills and culminating in learning credentials which motivate learners to baseline their proficiency and mastery.

Learning Platforms

In recent years, organizations have been transforming themselves from a training based culture to a learning based culture wherein the learning is more democratized, personalized, and is available anytime, anywhere, and on any device. This transformation is evident when we observe that instructor-led training is becoming increasingly niche

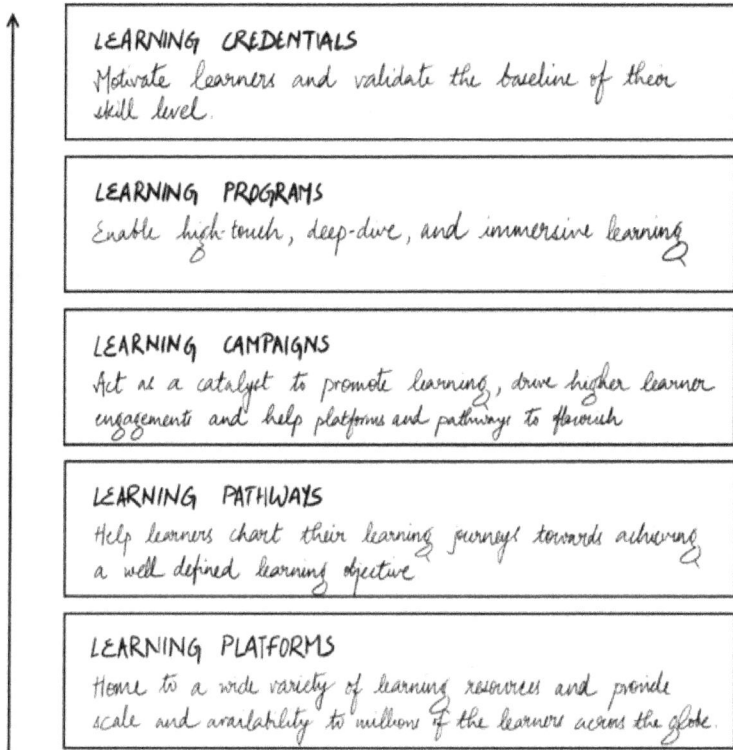

LEARNING CREDENTIALS
Motivate learners and validate the baseline of their skill level.

LEARNING PROGRAMS
Enable high-touch, deep-dive, and immersive learning

LEARNING CAMPAIGNS
Act as a catalyst to promote learning, drive higher learner engagement and help platforms and pathways to flourish

LEARNING PATHWAYS
Help learners chart their learning journeys towards achieving a well defined learning objective

LEARNING PLATFORMS
Home to a wide variety of learning resources and provide scale and availability to millions of the learners across the globe.

Fig 4.2: Reference Learning Architecture

and self-learning is becoming increasingly mainstream. Learning platforms are at the heart of this transformation.

Learning platforms are home to a wide variety of learning resources and provide scale and availability to millions of learners across the globe. The availability of these learning resources anytime, anywhere and on any device truly democratizes the way learning happens. Besides enabling self-learning, these platforms also promote a hybrid learning approach wherein self-learning is augmented with instructor-led touchpoints that further steer the learning through discussions on key concepts, and guidance from subject matter experts on the topic. Although learning platforms are transforming the learning styles and preferences of individuals, instructor-led training is and will continue to be an intrinsic part of any learning ecosystem. Such training holds merit and provides great benefits to efficiently deliver highly personalized, niche, targeted and time bound learning interventions.

There are numerous learning platforms for organizations and individuals to choose from and some of the popular players in this space (in no particular order) are Coursera, edX, Udemy, Udacity, O'Reilly, Pluralsight, Codility, Codecademy. Cumulatively, these platforms are estimated to host hundreds of thousands of hours of learning content which are consumed by more than 300 million users[204]. It is also interesting to note that the adoption of these learning platforms boomed significantly during and after the Covid-19 pandemic. The wide variety of learning resources offered by these learning platforms come in varying **pedagogies** - from bite-sized videos to full length textbooks; from simple interactive practice exercises to complex simulations; and from micro-credentials for instant gratification to professional industry certifications that assert proficiency. Organizations and individuals can choose from the plethora of learning platforms not just based on the pedagogy of the learning resources but also based on the various other aspects offered by them, as depicted in Fig 4.3.

The **breadth** of the catalog of learning resources offered by the learning platform is a key factor that organizations and individuals should consider while choosing among multiple platforms. The breadth is typically compared with the organizational skill taxonomy which defines the range and hierarchy of skills required by the enterprise. While some platforms may boast a wide catalog covering multitude of skills, some others may specialize in providing learning resources for a niche segment. For example, some of the learning platforms may offer a wide variety of content in technologies like data science, full stack web development, etc. but may not contain a comprehensive library of content in other areas such as business domain or process. On the other hand, there could be some platforms that exclusively

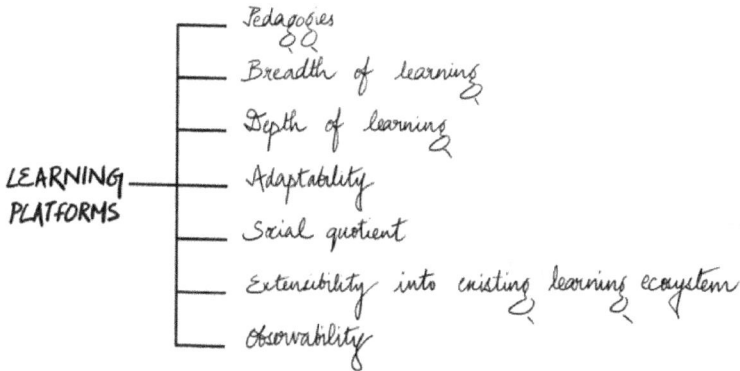

Fig 4.3: Features of Learning Platforms

provide content in a specific domain or set of processes. Enterprises have to evaluate the breadth of the learning catalog that the platform offers against their skill taxonomy and future skills plans. It is important to note that the learning resources from platforms may need to be further augmented with the internal knowledge repositories of the enterprise to provide context about how the skills are used within the organization. Enterprises should choose the right combination of learning platforms that comprises a wide variety of learning resources to arrive at the desired breadth of learning.

Learning platforms enrich the learning experience of individuals by providing immersive learning resources that help the users engage **deeply** with them. Several learning platforms provide technology sandboxes so that learners can practice technology skills in an interactive manner using a learn-by-doing approach. These environments can be interwoven with other learning resources for learners to practice the concepts they learn, promote incremental progress, and encourage learners to experiment as they acquire new skills. For example, if one has to learn programming languages such as Python, one can spin-off a Python sandbox provided by the learning platform to start with trying-out the language's basic syntax and grammar and eventually leverage the sandbox to experiment with some of Python's advanced programming libraries. On the other hand, for behavioral and leadership skills, learning platforms offer case study based simulations. For example, to build critical thinking and innovative problem solving skills one may engage with interactive case-studies that stimulate creativity and ingenuity. These learning resources also need to be paired with internal deep-dive learning environments (systems/sandboxes) that help individuals contextualize their advanced skills for the enterprise and realize the desired depth of learning.

The **adaptability** aspect represents how the learning platform transforms its user experience to suit the learning style and needs of its users. Most learning platforms offer users the flexibility to create a profile and choose their areas of interest upon initial sign-up. Further, as users engage with the platform, they receive personalized learning recommendations that consider both their preferred pedagogy and their current skill level. Learning platforms continuously analyze and derive insights from user engagement data and collect feedback to continuously improve their offerings, the user experience, and in turn the adaptability.

Contrary to the belief that learners may feel alienated as they start consuming learning resources in self-learning mode; learning platforms actually help develop a community of learners and SMEs (Subject Matter Experts) across the globe who support each other along the learning journey, by providing a host of social features such as learning groups, Q&A forums, user-curated learning playlists, etc. These features have been inspired from the experience of social media platforms and the unprecedented levels of engagement and size of communities they create. These **social features** not only benefit individual learners, but also benefit teams within the enterprise where they can customize, share and track the learning to suit their project/pod learning style and needs. The adoption and propagation of such social features helps enterprises build a strong community of learners who aid in fostering a learning culture.

Extensibility refers to the ability of the learning platform to be smoothly integrated with the existing platforms and be flexible enough to be hosted within the enterprise's environments. Learning platforms that provide the ability to address the needs of an enterprise beyond the standard offerings provided by default, are even more sought after. For example, some learning platforms provide the ability for enterprises to author, host and serve custom content that is exclusive to the organization; and some platforms partner with organizations to tailor the content and features to suit the enterprise's context. Further, platforms should also be extensible to adapt to the changing needs of the enterprises with respect to regulations and governance as they grow and scale across geographies over time. For example, the learning platform should clearly define the various mechanisms using which it supports the protection of the Intellectual Property of any organization that authors and/or hosts content on it. It should also ensure to follow the appropriate regulations such as GDPR to protect the data of the learner's and maintain their privacy.

Learning platforms support the enterprise's transition from training based culture to learning based culture. Enterprises and learning teams may stay in a comfort zone and believe that they are a learning organization just because they deliver training to the individuals and teams when required. However, a true learning organization thrives when individuals and teams adopt a proactive approach to learning and leverage learning platforms and resources to acquire skills and become fit for the future. Introducing learning platforms into the learning ecosystem can help enterprises and learning teams move towards a learning based culture. The observability related features of learning platforms can help collect, analyze and monitor the learning patterns of the learners. These insights can be used by enterprises and learning teams to make informed decisions which help keep the learning trajectory of individuals and teams aligned to the broader objectives of the organization.

Having understood the different features of learning platforms you may now be able to visualize how a learner engages with these platforms to acquire skills. You might also have some first hand experience with some of these platforms and may have gone through a few courses on them already. As a learner, you are typically presented with a catalog of learning which adapts to your learning preferences and activities on the platform. You are also recommended courses based on the interests that you indicated when signing up and your browsing/learning activities on the platform. When you make progress in your learning, you are able to share your progress with your friends on social media, you also receive notifications when they make progress, and you have access to a community of learners who you can exchange ideas with.

Looking from the perspective of an enterprise, you should now be able to appreciate the importance of having such learning platforms in the learning ecosystem. Learning platforms are foundational to building a robust learning architecture that supports a thriving learning ecosystem. Enterprises that are in the nascent stage of building a learning ecosystem can start by investing in a single learning platform in order to germinate the learning culture. They should choose a platform that caters to their critical mass of employees, offers a wide catalog relevant to their learning goals, provides deep-dive learning resources, facilitates social features, allows extensibility, adaptability and observability. With time, as the learning needs and learning maturity evolves, enterprises can incorporate several more learning platforms to lean on a multi-platform strategy for learning to further strengthen the breadth and depth of learning for a wider range of personas across the organization. In a multi-platform strategy, to provide a consistent and unified learning experience for employees, organizations can invest in Learning Experience Platforms(LXPs) such as Degreed, Cornerstone EdCast or Docebo. These LXPs typically provide a single interface that acts as a gateway to the wide catalog of learning resources provided by the various underlying learning platforms.

Learning Pathways

Learning platforms typically host a large repository of learning resources which could overwhelm learners, especially those who are just beginning their learning journey. By integrating learning pathways into the learning ecosystem, enterprises can bring a method to the madness by providing a guide to navigate their learning journey in the giant labyrinth of learning content and help them stay focussed. Learning pathways consist of learning resources structured in a gradational manner to help learners develop their knowledge and skills progressively. These can help promote self-learning to individuals and teams and thus bolster an enterprise's efforts to shift from a training based culture to a learning based culture.

Learning pathways are typically designed to help learners chart their learning journey towards achieving a well defined learning objective such as to learn a new skill, enhance the knowledge level in a topic, or develop a suite of capabilities that are required to progress in a role. They contain a combination of relevant learning resources such as videos, articles, courses, books, sandbox environments, and self-assessments, organized in a gradational manner. These pathways not only serve as a guide for the uninitiated but also help all learners ensure that they stay on track towards achieving their learning goals.

Learning pathways may be designed and hosted either on learning platforms directly, if they provide the capability to, or on the learning experience platforms (LXPs) that provide the capability to aggregate content from a multitude of learning platforms; or both. Irrespective of where they are designed and hosted, a comprehensive learning pathway should address five key aspects, as depicted in Fig 4.4.

Defining the **learning goal** is a vital aspect of designing and implementing learning pathways. Typically learning pathways are designed as either Skill development pathways which enable learners to acquire and/or enhance skills in order to bolster their knowledge

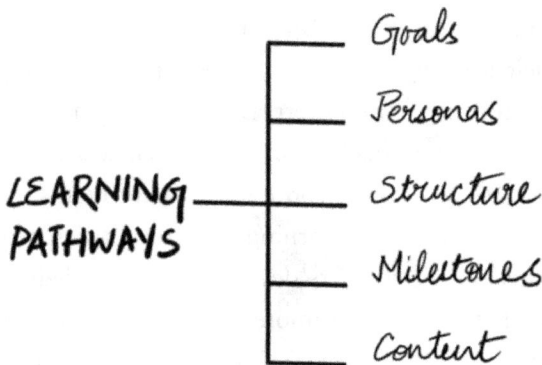

Fig 4.4: Key Aspects of Learning Pathways

and skill-set, or as Role based pathways which equip the learners with a suite of capabilities that may be required to perform a role in the organization. Skill-development pathways may be atomic in nature and focus on acquiring/enhancing knowledge in a single skill such as learning a new programming language (JavaScript), learning a new software framework/library (Angular), or becoming empathetic. Role based pathways are typically composite in nature and focus on a suite of skills that are required for the role. For example, a role based pathway to become a full-stack web developer guides the individuals to learn a suite of skills such as UX Design, Empathy, JavaScript, TypeScript, Angular, MongoDB, Express, Node, Git, Jira, Jenkins, Cloud platforms/services, etc.

The design and implementation of learning pathways is intricately connected with the **persona of its learners**. Recall that enterprises comprise of individuals broadly categorized into various personas such as decision makers, influencers and implementers, and each of these personas have different learning needs in terms of its breadth, depth, pedagogy, size, complexity, and knowledge level. For example, a learning pathway for decision makers on a technology such as AI would be tailored to help them drive the adoption of the technology and initiatives within the enterprise. The pathway may broadly cover topics such as fundamentals of AI, how to create an AI strategy, ethical and legal considerations, implementing AI within existing systems, and risk management. On the other hand, a pathway on AI for implementers would focus on getting them to build AI solutions. This pathway may include topics such as fundamentals of AI, data processing and feature engineering, machine learning, supervised and unsupervised learning algorithms, deep learning, evaluating models, deploying models, ethical considerations, data privacy, reducing bias, AI explainability, and various real-life case studies. Identifying and defining the persona of the learners is critical to ensuring that the learning resources included in the pathway are attuned to their needs.

The **structure or anatomy** of learning pathways should be designed by considering both the goal and the persona of its learners. Learning pathways are designed to be gradational in nature where the size and the complexity of the modules included in it grows as the learning progresses. Both skill-based and role-based pathways typically begin with modules that cover foundational aspects such as 'starting with the why (of the skill or role)' and 'exploring the world of possibilities (for the skill or role)' in order to entrance the learners and arouse their curiosity. The pathway then progresses into various modules that are strung together in a well defined structure to guide the learner further into the skills that they want to master or ace the role that they play.

Learning pathways should include **milestones** as a way for its learners to track their progress and validate their learning along their learning journey. Periodic notifications not only help learners to know how far they have progressed along their learning journey but also nudge learners to get back on track whenever required. The inclusion of self-assessments at various stages of their learning journey helps learners validate the skills that they have acquired using the pathway.

The **content** of the learning pathway is of course its most essential aspect. It is curated into the learning pathway by considering all the aspects mentioned earlier- learning goal, learner persona, and the structure & milestones of the pathway. These aspects help determine the pedagogy of the learning resources that is most appropriate for the learners in the given context. The content of the learning pathway should seek to nurture the three elements of the learning triad - logic, data and imagination, while keeping the learning goal, the learner's persona, and the pedagogy in consideration.

Learning resources that 'start with the why (of the skill or role)' and 'explore the world of possibilities (for the skill or role)' play a key role in fueling the imagination of the learners. For example, a learning pathway for decision makers to learn AI should begin by emphasizing the potential of AI to solve business problems and highlight real world examples of where AI has been employed to create new or better outcomes. The pathway should then progress towards enabling learners to understand the core aspects of how data, logic and imagination interplay in the context of the skill or the role they seek to learn. In the example of the AI learning pathway, this means including resources on how data influences AI systems, how programming helps build algorithms that interplay with data to create models, and how imagination helps conceptualize enhancements to digital experiences that leverage AI.

In order to explore the nuances of this interplay, learning resources that promote experiential and iterative learning using principles of systemic thinking and design thinking approaches should be included. Content that promotes experiential learning via systemic thinking helps learners deconstruct the system to understand its parts and (re)construct it to understand the whole. For example, one could deconstruct an AI system and understand its various components such as its capabilities, the data used to build the system, the underlying algorithms, the model learnt from the data, and the parameters to the model. Then, one could rebuild or retrain the model using a similar set of data and algorithms to better understand how it can be constructed and in the process learn to imagine how the model can be enhanced. Similarly, learning resources that are centered around fostering a design thinking mindset not only enrich the learner's understanding of the interplay between the elements of the triad but also help them gain a better understanding of the skill or role they seek to learn as they empathize, ideate, prototype and test along their learning journey. In the AI example, this refers to having learning resources such as exercises/case studies which help with empathizing with the users to identify the problems they face, ideating solutions where AI could be used to alleviate the pain points, building prototype models, and testing them for the efficacy in solving the problems.

Learning pathways are a key component of the learning architecture and are effective in promoting a self-learning culture within the organization. In order to accelerate the learning and development journey of employees, enterprises should first identify the most critical skills and roles that are relevant to them and then curate appropriate learning pathways to meet the demand. Over time, enterprises should create (and refresh) a comprehensive repository of learning pathways that cater to the roles performed by their employees and the various skills they use across the board.

Learning Campaigns

Undoubtedly, establishing learning platform(s) and publishing learning pathways is key to laying the foundation of the learning ecosystem; platforms provide the learning resources and pathways help organize the learning. However, large enterprises typically struggle with keeping up a culture of continuous learning using these platforms and pathways alone. Learning campaigns are crucial here and help enterprises nudge individuals and teams to start/restart their learning journey, and in turn help sustain the learning momentum.

Learning campaigns typically provide a series of learning experiences over time that act as a catalyst to promote learning, drive higher learner engagements, and help platforms and pathways to flourish. They are designed with a specific objective such as promoting the learning platforms/pathways/resources associated with a specific role/ skill, influencing learning behavior, encouraging social or informal learning and knowledge sharing, or evoking curiosity and fostering innovation. In addition to having a **well defined objective**, learning campaigns should also exhibit the attributes depicted in Fig 4.5.

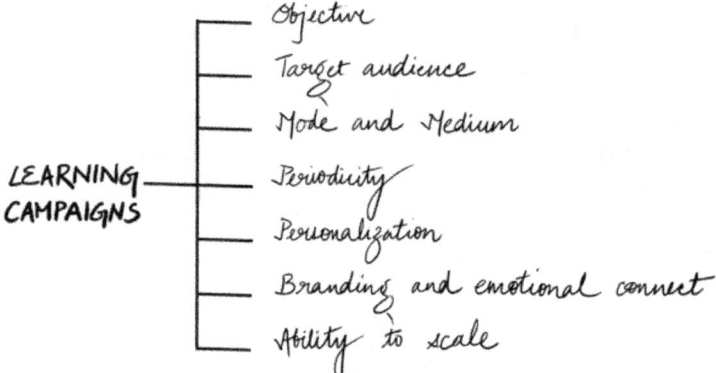

LEARNING CAMPAIGNS
- Objective
- Target audience
- Mode and Medium
- Periodicity
- Personalization
- Branding and emotional connect
- Ability to scale

Fig 4.5: Key Attributes of Learning Campaigns

Identifying the right **target audience** is critical to the design of any learning campaign. The objective and the content of the learning campaign should be best suited to match the profile of the target audience. For example, it would be prudent to target individuals who are web developers / backend engineers / API developers as the audience for a learning campaign that promotes a full stack developer learning pathway because their current skills are adjacent to the skills of a full stack developer. On the other hand, learning campaigns such as hackathons that foster innovation could target individuals with diverse skill-sets and help them come together to learn collaboratively.

Learning campaign experiences could be delivered to the target audience in either **synchronous or asynchronous mode**. Synchronous experiences are highly engaging and promote spontaneous interaction/exchange among participants in a given context. For example, fireside chats, live sessions, conferences, etc. are some of the synchronous experiences that form part of campaigns that aim to promote the adoption of new skills or evoke curiosity among learners. Asynchronous experiences are flexible, low touch, and are typically used to influence learner behavior or continue to keep the learners engaged over the length of a campaign. For example, newsletters, podcasts and blogs are some of the asynchronous experiences that are delivered to the learners for them to consume at the time of their choosing.

Timing and periodicity play a crucial role in the delivery of impactful learning campaign experiences. Typically continuous learning organizations have a variety of learning initiatives and programs running across regions, business lines, teams, etc., so it is critical to get the timing right when launching a learning campaign so that it garners maximum attention and produces the desired outcomes. Getting the timing right is only the first step. In order to build and sustain the rhythm throughout the lifecycle of the campaign, its experiences need to be delivered with the right periodicity. For example, to run a successful campaign that helps learners embrace a new learning platform, the campaign events/experiences have to be triggered at opportune moments and in a manner that gives the audience sufficient time to be enthused about the platform, embark their learning journeys with the platform, and finally sustain a healthy and periodic engagement with the platform.

Personalization is key to designing and delivering learning campaign experiences to sustain the right amount of rhythm and ensure that the audience remains connected with the campaign throughout its lifecycle. While the initial campaign experiences could be generic, as time progresses the subsequent experiences may be adapted to become more specific and personalized to individuals based on their journey with the campaign so far. For example, a typical learning campaign to influence learning behavior may start with a common launch experience that is addressed to everyone, but as time progresses the campaign experiences can get more personalized such as differentiated timing and periodicity, or differentiated modes of the campaign experience, or both based on the behavior demonstrated by the individuals during the preceding campaign experiences.

Establishing a strong **emotional connect** with the audience is critical to learning campaigns and goes a long way in ensuring its success. All learning experiences of a campaign, irrespective of mode, timing, periodicity, or personalization, should be designed and delivered in a manner that makes it easy for the audience to instantly connect them to the brand of the campaign.

Finally, learning campaigns and its experiences should be designed and delivered in ways that maximize **(scale)** both the reach and the results. Learning campaigns should grow over time to garner interest from wider communities. For example, in order to reach learners located in different regions, the learning experiences could be adapted to the popular language(s) of those regions. Similarly, learning experiences should be delivered using the right set of tools which make it easy for learners to consume them. Choosing the right set of tools includes choosing the right messaging medium, right learning platform(s) which host the content, and right tools to measure the impact/outcomes. Achieving the right mix of mode, timing, periodicity, personalization, and branding is key to maximizing the results.

Learning campaigns are crucial to a robust learning architecture. They help learners stay on track with their learning journey and reassure them of their learning intent. Now that you have understood the various aspects of a learning campaign, you can visualize how it may play out in an enterprise. For example, a campaign to promote a new learning platform in order to bolster the learning would have several touchpoints and progressively measure the adoption and usage of the new learning platform. At the beginning of the campaign, learning teams may publish news and updates about the platform via emails and newsletters giving a teaser of what's coming. They may then follow it up with a launch event such as a webinar to announce the inclusion of a new platform into the ecosystem and walk through its catalog and features. Further, there could be challenges or events to encourage people to learn more from the platform, and periodic reminders/nudges to help individuals leverage the learning resources on the platform. Finally, a key part of this campaign could be various leaders in the enterprise not only endorsing its use but also setting the trend with learning on it and bolstering its adoption.

Enterprises and learning teams need to be creative as they design and deliver the learning campaigns and experiences over time in order to sustain the learning momentum. Exploring newer modes, experimenting with different timing/periodicity, and establishing the brand reputation are continuous pursuits that enterprises and learning teams need to go through. Further, they should also have campaigns that celebrate and reward learners for demonstrating the right learning behaviors, achieving their learning goals, and staying on track with their learning journey.

Learning Programs

Learning campaigns, ably supported by learning pathways and underlying learning platforms help propagate the breadth of learning by enabling individuals to engage with a wide variety of skills and knowledge areas. These layers are essential to building a learning culture where individuals take control of their learning journeys which are largely self-motivated, self-directed, and self-paced. They are particularly effective in situations where time is not a constraint and the learning outcomes can be achieved by the individuals with minimal support or intervention. However, to accelerate the skill acquisition, bolster role progression/maturity, or channelize the learning journeys of individuals, enterprises typically institute learning programs.

Learning programs put the individual learners in touch with highly skilled facilitators and subject matter experts (SMEs) in real-time to enable interactive, deep-dive, and immersive learning. To get an idea about these learning programs you can think of any training that you may have attended - either in-person or virtually. At the start of your career, you may have attended training in foundational skills that are required for you to get up to speed with your role. If your role was technical and involved writing software code, you may have gone through deep dive training programs in a programming language or a framework. You may remember these learning programs as typically high-touch, highly adaptive in nature, and observed that they can be dynamically modified on-the-fly to suit the needs and the pace of the learners based on real-time interactions and feedback. These learning programs help rekindle the minds of learners and reinforce their learning which technology based self-learning solutions may only be able to provide partially at best. Learning programs typically exhibit the following key attributes, as depicted in Fig 4.6. While you may observe that some of these attributes may be broadly similar to that of learning pathways, the difference lies in how these attributes are dealt with in the context of learning programs.

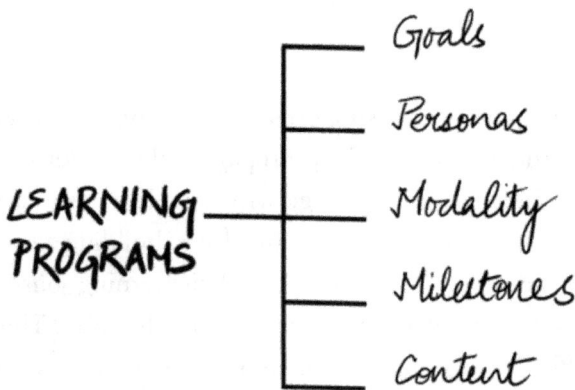

Fig 4.6: Key Attributes of Learning Programs

Identifying and articulating the **goals and objectives** of the learning program is one of the crucial aspects involved in instituting learning programs. Typically learning programs are designed to either accelerate the skill acquisition or bolster role progression/maturity. Skill development learning programs are commonly employed to help accelerate individuals in their upskill/cross-skill learning journeys in a time-bound manner through the guidance of highly-skilled SMEs and facilitators. Learning programs that are aimed at supporting the role progression/maturity primarily focus on preparing individuals to learn behavior and skills that are required for the role that they aspire for, and help accelerate the achievement of their goals in a structured manner.

Learning programs should be designed and implemented by keeping the **persona of the learners** at the center. Recall that there are three broad categories of learners, defined earlier, viz. decision makers, influencers and implementers; and each persona would have different learning needs and expect different outcomes from the learning program. It is critical to calibrate the breadth, depth, pedagogy, size, and complexity of the various elements of the learning program to suit the persona of the learners. The duration of the learning programs may also need to be calibrated based on the persona of the learners. For example, while decision makers may prefer to engage with high impact learning programs for a shorter duration, implementers may be willing to engage with longer duration deep dive learning programs that boost their skills.

The success of learning programs hinges on how its various components are structured and delivered. Choosing the right mix of the **modality** (guided or self-paced) of learning components is critical to ensuring the effectiveness of the program. Based on the goal of the program and the persona of the learners, programs can have varying degrees of guided learning components such as face-to-face time with SMEs/instructors for knowledge sharing, mentoring, hands-on coaching, and peer learning; and self-paced learning components such as learning pathways, assignments/exercises, and self-assessments. For example, a skill development program for entry-level "implementers" could have a high degree of guided learning components whereas a role maturity program for "influencers" may have a balanced mix of guided and self-paced learning components.

Learning programs should be continuously steered to stay on track towards its goal by measuring the progress at various **milestones** and analyzing the feedback along the learning journey. Learners can keep a track of their learning progress through various assignments/ exercises, assessments, and feedback from facilitators/SMEs; and the program can be calibrated to be more effective by seeking and understanding the feedback from the learners at regular time intervals.

The **content** of learning programs should not only be designed to meet the goals and objectives of the program but it should also be delivered in a manner that caters to the higher levels of engagement and immersiveness that learning programs are uniquely positioned to offer. The content may be delivered through a combination of various learning elements such as discussions, quizzes, and collaborative hands-on assignments; either synchronously or asynchronously. All content must aim to nurture the three elements of the learning triad - logic, data, and imagination, and promote a holistic understanding of the elements and the interplay among them.

The anatomy of the learning resources that form the content of learning programs are broadly similar to that of learning pathways. The resources should 'start with the why (of the skill or role)' and 'explore the world of possibilities (for the skill or role)' and emphasize the goals and outcomes. Further, the content should contain elements that enable the learners to understand the core aspects of how data, logic and imagination interplay in the context of the skill or the role they seek to learn. Resources that promote experiential and iterative learning using principles of systemic thinking and design thinking approaches should be included to explore the nuances of this interplay. Recall that content that promotes experiential learning via systemic thinking helps learners deconstruct the system to understand its parts and (re)construct it to understand the whole. Similarly, learning resources that are centered around fostering a design thinking mindset not only enrich the learner's understanding of the interplay between the elements of the triad but also help them gain a better understanding of the skill or role they seek to learn as they empathize, ideate, prototype and test along their learning journey.

Learning programs are key to accelerating skill acquisition, bolstering role progression/maturity, and channelizing the learning journeys of individuals. The guided training provided through these learning programs act as a booster amidst the various self-learning layers of the learning ecosystem. A balanced mix of guided training and self-learning components delivered through learning programs helps create a robust learning ecosystem that is equipped to support a thriving learning culture.

Learning Credentials

As individuals and teams progress on their learning journeys using the learning platforms, pathways, campaigns and programs, they may seek a way to not only stay motivated but also to validate their learning. Learning credentials take care of this aspect and in turn completes the entire stack of the learning architecture. Credentials provide learners with milestones to follow along the learning journey which keeps them motivated, helps them stay on track, and may serve as a baseline of their skill level.

The spectrum of learning credentials is diverse as they come in varying size and shapes. They may range from bite-sized micro-credentials such as learning badges and nanodegrees to industry/professional certifications that are typically achieved through rigorous study, practice, and a formal assessment. They may also be found in the form of accreditations such as degrees/diplomas from formal learning institutions, or as publications in the form of whitepapers, books or patents. This variety of learning credentials that learners may seek to achieve is depicted in Fig 4.7

Fig 4.7: Variety of Learning Credentials

Micro-credentials recognize learners' achievement of very specific learning outcomes that are accomplished by performing a relatively short duration learning activity such as completing a course or an assessment/project. These micro-credentials validate the competency of the learner in the specific skill and are typically represented as badges/certificates of completion. These may be issued as either a record of attendance alone or as a record of completing a reliable assessment at the end of the learning activity. Such credentials are commonly issued by learning platforms but can also be associated with learning pathways, campaigns and programs.

Industry/professional certifications are typically awarded by credentialing institutions after a learner demonstrates significant expertise by way of qualifying in standardized assessment(s). These certifications are highly reputed as they are backed by trustworthy institutions which are relied upon to continuously set high standards of training content and assessments. Although certifications may be of varying degrees of complexity and may not be comparable to one another, they provide assurance of the learner's competence in a set of specific skills that are linked to the readiness for a job role. Enterprises may have their own internal certifications when there is a need to accredit the competence of an individual exclusively within their context. On the other hand, for accrediting the competence in industry-wide skills/roles enterprises may rely on external bodies - it could either be product specific such as Google Cloud Certified Professional Data Engineer or Oracle Certified Professional Java Programmer; or be related to a profession such as Certified Financial Analyst, Project Management Professional or Professional Scrum Master.

Higher educational degrees/diplomas offered by learning institutions serve as widely accepted certificates of knowledge and skill of individuals across enterprises. Enterprises encourage the individuals to enroll for these higher education programs in order to boost their knowledge and skills. Enterprises may offer individuals off-the-shelf programs that are directly offered by learning institutions such as universities, or co-create bespoke programs which bake in the enterprise context.

Publishing **whitepapers, research papers, books, or patents** represents a class of credentials that reflects an individual's credible expertise in a particular knowledge area. Enterprises should encourage individuals to pursue these credentials, provide appropriate support to enable them, and reward the distinguished ones.

Learning credentials however big or small represent the achievement of learning goals, and help individuals stay motivated along their learning journeys. Earning these credentials not only boosts the profile of an individual but also contributes to bolstering the brand of the enterprises. Enterprises and learning teams should include a wide range of credentials for individuals to strive for and celebrate their achievements along their continuous learning journey.

So far, we have visualized the learning architecture with a perspective of deconstructing it into 5 layers - learning platforms, learning pathways, learning campaigns, learning programs and learning credentials, and explored the key components within each of these layers. Enterprises may construct their own learning architectures by combining the components within these layers in a form that best suits their learning needs and style. Ultimately any learning architecture should be built to support a holistic learning ecosystem that not only caters to the adequate breadth and depth of learning leading to the mastery of the learning spectrum, but also instills the virtues of our learning fractal viz. perseverance, discipline and curiosity, which are the key tenets of a progressive learning culture.

Learning Culture

Individuals and enterprises are continuous learning organisms supported by learning ecosystems that continuously evolve with time. The progress and success of a learning ecosystem to support its learners can be predominantly attributed to the learning culture that it nourishes. Individuals, enterprises and learning teams all contribute to the learning culture within an enterprise. Individuals consume learning and further their skills, enterprises sponsor learning and create the learning ecosystem, and learning teams work towards the upkeep of the learning momentum. The leaders within an enterprise have a key role to play in creating and sustaining a healthy learning culture. They should not only sponsor the various learning activities but also be visible and active learners themselves to inspire their teams and emphasize the importance of learning. The learning culture plays a dual role in the overall learning ecosystem. On one hand, it helps individuals and enterprises adapt to the changes that come with evolution, and on the other, it also supports the transformation of the learning ecosystem to suit the tides of time. It plays both ways!

While one may have observed that the learning culture changes (and has changed) over time, however, what remains constant (and has remained so since time immemorial) are the three timeless virtues of the learning fractal - perseverance, discipline, and curiosity - which are essential for the culture to thrive. Recall that these three virtues are inspired from the fundamental characteristics of fractals viz. eternal, connected, and self-organized, as depicted in Fig 4.8.

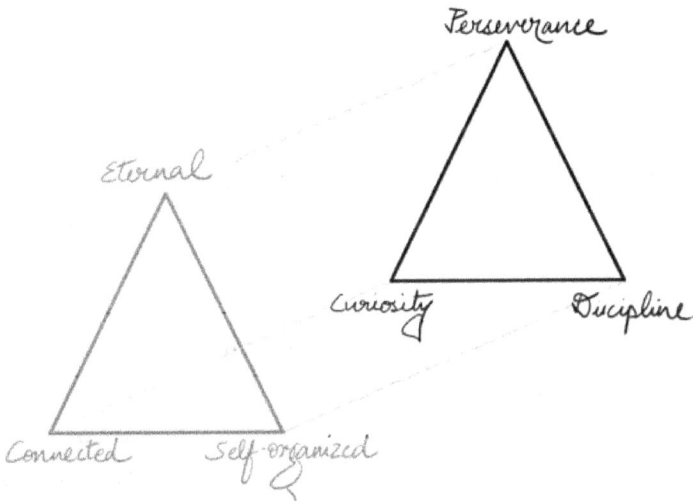

Fig 4.8: Virtues Required for a Thriving Learning Culture

Perseverance reflects the eternal nature of learning which learners should imbibe by consistently investing in learning for their sustained growth. Enterprises and learning teams can help learners cultivate this virtue by helping them calibrate their learning goals, providing a fail-safe environment that challenges them periodically, and putting their failures into a growth perspective. Further, learners should be appreciated for their effort as they progress in their learning journey in order to help them focus on their strengths, and stay motivated.

Enterprises and learning teams can foster perseverance within the learning architecture by including fail-safe components such as sandbox environments and simulations in the learning platforms and learning programs. These components allow learners to experiment freely without the fear of failure and learn from their mistakes. Further, gamifying the learning and rewarding learners with micro-credentials such as badges may help keep them motivated as they pursue their learning goals.

Discipline reflects the self-organized nature of learning. It is the bridge between the learning goals that are defined and the outcomes that are accomplished. This virtue helps learners create and sustain new learning habits, stay focussed on their goals, and overcome discomfort and persist when faced with challenges. Learners should cultivate it by striving to learn diligently, ardently honing their skills, and applying their learning repetitively along their learning journey.

Enterprises and learning teams can help learners inculcate discipline in their learning through positive reinforcements and timely nudges delivered along the learning journey both through learning platforms and mentors/coaches/learning communities. They can also run periodic learning campaigns to build a rhythm, uplift learner engagement, and leave no one behind. Individuals should set aside time each day exclusively for learning and diligently follow it to make strides towards their learning goals.

Curiosity is closely knit with the connected nature of learning and fostering this virtue helps accentuate the imagination of the learners. Staying curious not only enables learners to widen the breadth of their knowledge across the learning spectrum but also acts as the seed for the ever expanding imagination spiral of the learning triad which leads to unearthing the depth of the learning spectrum. A curious mind always yearns to learn more, and the more you learn, the more you can imagine!

Enterprises and learning teams can encourage learners to stay curious and cultivate open mindedness by inspiring them to explore the world of possibilities. Including design thinking and system thinking techniques into learning programs and pathways further helps bolster the desire of learners to learn more and connect the dots as they learn. Enterprises and learning teams may also ignite the curiosity of learners through various learning campaigns that help learners discover new skills.

Both enterprises and individuals should have a bias for action that is required to sustain the learning culture. Individuals contribute to the overall culture by being open minded, staying curious, and demonstrating a desire to learn. Individuals should not be just passive consumers of the learning ecosystem but should rather be active creators who enable the ecosystem to thrive. Enterprises should sustain the learning culture by supporting the individuals to learn, encourage them to set learning goals and development plans, and celebrate their learning successes. Enterprises should sponsor learning teams focused on upkeeping the learning conscience of the organization and thereby upholding the learning culture.

Although learning teams may differ in how they are organized and how they operate within enterprises, their broad purpose is to be the conscience keepers of learning in the organization. They typically achieve this by envisioning learning coverage for all, conceptualizing the learning roadmap, communicating with key stakeholders and consulting on competency needs, collaborating with subject matter experts, and helping calibrate the learning rhythm.

The Learning Ecosystem

Johann Wolfgang von Goethe was an influential German writer, poet, playwright and polymath with works spanning multiple genres such as drama, poetry, prose, and scientific writing to his credit. He is credited with significant contributions in literature, anatomy, botany, and color theory, and remains one of the most influential and prominent figures in German Literature. In his timeless quote, "Knowing is not enough; we must apply. Willing is not enough; we must do", Goethe eloquently captures the importance of applying knowledge and taking action. This not only resonates with Aristotle's Nicomachean ethics where he emphasized the value of learning by doing, but also impresses that the crucial step to success lies in **taking action**.

In this chapter, we have explored the importance of learning by doing for individuals, enterprises and learning teams in the context of mastering digital skills. We discussed the importance of learning ecosystems in enabling learners to acquire skills through practice, encouraging them to make incremental progress, and instilling the virtues of perseverance, discipline and curiosity to support their lifelong learning journey. We also delved into the nuances of a reference learning architecture that enterprises and learning teams can use as a blueprint to build a learning ecosystem for themselves. In this chapter, we have also discussed that any learning ecosystem can thrive only if it is supported by a progressive learning culture. And we have seen the dual role that the learning culture plays i.e. it not only helps enterprises and individuals adapt to evolving trends, but also aids the transformation of the learning ecosystem itself.

To support the goal of becoming a continuous learning organization, enterprises and learning teams need to build and sustain a holistic learning ecosystem. This is a journey in itself in which they have to learn to do, by doing. They not only have to build the various components of the learning architecture to suit their context but also discover how they can instill the virtues of the learning fractal which can help sustain the learning culture in the process. Success on this journey comes from taking action. Individuals, enterprises and learning teams all must have a **bias for action** when it comes to fostering a learning ecosystem.

Fig 4.9 depicts the learning ecosystem as being composed of learning architecture and learning culture. It also symbolizes the influence that individuals, enterprises and learning teams have on ensuring that the learning ecosystem grows to support their learning needs and bolster their learning agility.

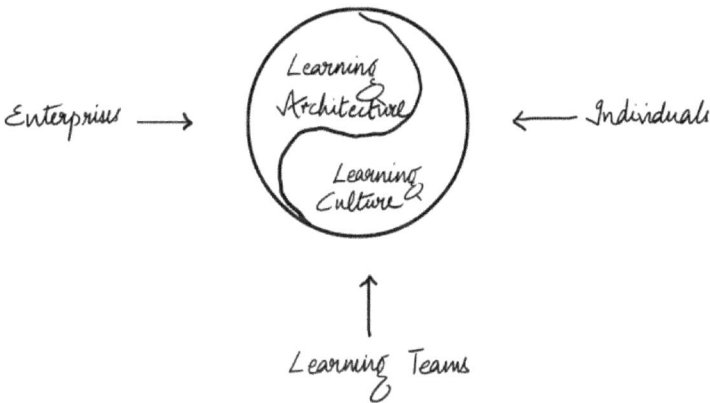

Fig 4.9: The Learning Ecosystem

The learning ecosystem forms the nurturing ground to grow the learning fractal. Enterprises that aim to become learning organizations should set up a holistic learning ecosystem which caters to the breadth and depth of the learning spectrum across various personas. The learning ecosystem should also help learners appreciate the fundamental fractal - the learning triad and instill virtues which lead to life-long learning. Individuals, enterprises and learning teams should evoke their innate desire for progress and manifest it in their acts of learning. Individuals should do so by exploring the breadth and depth of the spectrum to master their craft. Enterprises should sponsor learning, build and sustain the learning ecosystem, and promote a progressive learning culture. Learning teams being the conscience keepers, should be at the helm and steer the journey towards becoming learning organizations.

For enterprises who are in an early stage of setting up a learning ecosystem, we recommend they start by exploring their various learning needs to discover their learning goals and priorities. After they identify the breadth and depth of their learning needs, they should look at how to meet these learning needs. Learning platforms are a great starting point for the enterprises to enable individuals and teams with most common digital skills. Once they have a catalog of learning content, they should curate and contextualize it as learning pathways. These learning pathways could be as simple as a list of recommended resources circulated to individuals and teams, or could be hosted and tracked on learning platforms and/or learning experience platforms.

Augmenting their suite of learning offerings with learning programs is often the next step. These programs aid in emphasizing the digital skills that are priority for the enterprise and accelerating their talent pipeline. Overtime as learning activities flourish, the enterprises should use learning campaigns to garner interest towards the learning activities and promote their consumption. Finally, they should institute policies and processes that support individuals and teams to acquire learning credentials and assert their proficiency in digital skills.

For enterprises who already have different learning components in their learning ecosystem, we recommend that they start by evaluating how different components are being consumed and measuring their efficacy. They should optimize how to fulfill their learning needs by including a learning catalog that fits them, curating learning pathways for key skills and roles, offering learning programs to accelerate skill development, promoting learning agenda using campaigns, and instituting learning credentials to validate skill proficiency. These enterprises and learning teams need to calibrate their learning offerings for success by not only offering newer avenues for learning but also enhancing their existing stack and channeling the learning energy in the right direction.

Ultimately, fostering a continuous learning culture is crucial for enterprises to be learning organizations. And to do this, they have to adapt to the various forces that influence their learning behavior. Forces such as changing technology trends, evolving customer needs, and shifting learning preferences all influence the flow and rhythm of learning. In the next (and final) chapter, The Learning Rhythm, we will explore the various rhythms that individuals, enterprises, and learning teams encounter along their learning journey. We will also delve into the nuances of these rhythms and understand how channelizing the bias for action of individuals, enterprises and learning teams leads to harmonizing the overall learning rhythm. We will understand how the harmonious learning rhythm is the key to the blooming of the learning fractal, which is sowed and nurtured in the learning ecosystem.

Chapter-5
The Learning Rhythm

Everything in nature has its own vibration, including nature itself!

From the twirl of a subatomic particle to the motion of the expanding universe, and everything in between and beyond, the universe is full of vibrations. Pleasant sounds, such as the rustling of leaves and the chirping of birds, are produced by sound waves resulting from vibrations in the air. The pollination of flowers occurs when bees and other pollinators vibrate while collecting nectar, loosening pollen grains and facilitating their transfer from the stamen to the pistil of the flower. In humans, vibrations between our skin and other objects play a crucial role in perceiving the world. Sensory receptors on our skin provide valuable information about texture, temperature, and pressure.

Learning too exhibits vibrations.

From an individual reading a single page of a book, to a large enterprise fostering a continuous learning culture, and everything in between and beyond, is built around learning vibrations and moves with a learning rhythm. Learning activities such as exploring a subject by reading a book, interacting with the environment, technology, peers and instructors, and making connections with existing knowledge are all sources of learning vibrations. Similarly, when enterprises actively sponsor training programs, foster mentoring and coaching, create and/or curate learning offerings for individuals and teams, and encourage learning and sharing, they too produce learning vibrations. Learning vibrations arise from the actions that individuals, enterprises and learning teams take to channelize their learning energy.

The learning vibrations in individuals stem from their innate desire to learn, and manifests into learning either as a plain act of curiosity, or broadening their horizons, or honing their skills in a particular area to master their craft. These biases for action are central to individuals as they navigate the learning spectrum and explore the breadth and depth of the skills that are required to craft digital experiences.

The learning vibrations in enterprises originate from their desire to grow and thrive, and manifests into sponsoring enterprise-wide learning initiatives with both passion and purpose. These initiatives come to fore when organizations are deeply tuned into their desires and realize the value of learning in their path to success. This bias for action is crucial for enterprises to build and sustain a robust learning ecosystem that boasts a comprehensive learning architecture and fosters a continuous learning culture.

The learning vibrations in learning teams originate from their desire to be the conscience keepers of learning in the organization, and manifests into acts of connecting learning with business outcomes, envisioning learning coverage for all, conceptualizing the learning roadmap, communicating with key stakeholders, collaborating with subject matter experts, and eventually calibrating the overall learning rhythm. This bias for action leads learning teams to establish frameworks, policies and procedures that create an environment which is conducive for learning and drives the learning agenda.

Much like in nature where the vibrations are orchestrated in a rhythm that is crucial to the behavior and sustenance of the natural world, learning vibrations in enterprises too need to be synergised to form the learning rhythm. You may have observed that when natural rhythms deviate from their normal patterns, it can often have significant and far-reaching consequences, affecting everything from the behavior of individual organisms to the stability of entire ecosystems. Similarly, a harmonious learning rhythm is essential for any learning ecosystem to ensure that the individuals and enterprises learn and grow to their potential. When the learning rhythm is either unestablished or perturbed it may lead to a variety of scenarios such as innovation gap, inability to handle crisis, and loss of competitive edge. A harmonious learning rhythm ensures that the learning ecosystem thrives to nurture the learning fractal. The learning rhythm is composed by synergizing the learning vibrations arising from the bias for action of the three actors - individuals, enterprises and learning teams. It is the key to becoming a continuous learning organization and sustaining a progressive learning culture.

Synergizing the learning vibrations is all about harmonizing the timing, periodicity and intensity of the learning vibrations of the three actors in unison. Timing refers to tuning the learning efforts of individuals in synchronization with the organization's skill needs. Periodicity refers to keeping up the learning momentum of the individuals and teams so as to ensure continuous learning. And finally intensity refers to calibrating the depth of learning that individuals and teams engage with. A harmonious learning rhythm ensures that the learning fractal blooms to life, and individuals and enterprises reach their highest potential as they progress on their digital journeys.

Fig 5.1 depicts our learning journey in this book so far. In the first chapter, we explored the fundamental characteristics of fractals, observed how learning too exhibits fractal patterns and discovered the timeless learning fractal and its virtues.

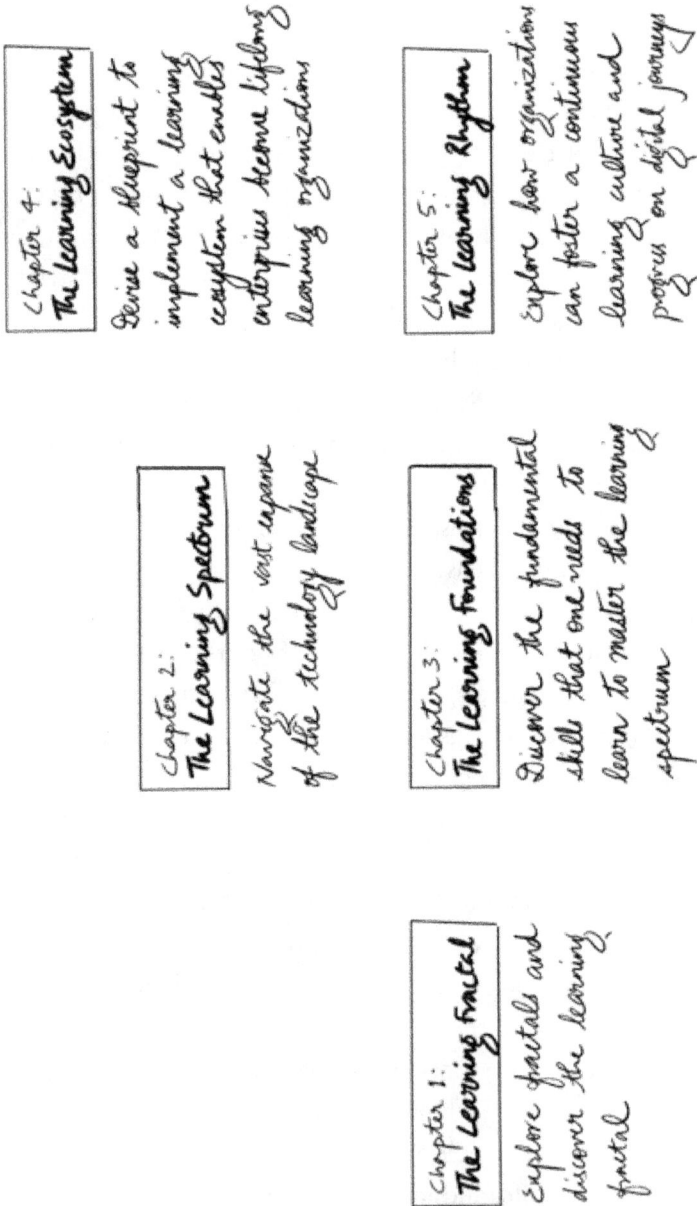

Fig 5.1: Learning Journey of this book

In the second chapter, we demystified our learning fractal - the learning spectrum, traversed across its breadth and depth to discover and piece together the connections between its various areas, and understood the plethora of digital skills that one encounters when crafting digital experiences. In the third chapter, we discovered the self-organized fundamental fractal of the learning spectrum - the learning triad, explored the interplay between the elements of the triad, and delved into the nuances of how to master the fundamentals of each element.

In the previous chapter, we understood the key aspects of a holistic learning ecosystem which enterprises must aim to build, delved into a reference learning architecture that serves as a blueprint for the learning ecosystem, and explored how the virtues of the learning fractal form the key aspects of a progressive learning culture.

In this concluding chapter, we will explore the various rhythms that individuals, enterprises, and learning teams encounter, delve into how they can tune into these rhythms to orchestrate the learning journey, and how harmonizing these rhythms creates the overall learning rhythm which blooms the learning fractal to life. We will understand how the learning rhythm augments the bias for action in individuals, enterprises and learning teams, and leads to success on their learning journeys.

The overall learning rhythm may at first seem to be abstract, but it can be appreciated by looking at the six different elements that come together to shape it, as depicted in Fig 5.2.

The learning spectrum rhythm signifies the rhythm with which individuals, enterprises and learning teams adapt to the expanding breadth and depth of the learning spectrum. The learning triad rhythm represents the consistency with which the fundamental fractal beats across the ever-changing and evolving learning spectrum. Learning architecture rhythm describes the adaptation of the blueprint of the learning ecosystem to stay relevant, contextualized, and true to the times. Learning culture rhythm symbolizes the rigor with which this blueprint is being implemented. Learning data rhythm quantifies the learning trends that are continuously observed along the learning journeys of individuals and enterprises. Finally, the learning operations rhythm describes how learning is orchestrated across the learning ecosystem (and beyond).

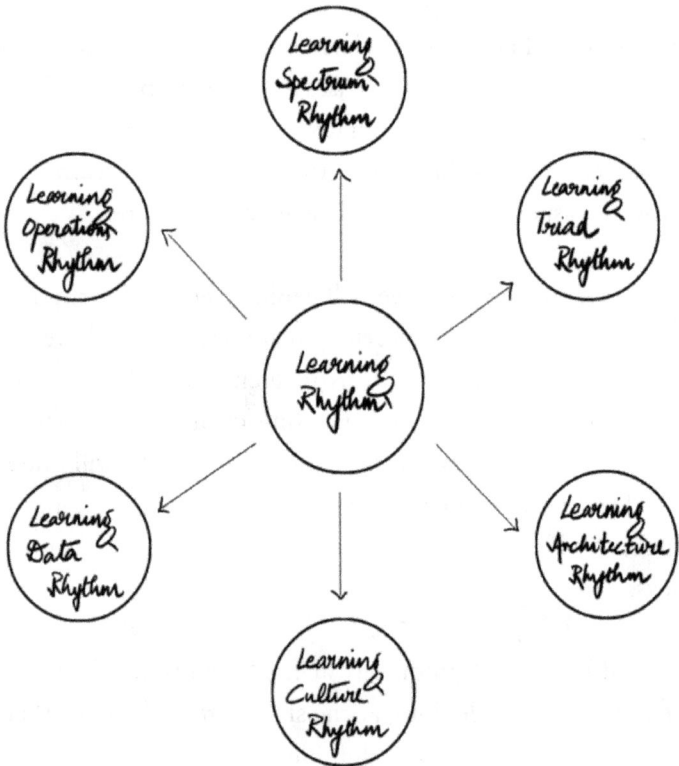

Fig. 5.2: Six Elements of the Overall Learning Rhythm

Learning Spectrum Rhythm

In chapter 2, we have explored the vast expanse of the learning spectrum across its visible and invisible parts. Recall that the visible part of the learning spectrum represents the digital skills required to build the aspects of digital experiences that users see and/or feel. In the visible part, we explored skills across web, mobile, conversational interfaces, and extended realities, which are used to build access points. Further, we also explored skills required to generate descriptive, predictive and cognitive insights, across the insights continuum. The invisible part of the learning spectrum comprises the digital skills that are employed under the hood to create the technology stack that performs the heavy lifting required for modern digital experiences. Here we explored a variety of technologies and skills in the areas of services, data, devops, cyber, and cloud. The overall learning spectrum is represented in Fig 5.3 for quick reference.

Recall that when we discussed the learning spectrum - our learning fractal, in the second chapter, we observed its eternal and connected nature as we traversed its breadth and depth. The eternal nature was evident when we observed how the learning spectrum grew with the inclusion of newer skills and technologies. And its connected nature was characterized by the interactions between its various areas. The learning spectrum rhythm can be observed when we notice the rhythm with which individuals, enterprises and learning teams respond to the eternal expansion and growing connectedness of the learning spectrum.

For example, when we look at the evolution of access points, we see how they've transitioned from the web to mobile to conversational interfaces and extended realities. Zooming into each of these areas, we can track the growth of the Web from Web 1.0 to Web 3.0, the continuous improvements in mobile device platforms, and the increasing sophistication of conversational interfaces and extended realities. It is also important to note that although these components

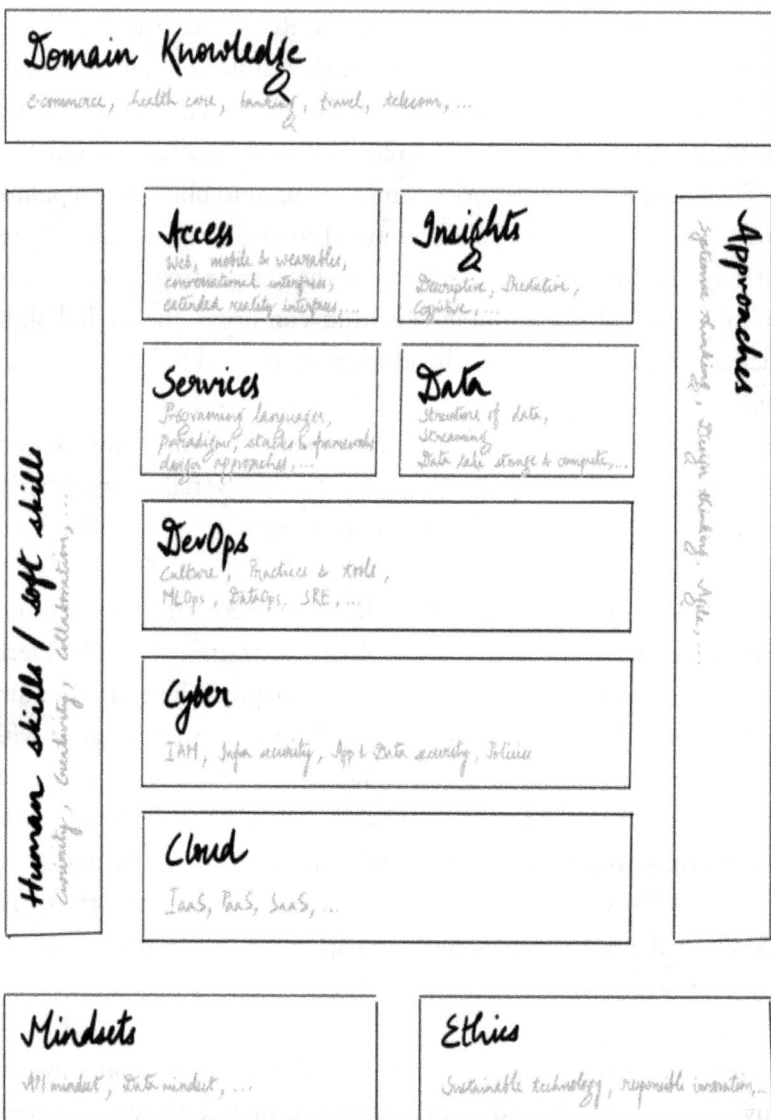

Domain Knowledge
e-commerce, health care, banking, travel, telecom, ...

Human skills / soft skills
curiosity, creativity, collaboration, ...

Access
Web, mobile & wearables,
conversational interfaces,
extended reality interfaces, ...

Insights
Descriptive, Predictive,
Cognitive, ...

Services
Programming languages,
paradigms, stacks & frameworks,
design approaches, ...

Data
Structure of data,
Streaming
Data lake storage & compute, ...

DevOps
Culture, Practices & tools,
MLOps, DataOps, SRE, ...

Cyber
IAM, Infra security, App & Data security, Policies

Cloud
IaaS, PaaS, SaaS, ...

Approaches
Systems thinking, Design thinking, Agile, ...

Mindsets
API mindset, Data mindset, ...

Ethics
Sustainable technology, responsible innovation, ...

Fig 5.3: The Learning Spectrum

may have evolved independently, they eventually all got connected to create the learning spectrum that we observe today.

Similarly, the insights continuum has evolved from descriptive to predictive to cognitive insights, delving deeper in each realm. Predictive insights have evolved with machine learning algorithms, while cognitive insights are advancing with deep learning applications in areas like computer vision, natural language processing, robotics, and reinforcement learning. They're even venturing into replicating human imagination through generative AI techniques. These evolving skills and technologies are integral parts of the broader learning spectrum.

The example of the cloud's evolution in the invisible part of the learning spectrum is particularly noteworthy. Initially, it provided distributed compute power and storage as a service but has since expanded to offer almost anything and everything as a service, including the access and insights discussed earlier. The cloud operates through models like SaaS, FaaS, PaaS, CaaS, and IaaS, enabling the creation of modern digital experiences. We can see that the growth of the cloud truly imbibes eternal and connected nature, and it may not be an overstatement to say that adapting to the evolution of the cloud is a key note of the learning spectrum rhythm.

Changes to the learning spectrum evokes the individual's bias for action which draws them towards learning new skills and further exploring how it all connects with what they already know. The learning spectrum rhythm for individuals can be observed when we notice how they adapt to the evolution in the various areas of the learning spectrum. We see that the rhythm in their learning follows a typical cycle from ignorance to mastery; and then starts all over again with the emergence of new skills and technologies. For example, consider an amateur programmer in the 1970s who learns programming with COBOL. She would have navigated an arduous learning journey from ignorance to mastery of COBOL, only to soon witness the shift in the technology to other programming languages and paradigms.

She then starts her learning journey all over again to move from ignorance to mastery in the next technology. It is worthwhile to note here that the latter learning cycles tend to get progressively shorter. It is often easier to learn a second programming language because the learner would be able to transfer some of the knowledge from her previous learning experiences. While the overall learning journey is eternal, just like the growth of the learning spectrum, an individual can accelerate their progress in each cycle, and from one to the next, by banking on the three virtues of the learning fractal viz. perseverance, discipline and curiosity. Curiosity helps them discover the evolution of the spectrum, perseverance enables them to strive to hone their skills, and discipline helps strike a balance between acquiring new skills and reinforcing existing capabilities. Individuals must also remember that learning is not just about consumption but also about creation. As they move from ignorance to mastery, they should learn to do so using experiential learning techniques and eventually apply their learning to create something - a throwaway prototype or a billion dollar product. Such creation eventually contributes back to the evolution of the learning spectrum and in-turn enhances the cadence of their learning spectrum rhythm.

For enterprises, the learning spectrum rhythm is all about how they adopt new skills to create products and services that embrace the evolving trends. Enterprises need to sync with the learning spectrum by staying abreast with the evolving technology trends and adopting the appropriate skills into their digital journey roadmap. This would in turn lead to strong sponsorship of enterprise-wide learning initiatives that focus on these skills and eventually enable individuals and teams to be future-ready.

Learning teams, being the conscience keepers of learning, should act as the catalyst to adapt to the evolution of the learning spectrum by being at the helm of orchestrating the learning spectrum rhythm within the organization. They should play a key role in incepting and implementing enterprise-wide learning initiatives that are influenced by changes in the learning spectrum, and steer the learning journeys of individuals and enterprises towards the future. This translates to partnering with learning platforms and other Subject Matter Experts (SMEs) to offer learning resources that go hand-in-hand with the evolving learning spectrum and designing learning pathways to help individuals up-skill themselves and/or prepare for new roles. They should also launch learning campaigns to promote these changes and boost their adoption. Further, depending on the enterprise's strategy and roadmap, learning teams may need to institutionalize learning programs to cultivate deep-dive skills in required areas.

The evolution of the learning spectrum fuels the bias for action of all the three actors - individuals, enterprises, and learning teams, and rouses the learning spectrum rhythm. Embracing this rhythm keeps them on their toes constantly and in turn enables them to achieve their highest potential as they learn and progress on their digital journeys.

Learning Triad Rhythm

In chapter 3, we drew inspiration from the self-organized nature of fractals to discover the fundamental fractal of the learning spectrum. We observed how the learning triad - the fundamental fractal of the learning spectrum, comprises three elements i.e. imagination, data and logic, and repeats across the breadth and depth of the learning spectrum. We not only learnt that the learning triad holds the key to mastery of the learning spectrum but also explored how to pursue the path to attain mastery of each element of the triad and the interplay among them. Fig 5.4 depicts the essence of each element of the learning triad, for quick reference.

Unlike the learning spectrum rhythm which is cyclical and moves from ignorance to mastery as new technologies and skills integrate into the learning spectrum, the learning triad rhythm is fairly consistent. The learning triad rhythm is a steady rhythm which provides

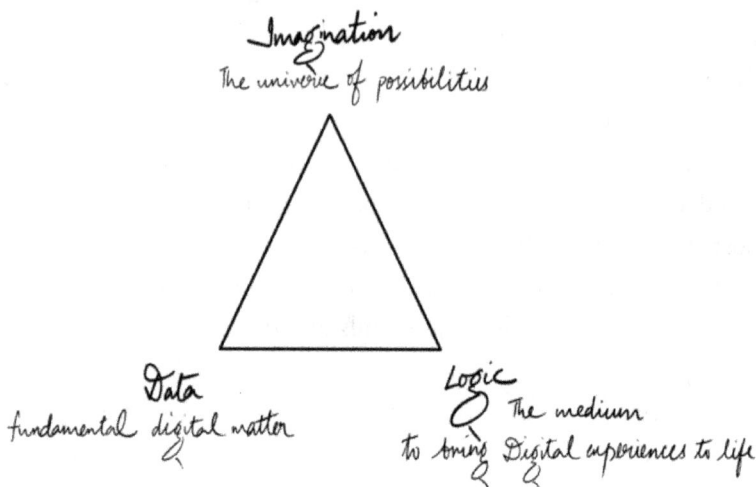

Imagination
The universe of possibilities

Data
fundamental digital matter

Logic
The medium
to bring Digital experiences to life

Fig 5.4: The Learning Triad and the Essence of Each of its Elements

the foundation to the continuous learning journey towards mastery of the learning spectrum. It mirrors the consistency with which the learning triad repeats across the breadth and depth of the learning spectrum. This rhythm emphasizes the importance of exploring the role of the fundamental elements of the triad and their interplay in the context of every new learning cycle.

For example, let us refer to the earlier scenario of a learner continuously navigating the evolving technologies in the area of web technologies. As the Web evolves from Web 1.0 to Web 3.0, the learner has to constantly stay abreast with new web standards, frameworks, and libraries, following the learning spectrum rhythm when encountering these skills and technologies. To accelerate each learning cycle, she can rely on the consistency of the learning triad and tune into the learning triad rhythm. In this scenario she will observe that the role of logic remains constant and translates to defining the elements of the web interface and describing their interactions with the user. She will observe that data continues to be the fundamental digital matter and gets consumed, generated, transformed and exchanged as it interplays with the logic. And finally she will observe the role of imagination in conceptualizing the use cases, designing the interface, and visualizing the flow of data. The learning triad rhythm offers guidance on navigating the new learning journey and bolsters her learning progress.

Similarly, in the example of the evolving insights continuum, we see that the learner can accelerate her learning journey by following the learning triad rhythm. Logic (as programming) plays a key role in the evolution of sophisticated algorithms and optimization techniques, preparation of data, use of frameworks and libraries for both development and deployment of insights, integration of these insights into the overall stack of the digital experience, and continuous improvement of AI models in real-time. Data, as the fundamental digital matter, changes along the structure, shape, and time dimensions as it interplays with the logic to get generated, transformed, exchanged, and consumed across these insights. And imagination is key to not only creating a data story or narrative and culling out insights but also to ensuring that the models are ethical and fair to everyone.

The learning triad rhythm is intrinsic to the learning spectrum rhythm and tuning into it is essential for individuals to accelerate their learning journeys. Appreciating the fundamental aspects of the learning triad not only helps them strengthen their learning foundations, but also inspires them to stay disciplined in their continuous learning pursuit.

For enterprises, the learning triad rhythm serves as a way to keep up with evolving trends and adopt new skills into their digital journey roadmap. The learning sponsors across enterprises can use this rhythm as a foundation on top of which they can build a future-ready skilled workforce.

Learning teams being the conscience keepers of learning should treat the learning triad rhythm as the true north and ensure that it consistently features across the enterprise-wide learning initiatives which they incept and implement. They should ensure that learning initiatives should help individuals and teams develop their logic, data and imagination skills and prepare them to master the learning spectrum. This is often achieved by including the key aspects of these three elements and their interplay into the design of the learning pathways and learning programs. For example, a learning pathway for learners to specialize in predictive insights should have resources such as case studies and pocket stories which peak their imagination on the potential use cases of such insights. It should delve into the nuances of how data is consumed, transformed, and analyzed to derive insights. And it should enable learners to get familiar with the logic and algorithms that help glean insights from the data. It is important to note the pathway should bind these aspects cohesively such that one feeds into the other, in order to establish the nuances of the interplay between these elements.

Learning Architecture Rhythm

In chapter 4, we explored the learning architecture, which is a collection of related components or structures that coexist in the enterprise to help individuals and teams navigate their continuous learning journey. The architecture serves as the master blueprint for guiding the enterprises towards building and sustaining a skilled workforce that is fit to meet the enterprise goals.

Recall that the reference learning architecture presented in Chapter 4, as depicted in Fig 5.5, is composed of 5 layers viz. Learning Platforms, Learning Pathways, Learning Campaigns, Learning Programs, and Learning Credentials. This architecture can be used as a guide for enterprises and learning teams to build a learning ecosystem that supports individuals and teams on their continuous learning journey. It lays out the components of a learning ecosystem in a well defined structure, with a strong foundation built on learning platforms to support the acquisition of knowledge and skills and learning credentials at the pinnacle to demonstrate proficiency and mastery.

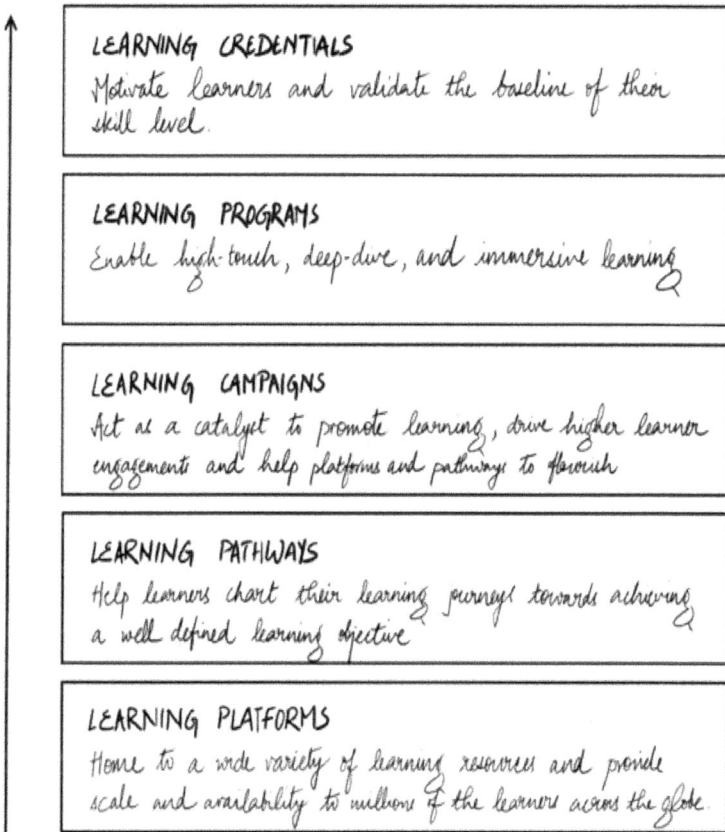

LEARNING CREDENTIALS
Motivate learners and validate the baseline of their skill level.

LEARNING PROGRAMS
Enable high-touch, deep-dive, and immersive learning

LEARNING CAMPAIGNS
Act as a catalyst to promote learning, drive higher learner engagements and help platforms and pathways to flourish

LEARNING PATHWAYS
Help learners chart their learning journeys towards achieving a well defined learning objective

LEARNING PLATFORMS
Home to a wide variety of learning resources and provide scale and availability to millions of the learners across the globe.

Fig 5.5: The Reference Learning Architecture

This learning architecture is robust enough to remain stable at a high level, while also nimble enough to adapt each component to the evolving learning needs and preferences of individuals and teams within an enterprise. The learning architecture rhythm tracks how these changing trends and needs evoke the bias for action of enterprises and learning teams and leads them to adapt the various components of the learning architecture.

In the learning platforms layer, we can observe changes in terms of the pedagogy, breadth of learning content, depth of learning content, adaptability features, social features, extensibility features, and observability features. The learning pathways layer eventually follows these changes and adapts to them such that these newer and better experiences are curated for the learners. As platforms themselves evolve to these changing trends, they also influence how individuals consume the learning resources they offer. Enterprises respond to changing trends by sponsoring platforms that offer enhanced capabilities and promote their integration into the learning architecture. Learning teams remain at the fulcrum of these changes and steer the incorporation of these features by adapting them into the design of learning pathways, learning campaigns and learning programs and influence the overall learning within the enterprise.

The learning campaigns layer too continuously evolves to meet the evolving learning needs and trends. The changes in how campaigns are designed and delivered are not only reflective of the changes in the learning behaviors of learners, but also of the changes in the learning spectrum rhythm, at large. Campaigns help drive the learning agenda forward by engaging more learners to the cause of learning to eventually help make progress towards the overall learning goals of the enterprise. For individuals, campaigns help them discover new areas of the learning spectrum, engage with newer learning pedagogies and experiences, and get inspired by/draw energy from other learners. Learning teams help organize and track these learning campaigns as they implement the learning architecture and strive to drive the learning agenda forward.

Learning programs and learning credentials layers help establish the depth of learning for individuals and enterprises. Changes to these layers are often in response to the growing need for highly skilled versatilists and take shape with the launch of newer learning programs, or increasing penetration of existing programs, or with encouragement and support to acquire learning credentials that bolster the overall skill quotient. For individuals, these changes reinforce their need for up-skilling and/or cross-skilling, thus progressing towards their career goals and eventually becoming fit for the future. For enterprises, providing impetus to these layers is crucial to accelerate their digital journeys, and for learning teams it is the act of conscience keeping by making sure that there is a healthy supply chain of talent to meet the demands of the business.

Overall, the learning architecture rhythm tracks the changes to the enterprise's learning landscape in response to the evolving learning needs and trends which evoke the bias for action of individuals, enterprises and learning teams. The synergy between this rhythm and the learning culture rhythm, which we will see next, is key to building and sustaining a holistic and thriving learning ecosystem which is essential for enabling a future-ready workforce

Learning Culture Rhythm

In chapter 4, we understood that the learning culture is the foundational aspect of any learning ecosystem, and is key to the progress of individuals and enterprises on their life-long learning journeys. We also learnt about the dual role that the learning culture plays in the overall learning ecosystem wherein it not only helps individuals and enterprises adapt to the changes that come with the evolution, but also enables the learning ecosystem to transform itself to suit the tides of time.

Recall that, although the learning culture evolves with time, its essence fundamentally hinges on the learning fractal. The three timeless virtues of perseverance, discipline, and curiosity which are inspired from the three fundamental characteristics of fractals viz. eternal, self-organized and connected, as depicted in Fig 5.6, hold the key to building a progressive learning culture which ensures that the learning ecosystem thrives.

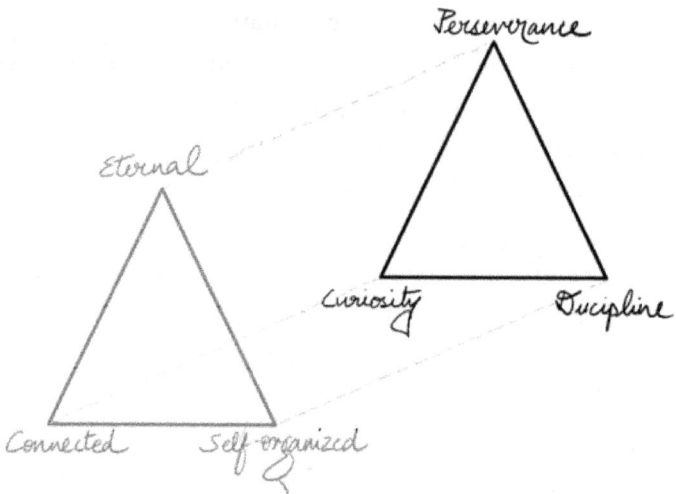

Fig 5.6: The Learning Fractal

The learning culture rhythm is intrinsic to the learning architecture rhythm and it symbolizes the rigor with which the learning ecosystem is being implemented and sustained. This rhythm centers around the three timeless virtues of the learning fractal and tracks the acts of learning of individuals, enterprises and learning teams along these virtues.

Perseverance reflects the eternal nature of learning which individuals, enterprises and learning teams should imbibe by consistently investing in learning for their sustained growth. Imbibing this virtue requires all three actors to ask themselves the pertinent question - "are we learning enough?" and put relentless effort to sustain their learning journeys. For individuals, this translates into engaging with continuous learning and making the best use of the learning ecosystem within the enterprise, and beyond. For enterprises this translates into exhibiting a strong commitment and striving towards establishing a robust learning ecosystem. For learning teams, as conscience keepers of learning, this translates into their persistence in providing learning resources that can vouch for the variety and volume of learning that individuals and enterprises require to navigate their eternal learning journeys.

Discipline reflects the self-organized nature of learning. It is the bridge between the learning goals that are defined and the outcomes that are accomplished. Imbibing this virtue requires individuals, enterprises and learning teams to ask themselves the question - "are we consistent in our learning?" and to perform learning acts with rigor and diligence. For individuals, this virtue translates into engaging in experiential learning and putting their skills to practice. For enterprises, it translates into defining their skill taxonomy and creating a learning roadmap, and consistently measuring the learning progress. Learning teams play a key role in helping individuals and enterprises cultivate learning habits that lead to consistent and disciplined learning efforts along the journey.

Curiosity is closely knit with the connected nature of learning and is essential to help accentuate the imagination of individuals and enterprises. It is fostered when individuals ruminate on the question - "what should I learn next?" and explore everything that they come across to eventually connect the dots, and appreciate how everything connects with everything else. Enterprises and learning teams need to create a fail-safe environment that encourages individuals to experiment and unearth the potential of the visible and invisible parts of the learning spectrum.

The learning culture rhythm is central to ensure that the learning fractal blossoms and grows, as other rhythms such as the learning spectrum rhythm and the learning architecture rhythm evolve. This rhythm is essential to embrace the perennial duality of "renew and new" that individuals, enterprises and learning teams face as they come to terms with evolving technologies, consumer demands and learning styles.

Learning Data Rhythm

Learning data rhythm is a unique rhythm that brings in observability to the other learning rhythms and provides insights into how these rhythms are flowing. It helps quantify the learning trends that are continuously observed along the learning journeys of individuals and enterprises, and eventually provides a way to monitor and calibrate the state of learning.

The learning data rhythm can typically be observed from five key insights derived from the learning data of individuals and teams. These insights help answer the key questions - how much are we learning, is everyone engaged in learning, what is being learnt, are we learning enough in key strategic areas, and how effectively learners are leveraging the learning ecosystem; as depicted in Fig 5.7.

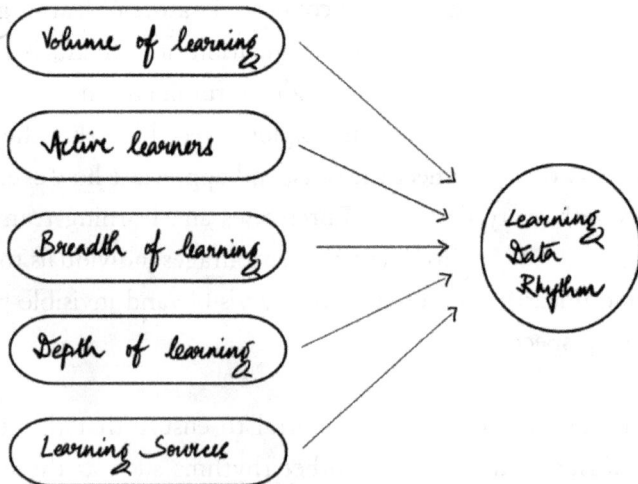

Fig 5.7: Observable Insights that form the Learning Data Rhythm

The volume of learning insight helps observe how much individuals and teams are learning. It throws light on how the learning culture rhythm is nurturing the learning within the enterprise. It is typically measured using metrics such as 'Total learning hours (accumulated over a time period) ' and 'Average learning hours per individual (over the defined time period)', as represented in Chart 5.1. Both these metrics are typically compared against the industry benchmarks (of the segment in which the enterprise operates) to help the leaders and the learning teams of the enterprise to encourage individuals and teams to continuously progress on learning; and stay on track with their learning goals. Learning teams should periodically measure and report how the volume of learning is trending within the enterprise to correlate it with various events and circumstances in the enterprise's context.

Volume of Learning (Monthly)
Note: Sample data used only for illustration

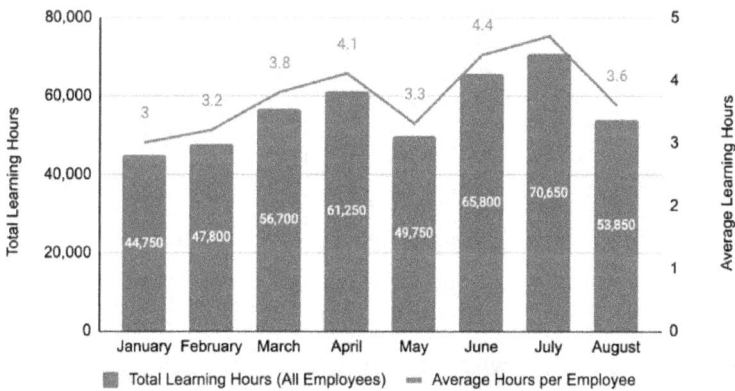

Chart 5.1: Volume of Learning

The active learners metric helps observe how many individuals and teams are actively engaged in their learning journeys. This metric in tandem with the volume of learning metrics provides a holistic view of the impact of the learning culture rhythm on the overall learning within the enterprise. It is typically measured as the 'percentage of learners' who are engaged with learning in a given period of time, as represented in Chart 5.2. It is imperative for the leaders and the learning teams to ensure that as many learners are engaged and making progress on their learning journeys. Leaders and learning teams can aim to boost the active learners by promoting learning platforms and pathways through learning campaigns and encouraging them to explore the wide catalog of learning available to them.

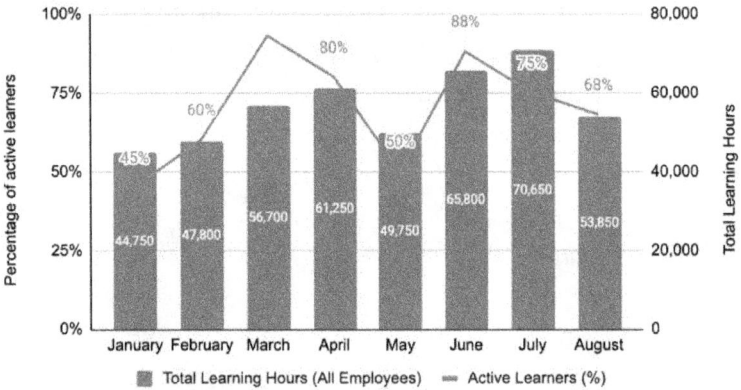

Active Learners (Monthly)
Note: Sample data used only for illustration

Chart 5.2: Active Learners

The breadth of learning insight helps peek into what individuals and teams are learning across the various areas of the learning spectrum. It helps in observing how much the individuals, enterprises and learning teams are in tune with the learning spectrum rhythm. It is typically represented using "learning pie(s)" that indicates the volume of learning and active learners across the strategic learning areas, as represented in Chart 5.3. This insight helps leaders and learning teams nudge individuals and teams to be more curious about the areas of the learning spectrum that are key to the enterprise's strategy along its digital journey. To accelerate the learning in any given area of the spectrum and bolster the progress towards the enterprise's goals, learning teams can run specialized learning campaigns or institute deep dive learning programs in specific areas.

Learning (by volume) across key areas

Note: Sample data used only for illustration

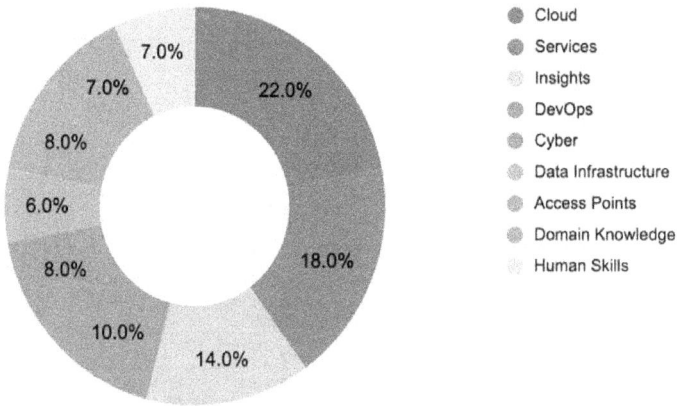

Legend:
- Cloud
- Services
- Insights
- DevOps
- Cyber
- Data Infrastructure
- Access Points
- Domain Knowledge
- Human Skills

Values shown: 7.0%, 7.0%, 22.0%, 8.0%, 6.0%, 18.0%, 8.0%, 10.0%, 14.0%

Chart 5.3: Breadth of Learning (learning pie) across Key Areas

The depth of learning insight is also connected to the learning spectrum rhythm and provides an enhanced understanding of whether individuals and teams are learning enough in the key strategic areas. It is key to creating learning programs that help build the future-ready skilled workforce. It is typically measured by tracking the number of individuals who have successfully completed specialized deep-dive learning programs and/or achieved learning credentials, as depicted in Chart 5.4. Using these insights, leaders and learning teams can not only efficiently perform strategic workforce planning but also help individuals navigate their career within the enterprise.

Finally, the learning sources insights are derived from measuring how individuals and teams are engaging with the various components of the learning ecosystem. These insights are gleaned from observing the volume of learning and active learners metrics in various layers of the learning architecture, as represented in Chart 5.5. This observability helps learning teams to reflect on what is working well and what needs to be improved across the different components of the learning ecosystem.

Depth of Learning across key areas

Note: Sample data used only for illustration

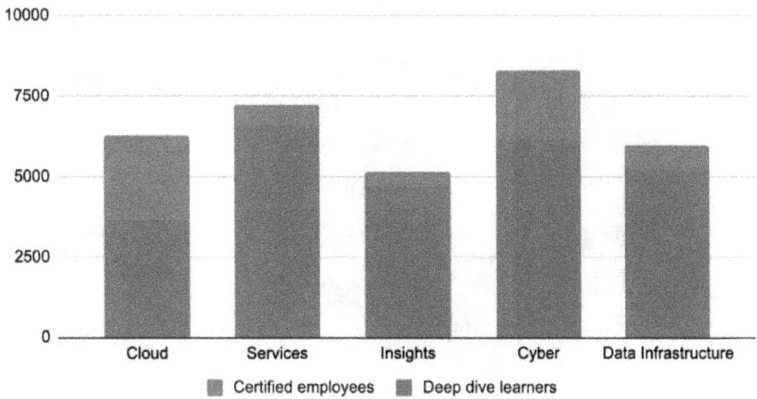

Chart 5.4: Depth of learning/Deep dive learners

Volume of learning by learning source/activity

Note: Sample data used only for illustration

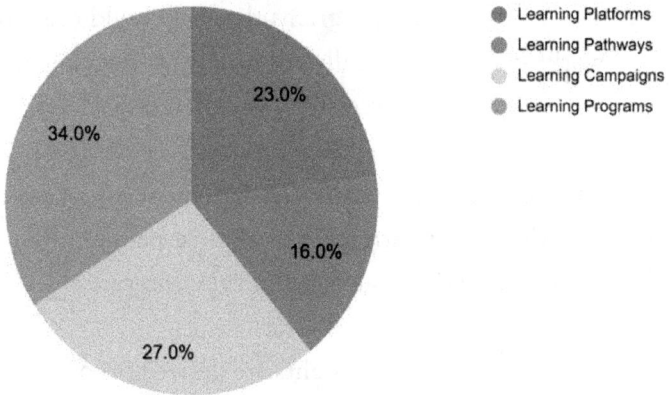

Chart 5.5: Learning sources insights

Ultimately, the learning data rhythm helps measure the overall learning activities across the enterprise, connects them to the relevant business outcomes, and articulates the role of learning along the enterprise's digital journey for key stakeholders.

Learning Operations Rhythm

The learning operations rhythm is a key rhythm that describes how learning is orchestrated across the enterprise's learning ecosystem. This rhythm is not only pivotal to operationalize the learning at the enterprise and synchronize the learning efforts of individuals, enterprises and learning teams, but also to build the learning momentum and sustain the rigor required along the learning journeys.

Although individuals, enterprises and learning teams all have a role to play in building the learning operations rhythm, it is most amplified by the bias for action of the learning teams who aim to be conscience keepers of learning within the enterprise. The learning operations rhythm is strongly influenced by their acts of establishing frameworks, policies and procedures to create an environment that is conducive for learning and helps drive the learning agenda forward. The rhythm is further supported by the bias for action of enterprises where-in its leaders act as strong proponents of learning and sponsor enterprise-wide learning initiatives with passion and purpose. And ultimately, individuals are always at the heart of this rhythm because eventually their bias for action leads them to leverage various learning avenues in order to take control of their learning journeys and reach their highest potential.

The learning operations rhythm is strung together when learning teams (with the help of enterprises and individuals) connect with business outcomes, conceptualize the learning roadmap, envision learning coverage for all, collaborate with subject matter experts, communicate with stakeholders, and calibrate the learning success and overall learning rhythm; as depicted in Fig 5.8.

Connecting with business stakeholders is key for learning teams to gather the priorities of the business and understand the roadmap for the enterprise's digital journey. This helps learning teams discover the competency needs of the enterprise and also helps them tune into the

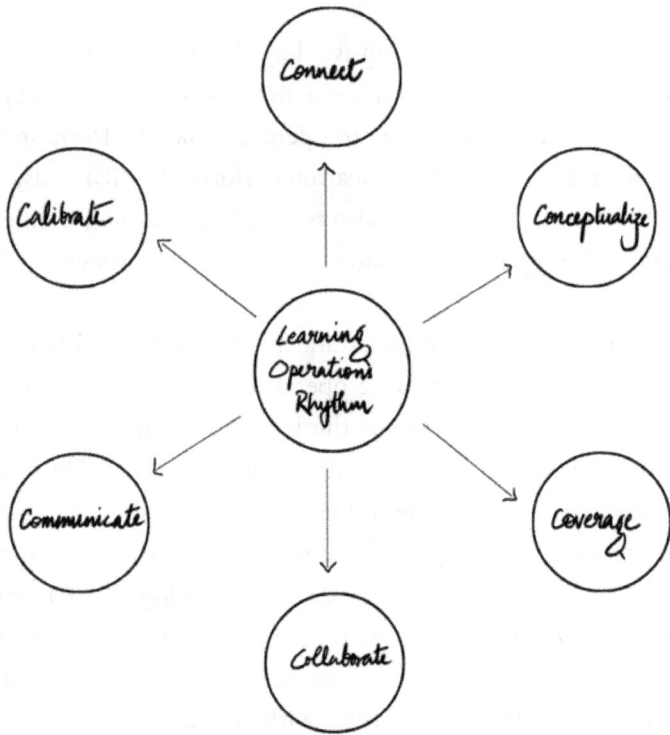

Fig 5.8: Elements of The Learning Operations Rhythm

state of the learning spectrum rhythm within the enterprise. Learning teams should typically connect with the leaders of the enterprise to understand the business outcomes not only for the enterprise as a whole, but also within the different parts of the enterprise, and gather the current and future demand for skills and competencies at both macro and micro levels.

Learning teams need to conceptualize the roadmap for the learning ecosystem in alignment with the enterprise's digital goals. They need to clearly articulate the learning architecture that is being established and further chalk out how the different layers of the learning architecture are being implemented. For instance, learning teams need to establish policies and procedures to periodically evaluate new learn ing platforms, review existing platform offerings and integrate multiple learning platforms into the ecosystem as enterprises traverse their digital journey. Similarly, they should also plan out the launch of various learning campaigns in order to encourage individuals and teams to foster a culture of learning. Ultimately, learning teams should ensure that the roadmap of implementing the learning ecosystem resonates with the learning architecture and learning culture rhythms.

Ensuring that the learning ecosystem and its offerings provides learning coverage for all personas in the enterprise is key to maintaining the overall momentum of learning; and learning teams have a key role to play here. Recall that we categorized the individuals within an enterprise into three broad personas - decision makers, influencers and implementers from a learning perspective. Since the learning needs of each of these personas vary significantly, it is typically challenging to offer a single learning solution that fits them all. While customizing the learning solutions for these personas, learning teams should tap into the learning triad rhythm and ensure that the learning solutions for each persona covers the three key elements of the learning triad - logic, data and imagination; to an appropriate degree. The offerings should not only cater to learning the individual element of the triad in the context of the learner but also enable them to understand the nuances of the interplay between these elements to appreciate the simplicity that underpins the seemingly complex learning spectrum.

As learning teams implement the learning ecosystem and continuously adapt to changes in the other rhythms they should collaborate with subject matter experts (SMEs) to contextualize the learning solutions for individuals. This collaboration is essential to ensure that learners are attuned to the principles and practices of the enterprise and are in sync with how the enterprise is responding to the learning spectrum rhythm. Some examples of collaboration include seeking SME support to co-create and/or vet learning pathways, host knowledge sharing sessions as part of learning campaigns, and engage with SMEs to deliver learning program modules. This collaboration is a key aspect of fostering a healthy learning culture within the enterprise.

Learning teams aim to be the conscience keepers of learning and drive the learning agenda forward. For this they need to proactively and periodically communicate with both internal and external stakeholders on the state of learning. Their interactions with key stakeholders is pivotal in garnering the required support for achieving the learning goals and in turn the business outcomes of the enterprise. Learning teams need to communicate with the leaders of the business to appraise them about the learning trends, seek sponsorship for learning avenues, and exchange perspectives that help them align the learning avenues better to the enterprise's digital goals. They also need to communicate with internal teams of learning consultants and learning advocates to further promote the cause of learning, share experiences and best practices, and build a community of individuals passionate about learning who eventually help the learning culture thrive. Learning teams must also communicate with other functions such as Recruitment, Talent Fulfillment, and Organization Development to ensure that enterprises foster a positive learning environment where learning is acknowledged and rewarded, and thus encouraging more individuals to learn and progress. Communication with stakeholders is key to upkeep the tempo of the learning culture rhythm within the enterprise.

Finally, learning teams have to calibrate the success of the various learning offerings and in turn sync with the learning data rhythm. They should put in place processes to record the data pertaining to various learning activities and periodically glean insights from them. Further they should seek regular feedback from individuals and teams engaged in learning to calibrate the learning offerings and ensure that the best learning avenues are made available for everyone. Learning teams should tap into the learning data rhythm to adopt data driven decision making practices and steer the course of learning within the enterprise.

In a nutshell, learning teams must put in place various activities to effectively orchestrate the learning within the organization. They must always stay up-to-date with the enterprise's digital strategy by connecting with business leaders. This would help them charter the roadmap of how individuals and teams will acquire and strengthen their skills along the journey. To this, they should design various pathways, campaigns and programs. They must also institute various policies and processes to administer these components of the learning architecture and strongly advocate for learning within the enterprise. They should embrace the virtues of collaboration and communication to build a growing community of learning enthusiasts who further ensure that learning permeates within the enterprise. Finally, they have to track, monitor, and communicate the learning progress, and periodically review the learning activities to calibrate the learning ecosystem for growth.

The learning operations rhythm is central to tuning the overall learning rhythm by harmonizing and orchestrating all the other rhythms. The role of learning teams as conscience keepers of learning comes to the fore when they act with passion and purpose to operationalize the learning activities and steer the enterprise towards becoming a continuous learning organization. This rhythm is the most critical factor in ensuring that organizations become life-long learning organizations and nurture a thriving learning ecosystem for perpetual learners.

The Learning Rhythm

So far, in this chapter, we have seen that individuals, enterprises and learning teams generate learning vibrations through their bias for action and that these learning vibrations assemble into the learning rhythm. Learning vibrations in individuals arise within, when they act on their innate desire to learn and navigate the vast expanse of the learning spectrum. The learning vibrations of enterprises manifest when they sponsor enterprise-wide learning initiatives that help build and sustain a robust learning ecosystem. And that of learning teams comes to the fore when they take the center stage in driving the learning agenda forward by establishing relevant frameworks, policies and procedures to create an environment that is conducive for learning. We further discussed that the synergy of these learning vibrations produces the overall learning rhythm which can be observed as being composed of six rhythms viz. learning spectrum rhythm, learning triad rhythm, learning architecture rhythm, learning culture rhythm, learning data rhythm, and learning operations rhythm, as depicted in Fig 5.9 for quick reference.

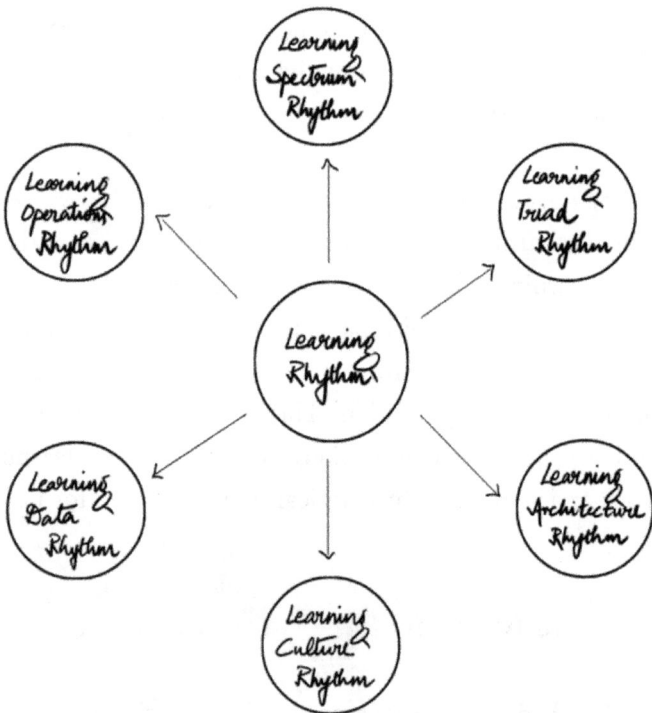

Fig. 5.9: Six Elements of the Overall Learning Rhythm

These individual learning rhythms represent different aspects of learning for individuals, enterprises and learning teams, and orchestrating them together into a harmonious learning rhythm is key to creating a thriving learning ecosystem that nurtures the learning fractal. Nurturing the learning fractal leads to the inculcation of its three virtues viz. perseverance, discipline and curiosity in individuals, enterprises and learning teams. It is interesting to note how the individual rhythms and the overall learning rhythm nurture the virtues of the learning fractal and help make progress towards mastering the learning spectrum.

The learning spectrum rhythm signifies the evolution of the breadth and depth of the learning spectrum and tuning into it helps individuals, enterprises, and learning teams foster the virtue of curiosity. Delving into this rhythm with curiosity not only provides a view of how the landscape of skills is evolving, but also helps learners explore how things connect with one another which ultimately puts them on the path of continuous learning and growth. For enterprises, this rhythm fosters their curiosity to explore and ideate how they can enhance their suite of digital experiences and create newer or enhanced experiences that enjoy advocacy from their consumers. For learning teams, drawing inspiration from the learning spectrum rhythm to enhance their curiosity not only helps them adapt their learning offerings to the changes in the learning spectrum, but also enables them to offer enhanced digital learning experiences for the learners to engage with.

The learning triad rhythm paves the way for individuals to stay disciplined on their learning journey. The learning triad rhythm which represents the consistency with which the fundamental fractal beats across the learning spectrum offers individuals with the master key to relentlessly pursue the mastery of the learning spectrum. The learning data rhythm brings in observability into the learning progress from insights such as - how much are we learning, is everyone engaged in learning, what is being learnt, are we learning enough in key strategic areas, and how effectively learners are leveraging the learning ecosystem. These insights coupled with a data driven mindset aids enterprises build discipline into their pursuit of becoming a learning organization. A healthy learning operations rhythm is the epitome of learning teams practicing discipline to meet their purpose of being the conscience keepers of learning in the enterprise. The rigor with which learning teams implement the various frameworks, policies and practices to support and drive the learning agenda reflects their passion, commitment and discipline to live up to their purpose.

The learning architecture rhythm, which describes how the blueprint of the learning ecosystem is implemented, is a key driver to providing learners with the necessary platform to persevere in their learning pursuit. Individuals can leverage the various layers of the learning architecture to persist in their learning. Through learning platforms, learning pathways and learning campaigns, they explore the breadth of the learning spectrum, and through learning programs and learning credentials they deep-dive into various areas of the learning spectrum. This coupled with the learning operations rhythm which learning teams drive to harmonize the learning across the learning ecosystem enables individuals to persist in their learning journeys.

By now you may have observed that the various learning rhythms help nurture the virtues of perseverance, discipline and curiosity, which in turn resonates with the learning culture rhythm. The learning culture rhythm represents these virtues in action and is the ultimate force which ensures that the learning fractal blossoms and thrives to help build and sustain a life-long learning organization. Just like how a simple process underpins the complexity that is found in fractals, the three virtues of the learning culture underpin the complexity inherent in creating a learning ecosystem which enables individuals, enterprises and learning teams to master the learning spectrum and supports them in their perpetual learning journeys.

In a nutshell, the bias for action of individuals, enterprises and learning teams generates learning vibrations which synergize to form the various learning rhythms. These different learning rhythms not only form the overall learning rhythm but also amplify the learning culture rhythm to generate the momentum that bolsters the inculcation of the three virtues and in turn nurtures the learning fractal, as depicted in Fig 5.10. Ultimately, these virtues form the core of life-long learning journeys of individuals and enterprises, which like fractals are eternal, self-organized and connected.

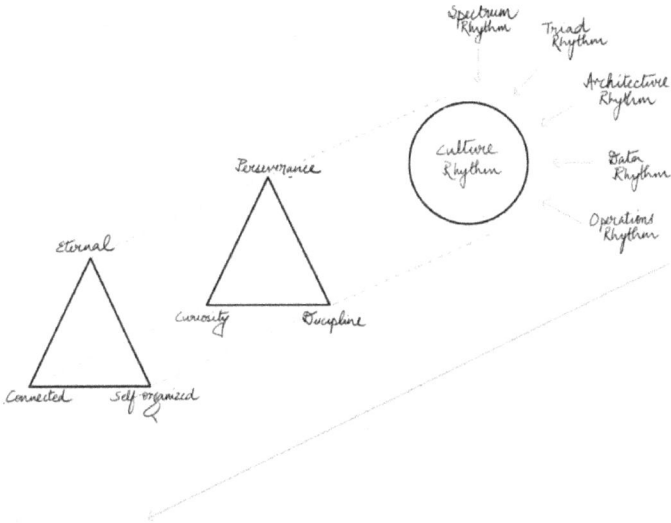

Fig 5.10: How Bias for Action leads to The Learning Fractal

Looking back at our learning journey in this book, you should now be able to see the various aspects of our learning fractal - the learning spectrum. In this journey, we crafted the prism of digital experiences to view our learning fractal, explored its vast expanse, and the connections between its various areas. We then zoomed into the learning spectrum to discover its fundamental fractal - the learning triad, and observed how its three elements (logic, data and imagination) and the interplay among them prevail across the breadth and depth of the spectrum. We then addressed the challenges of building a learning ecosystem that supports individuals and enterprises along the journey to master the learning spectrum. To do this, we designed a reference learning architecture and explored the nuances of how to cultivate a progressive learning culture within an enterprise. Finally, we tuned into the various learning rhythms which need to be orchestrated to make strides in learning and nurture the learning fractal.

Throughout this book, we observed the beauty of our learning fractal as we navigated its vast landscape, were pleasantly surprised to discover the ubiquitous learning triad that repeats across its expanse, and marveled at the creativity that it inspires, leading to the creation of compelling digital experiences. Undoubtedly, akin to any fractal, natural or simulated, our learning fractal - the learning spectrum - too is a **source of beauty, creativity and surprise**!

Epilogue

Dr. David Knott

CTO for UK Government

https://www.linkedin.com/in/david-knott-3a39085/

It took me a long while to learn to love learning.

This book provides a rich, deep way of thinking about learning. What does it look like when applied to a life? Perhaps I can use my own story as an illustration.

Up until the age of sixteen, I was an enthusiastic, avid and successful learner. I didn't enjoy every aspect of school: I had the same struggles to find my voice and identity, to find the groups I belonged to (and the groups I didn't) as everybody else. But I had friends, and I enjoyed several subjects, particularly English and the sciences. I read broadly, and I did well at exams.

Something changed around the ages of seventeen and eighteen - a particularly critical time if you want to prepare well to go to University and have an academic career. I didn't experience the turbulence of many teenagers in those years: I was mild rather than wild. But I grew disillusioned with structured, full time learning. The way my school worked meant that I had to choose English or Sciences, not both, and I had chosen sciences. Perhaps it was the wrong choice. I found study of science at that level to be frustrating: detailed enough that you had to pay attention and memorise long lists of facts and formulae, but not advanced enough to engage with the true frontier. Physics, for example, was more concerned with the acceleration of a trolley down a slope, than with the mysteries of relativity and quantum physics.

I was a bad student in those years. Not disruptive, just bored and uninterested. I did just enough to scrape some bare passes in my exams, and got an offer to study Biology at a respectable University. The question was, should I take it? To complicate matters, I was much happier in my personal life than my academic life. I had met the woman who would become my future wife, and I had friends and hobbies that I found much more interesting than school.

Eventually, I chose to take a year off before taking up my place at University. I think I knew then, even as I explained my choice to my disappointed parents, that I did not intend to return to full time education. In that year, rather than travelling the world, I got a job as an analyst/programmer for the UK Civil Service. I loved it. Alongside my school life, I had been a programmer since the age of eleven. I was fortunate enough to grow up alongside the first generation of affordable microcomputers: the ZX81, the ZX Spectrum, the Acorn Atom, the BBC Micro and so on. I had a succession of machines, and spent most of my spare time learning to program them; typing in code from magazines or writing my own games. I spent much more time on computers than I did on my homework, but I did not think of it as work, or as learning. It was *fun*.

And now, in my adult life, I was being paid to do what I enjoyed in my spare time. What is more, I was good at it. That initial entry level programming job led to a career in technology which has now lasted over three decades. If I look back on the way I have engaged with learning and digital skills over those three decades, I can divide my experience roughly into three periods.

First, I was a reactive learner. On my very first day in my very first paid programming job, I was enrolled in an eight week COBOL course, an impressive investment in my skills. I already knew how to program in BASIC, so the new language was quite easy for me to pick up. But I also learnt new, more difficult skills, such as how to work as part of a team, how to contribute my code to a bigger project, and how to use enterprise scale infrastructure. For several years, this was the pattern of my learning: my employer needed people with a new set of skills, and I was sent on a course to learn them.

Second, I became a proactive learner. This coincided with my progression to management and leadership roles, where I experienced the common paradox that, in technology, if you are good at something, you get promoted to the level where you can't do it any more. In theory, I no longer needed practical, hands–on technical skills as part of my job: I just needed to make sure that those skills were well represented in my team. However, I soon found that I was becoming detached from the technology, and sought out opportunities to learn new, deeper technical skills. This was particularly important as this period coincided with the early days of the commercial Internet, and the explosion of innovation that brought. I realised that it wasn't possible to be a digital leader if I didn't understand the digital landscape.

Third, I like to believe that I became a learning leader, albeit an imperfect one. Living through decades of rapid technology change taught me that digital organisations must be learning organisations. I took greater control of my own learning, and also strove to create the organisations and structures that would help my team and those around them to embrace learning as part of their everyday lives. This was all done in collaboration with one of the authors of this book.

Alongside all this, I rediscovered a passion for continuous further education that had nothing to do with technology (at least not to start with). Early in my programming career, one of my teammates asked me why I hadn't gone to university. When I answered with a shrug, he suggested that I look at the courses offered by the Open University, a wonderful UK institution for adult learners. At first, I was unenthusiastic about the prospect of more structured learning, remembering my lacklustre experiences in the final years of full time education. But my friend persuaded me to try an initial course, and I am very glad that he did. Through the OU arts curriculum I was introduced to philosophy, particularly ethics, and it gave me a whole new way of looking at the world.

I am sure that many people have a similarly haphazard and random experience of learning through their lives, especially working in the digital field, where new ideas are always emerging, and the path to grasping them is unclear. How might my personal learning journey have been different if I had the advantage of the ideas in this book? How does it look when viewed fractally?

First, I believe that I would have approached learning differently if I had understood **the learning fractal** described in Chapter 1. For a long time, I thought of the school work that bored me separately from the computing I did in my spare time, and my technical courses separately from my studies with the Open University. Now, viewed fractally, and with the benefit of hindsight, I can see how the science I learnt at school is **connected** to the fundamental nature of computing, how the **eternal** ongoing debate of philosophy now includes questions at the frontier of AI ethics, and how all of these topics have **self-organised** themselves into my own unique learning experience. I can now also see where I have displayed **perseverance, curiosity and discipline** - and where I have yet to display these virtues. The end of my school years made me suspect that I lacked these virtues, but looking back I now see where I have spent hours persevering with difficult topics, have organised my life with sufficient discipline to give me those hours, and been driven by curiosity to the point where none of that learning felt like work.

Second, I have had the privilege of working in computing for a few decades, and have witnessed its development from isolated mainframes serving large organisations, to a globe-spanning network that is a deep part of the lives of billions of people. I have seen the components of the **learning spectrum** as described in chapter 2 appear, and have seen the different aspects of the prism of digital experiences come into being. I doubt that anyone would have described the green-screen, character-based programs I wrote in the late 1980s as **intimate, immersive, immediate, intuitive, intelligent or insightful** - but they were **interactive**. One colour of the spectrum was there, and even though it has taken a long while for the others to show up, they have appeared. If I had possessed the concept of the learning spectrum from the outset, then it would have been easier for me to recognise that, just like a fractal, there are no finite boundaries to digital learning - and that we can discover new frequencies at the edge.

Third, in my personal life and my professional life, I have often felt overwhelmed by the depth and breadth of my ignorance, and the rate at which new concepts arrive. When I finally enrolled for an undergraduate degree, I realised that there were whole realms of learning which I had not explored. And just as I thought that I had achieved some degree of mastery of a field, I progressed to postgraduate studies, and found that I was still in the foothills of knowledge. As a programmer in the early stages of my career, I became expert in a particular type of mainframe, and the operating system and coding languages that worked with that mainframe - only to find that the action was shifting to PCs, and I had to learn a whole new set of skills. Since then, I do not think that a week has passed where I have not heard of a concept or technology that is new to me. It has taken a long while, much self-doubt and reflection to arrive at the belief that, despite this overwhelming pace of change, there are constants: as described in chapter 3, the foundations of **imagination, data and logic** always apply. However sophisticated they become, computers are machines that use logic to manipulate data - and the power that simple capability unleashes is only limited by our imagination. If we hold onto those foundations, all things are possible.

Fourth, for much of my personal learning journey, I felt alone. In my later years at school, I had grown disaffected with my studies, and struggled to connect with my peers who were still enthusiastic. But I was not nihilistic or rebellious, and also found little connection with those who had given up altogether. When I studied for my under graduate and postgraduate degrees, I had the support of a wonderful institution, the Open University - but still studied remotely, interacting with books and study guides rather than people. In my professional life, it was rare to find an organisation that genuinely invested in digital learning, and created the environment for people to refresh and enhance their skills - everybody wanted expert staff, but struggled to create the organisation that would build that expertise. That's why, when I worked at a company with one of the authors of this book, we endeavoured to establish the **learning ecosystem** and **learning architecture** described in chapter 4 - to set up **platforms**, **pathways**, **campaigns** and **programs** that enabled people to gain **credentials**. If such an architecture had existed in other organisations earlier in my career, then I would have learnt more faster.

Finally, over time, I have eventually settled into a pattern and habit of learning which works for me. I have organised the assets available to me and my team into a learning architecture, have fundamental foundations on which I can anchor, think about the digital world using a mental map that resembles the learning spectrum, and attempt to build time into my schedule and the schedule of my team to exercise perseverance, curiosity and discipline. I have also found that, like most virtues, these practices are habit forming: the more I do, the easier I find it, and the more I want to do. However, it took me decades to find these practices, through trial and error: one of the many virtues of this book is that it crystallises the experience of learners and learning leaders into a set of habits, practices and concepts that can help you at any stage of your learning career.

Just like a fractal, the digital world, when viewed in detail, can feel overwhelming: there seems to be no end to it, and there are always more layers. But, just like a fractal, there is an organising principle, a logic and harmony which, if grasped, makes the world accessible - and even more beautiful.

Dr. David Knott
London, 2024

About the Authors

Anubhav Pradhan

Anubhav is a global learning leader, tech evangelist, and author with over 26 years of experience in learning/education services in EdTech, FinTech, and InfoTech industries. He has designed and delivered several large-scale learning initiatives and competency development programs for the benefit of diverse and multi-cultural learners across the globe. He presently heads the learning and development for HSBC Technology's global workforce and leads the charge on developing a curious, collaborative, and continuous learning organization that possesses the skills of today and aims for the skills of the future. He is also the author of several publications including Raising Enterprise Applications (Wiley, 2010) and Composing Mobile Apps (Wiley, 2014). He holds Master's degree in Mathematics.

Sekhar Subramanian

Sekhar is a learning strategist, consultant and tech educator for digital skills with over 13 years of experience across IT Services, Financial Services and Identity Verification industries. He is a specialist in designing technology learning programs which have so far impacted over 300,000 learners across enterprises. He presently manages product and technical enablement at Trulioo Information Services, Vancouver, Canada with a focus on supporting the go-to-market organization for Trulioo's products and services.

References

Preface:

1. LinkedIn Blog - The Learning Fractals: https://www.linkedin.com/pulse/learing-fractals-anubhav-pradhan/

Chapter 1:

2. Golden Ratio: https://en.wikipedia.org/wiki/Golden_ratio
3. Romanesco Broccoli image: https://unsplash.com/photos/GiudN8NZhGY
4. Ba-ila Housing: Fractals, Complexity, and Connectivity in Africa, Ron Eglash, Jan 2005: https://www.researchgate.net/publication/242428244_Fractals_Complexity_and_Connectivity_in_Africa, and Image in Fig 1.2a in spired by: https://csdt.org/culture/africanfractals/architecture.html
5. Shikharas of Khajuraho inspired by https://coloring-book.printon.pro/product/khajuraho-temples-madhya-pradesh/
6. Mandelbrot references Eiffel Tower and Katsushika Hokusai: https://www.ted.com/talks/benoit_mandelbrot_fractals_and_the_art_of_roughness
7. The Great Wave Off Kanagawa image: https://commons.wikimedia.org/wiki/File:Tsunami_by_hokusai_19th_century.jpg
8. Mandelbrot Set: https://en.wikipedia.org/wiki/Mandelbrot_set
9. Mandelbrot Set Image: Created by Wolfgang Beyer with the program Ultra Fractal 3. (https://en.wikipedia.org/wiki/File:Mandel_zoom_00_mandelbrot_set.jpg)
10. Koch Snowflake: https://en.wikipedia.org/wiki/Koch_snowflake
11. Sierpinski Triangle: https://encyclopediaofmath.org/wiki/Sierpi%C5%84ski_gasket
12. Julia Set: https://en.wikipedia.org/wiki/Julia_set

Chapter 2:

13. Image of Grand Canyon and Colorado river showing a fractal pattern: https://earthobservatory.nasa.gov/images/6929/grand-canyon
14. For example, The Grand Canyon's "Hurricane" segment is estimated to have formed 50-70 million years ago, whereas its "Marble Canyon" segment is estimated to have formed only 5-6 million years ago.
15. Boston Computer Exchange: https://en.wikipedia.org/wiki/Boston_Computer_Exchange
16. Amazon Website from 1995: https://www.versionmuseum.com/history-of/amazon-website
17. Learn more about HTML: https://developer.mozilla.org/en-US/docs/Web/HTML
18. Learn more about CSS: https://developer.mozilla.org/en-US/docs/Web/CSS
19. Learn more about JavaScript : https://developer.mozilla.org/en-US/docs/Web/JavaScript
20. Principles of RWD: https://alistapart.com/article/responsive-web-design/

21. Bootstrap: https://getbootstrap.com/
22. Zurb Foundation: https://get.foundation/
23. Single Page Applications: https://en.wikipedia.org/wiki/Single-page_application
24. Angular: https://angular.io/
25. React: https://react.dev/
26. Kotlin: https://kotlinlang.org/
27. Android: https://developer.android.com/
28. Swift Programming Language: https://www.swift.org/
29. Swift Documentation: https://docs.swift.org/swift-book/documentation/the-swift-programming-language/
30. React Native: https://reactnative.dev/
31. Google Flutter: https://flutter.dev/
32. Apple Watchkit: https://developer.apple.com/documentation/watchkit
33. Open AI's ChatGPT: https://openai.com/chatgpt
34. Apple Sirikit: https://developer.apple.com/documentation/sirikit
35. Alexa Skills Kit: https://developer.amazon.com/en-US/alexa/alexa-skills-kit#
36. Google Assistant: https://developers.google.com/assistant
37. Google Dialogflow: https://cloud.google.com/dialogflow/
38. Facebook's Wit.ai: https://wit.ai/
39. Microsoft Bot Framework: https://dev.botframework.com/
40. Unity: https://unity.com/
41. Unreal Engine: https://www.unrealengine.com/en-US
42. Vuforia: https://library.vuforia.com/
43. Google ARCore: https://arvr.google.com/arcore/
44. ARKit: https://developer.apple.com/augmented-reality/arkit/
45. Oculus Developer: https://developer.oculus.com/
46. R Language: https://www.r-project.org/
47. Python Language: https://www.python.org/
48. Java: https://www.java.com/en/
49. Scala Language: https://scala-lang.org/
50. Julia Language: https://julialang.org/
51. Microsoft Power BI: https://powerbi.microsoft.com/en-us/
52. D3.js: https://d3js.org/
53. Tableau: https://www.tableau.com/
54. Qlik: https://www.qlik.com/us/
55. Supervised Learning: https://en.wikipedia.org/wiki/Supervised_learning
56. Unsupervised Learning: https://www.ibm.com/topics/unsupervised-learning
57. Reinforcement Learning: https://en.wikipedia.org/wiki/Reinforcement_learning
58. NumPy: https://numpy.org/
59. Pandas: https://pandas.pydata.org/
60. Scikit-Learn: https://scikit-learn.org/stable/
61. TensorFlow: https://www.tensorflow.org/
62. PyTorch: https://pytorch.org/
63. Microsoft Azure Machine Learning: https://azure.microsoft.com/en-us/products/machine-learning/
64. Google Cloud Vertex AI: https://cloud.google.com/vertex-ai

65. Artificial Neural Network: https://en.wikipedia.org/wiki/Artificial_neural_network
66. Keras: https://keras.io/
67. LaMDA: https://blog.google/technology/ai/lamda/
68. GPT-4: https://openai.com/product/gpt-4
69. DALL-E: https://openai.com/product/dall-e-2
70. Stable Diffusion: https://stablediffusionweb.com/
71. Open AI Codex: https://openai.com/index/openai-codex/
72. GitHub Copilot: https://github.com/features/copilot
73. Apache Spark: https://spark.apache.org/
74. English SDK for Apache Spark: https://pyspark.ai/
75. C# documentation: https://learn.microsoft.com/en-us/dotnet/csharp/
76. Solidity: https://soliditylang.org/
77. Spring Framework: https://spring.io/
78. .NET (Dot NET): https://dotnet.microsoft.com/en-us/
79. MEAN stack: https://www.mongodb.com/mean-stack
80. MERN stack: https://www.mongodb.com/mern-stack
81. Eclipse IDE: https://www.eclipse.org/ide/
82. IntelliJ IDE: https://www.jetbrains.com/idea/
83. Visual Studio: https://visualstudio.microsoft.com/
84. Bitcoin whitepaper: https://bitcoin.org/bitcoin.pdf
85. R3 Corda: https://r3.com/products/corda/
86. Ethereum Development: https://ethereum.org/en/developers/
87. APIs : https://blog.postman.com/intro-to-apis-what-is-an-api/
88. REST API : https://blog.postman.com/rest-api-examples/
89. SOAP: https://blog.postman.com/soap-api-definition/
90. SQL Documentation: https://docs.oracle.com/en/database/oracle/oracle-database/21/sqlrf/Introduction-to-Oracle-SQL.html
91. MongoDB: https://www.mongodb.com/
92. JSON example: https://developer.mozilla.org/en-US/docs/Learn/JavaScript/Objects/JSON
93. BSON fundamentals: https://www.mongodb.com/basics/bson
94. XML: https://developer.mozilla.org/en-US/docs/Web/XML/XML_introduction
95. Neo4j: https://neo4j.com/
96. Redis: https://redis.io/
97. Apache Cassandra: https://cassandra.apache.org/_/index.html
98. Apache Kafka: https://kafka.apache.org/
99. Apache Hadoop: https://hadoop.apache.org/
100. Agile Manifesto: https://agilemanifesto.org/
101. Scrum: https://www.scrumalliance.org/about-scrum
102. Kanban Explained: https://www.atlassian.com/agile/kanban
103. Lean: https://en.wikipedia.org/wiki/Lean_software_development
104. SAFe: https://scaledagileframework.com/
105. Extreme Programming (XP): http://www.extremeprogramming.org/
106. Mural: https://www.mural.co/
107. Miro: https://miro.com/
108. Jira: https://www.atlassian.com/software/jira
109. Confluence: https://www.atlassian.com/software/confluence

110. Git: https://git-scm.com/
111. GitHub: https://github.com/
112. BitBucket: https://bitbucket.org/
113. Docker: https://www.docker.com/
114. Kubernetes: https://kubernetes.io/
115. Ansible: https://www.ansible.com/
116. Puppet: https://www.puppet.com/
117. Chef: https://www.chef.io/
118. Veracode: https://www.veracode.com/
119. SonarQube: https://www.sonarsource.com/products/sonarqube/
120. Jenkins: https://www.jenkins.io/
121. PagerDuty: https://www.pagerduty.com/
122. OpsGenie: https://www.atlassian.com/software/opsgenie
123. DataDog: https://www.datadoghq.com/
124. Splunk: https://www.splunk.com/
125. AppDynamics: https://www.appdynamics.com/
126. Grafana: https://grafana.com/
127. Pachyderm: https://www.pachyderm.com/
128. DVC: https://dvc.org/
129. MLFlow: https://mlflow.org/
130. Weights and Biases: https://wandb.ai/site
131. Kubeflow: https://www.kubeflow.org/
132. Tensorflow Serving: https://www.tensorflow.org/tfx/guide/serving
133. Seldon: https://www.seldon.io/
134. SailPoint: https://www.sailpoint.com/
135. CyberArk: https://www.cyberark.com/
136. Auth0: https://auth0.com/
137. Firewall: https://en.wikipedia.org/wiki/Firewall_(computing)
138. Intrusion Detection Systems: https://en.wikipedia.org/wiki/Intrusion_detection_system
139. OWASP: https://owasp.org/
140. OpenText Fortify: https://www.opentext.com/products/fortify-static-code-analyzer
141. Armitage on Kali Linux: https://www.kali.org/tools/armitage/
142. NMap: https://nmap.org/
143. Wireshark: https://www.wireshark.org/
144. John the Ripper: https://www.openwall.com/john/
145. GDPR: https://gdpr-info.eu/
146. HIPPA: https://www.hhs.gov/hipaa/index.html
147. PCI DSS: https://en.wikipedia.org/wiki/Payment_Card_Industry_Data_Security_Standard
148. AWS: https://aws.amazon.com/
149. GCP: https://cloud.google.com/
150. MS Azure: https://azure.microsoft.com/en-us
151. Twilio SendGrid: https://sendgrid.com/
152. Amazon Lex: https://aws.amazon.com/lex/
153. Azure Bot Service: https://azure.microsoft.com/en-us/products/bot-services/
154. AWS SageMaker: https://aws.amazon.com/sagemaker/
155. GCP App Engine: https://cloud.google.com/appengine/
156. AWS Elastic Beanstalk: https://aws.amazon.com/elasticbeanstalk/

157. Azure App Service: https://azure.microsoft.com/en-ca/products/app-service/
158. GCP DataProc: https://cloud.google.com/dataproc
159. Amazon EMR: https://aws.amazon.com/emr/
160. Azure Data Lake Analytics: https://azure.microsoft.com/en-us/products/data-lake-analytics/
161. Google Cloud Build: https://cloud.google.com/build
162. AWS CodeBuild: https://aws.amazon.com/codebuild
163. AWS CodeDeploy: https://aws.amazon.com/codedeploy
164. AWS CodePipeline: https://aws.amazon.com/codepipeline
165. Azure DevOps: https://azure.microsoft.com/en-us/products/devops/
166. GCP IAM: https://cloud.google.com/iam
167. AWS IAM: https://aws.amazon.com/iam/
168. Azure Active Directory: https://azure.microsoft.com/en-us/products/active-directory/
169. GCP Cloud Functions: https://cloud.google.com/functions
170. AWS Lambda: https://aws.amazon.com/lambda
171. Azure Functions: https://azure.microsoft.com/en-us/products/functions/
172. Google Compute Engine: https://cloud.google.com/compute
173. AWS EC2: https://aws.amazon.com/ec2/
174. Azure Virtual Machines: https://azure.microsoft.com/en-us/products/virtual-machines/
175. Google Cloud Storage: https://cloud.google.com/storage/
176. AWS S3: https://aws.amazon.com/s3/
177. Azure Blob Storage: https://azure.microsoft.com/en-us/products/storage/blobs/
178. GKE: https://cloud.google.com/kubernetes-engine
179. AWS EKS: https://aws.amazon.com/eks
180. AWS ECS: https://aws.amazon.com/ecs
181. Azure Kubernetes Service: https://azure.microsoft.com/en-us/products/kubernetes-service/

Chapter 3:

182. Jackson Pollock's Lavender Mist: https://www.nga.gov/collection/art-object-page.55819.html
183. Fractal analysis of Pollock's drip paintings: https://www.nature.com/articles/20833
184. Richard Taylor is currently the Head of Physics Department at University of Oregon. Read his blog for his publication and research related to fractals: https://blogs.uoregon.edu/richardtaylor/
185. Perceptual and physiological responses to Jackson Pollock's fractals: https://www.frontiersin.org/articles/10.3389/fnhum.2011.00060/full
186. Why Fractals Are So Soothing : https://www.theatlantic.com/science/archive/2017/01/why-fractals-are-so-soothing/514520/
187. Go Programming Language: https://go.dev/
188. Perl: https://www.perl.org/
189. Visual Studio: https://visualstudio.microsoft.com/
190. VS Code: https://code.visualstudio.com/
191. Eclipse IDE: https://www.eclipse.org/ide/

192. PyCharm: https://www.jetbrains.com/pycharm/
193. SonarQube: https://www.sonarsource.com/products/sonarqube/
194. Technical Debt: https://www.atlassian.com/agile/software-development/technical-debt
195. Microsoft Power Platform: https://www.microsoft.com/en-us/power-platform/
196. Appian: https://appian.com/
197. Mendix: https://www.mendix.com/
198. Webflow: https://webflow.com/
199. Glide: https://www.glideapps.com/
200. Makerpad: https://makerpad.zapier.com/
201. Designing Data-Intensive Applications: https://dataintensive.net/
202. WCAG: https://www.w3.org/WAI/standards-guidelines/wcag/
203. The Minard Map article on BigThink: https://bigthink.com/strange-maps/229-vital-statistics-of-a-deadly-campaign-the-minard-map/

Chapter 4:

204. Users of MOOCs: https://www.classcentral.com/report/moocs-stats-and-trends-2021/ (Note: the data is as of 2021 and excludes some of the platforms listed in our text)

www.ingramcontent.com/pod-product-compliance
Lightning Source LLC
Chambersburg PA
CBHW050503210326
41521CB00011B/2300